DECISIVE BATTLES OF
HITLER'S WAR

DECISIVE BATTLES OF
HITLER'S
WAR

EDITED BY ANTHONY PRESTON

**Eagle
Editions**

A QUANTUM BOOK

Published by Eagle Editions Ltd
11 Heathfield
Royston
Hertfordshire SG8 5BW

Copyright ©MCMLXXVII Quarto Publishing Ltd

This edition printed 2000

ISBN 1-86160-356-8

QUMHIT

This book is produced by
Quantum Publishing
6 Blundell Street
London N7 9BH

Printed in Singapore by
Star Standard Industries Pte Ltd

CREDITS
Maps: Arka Cartographics
Technical drawings: Helen Downton and Pilot Press
Special illustrations: Christy Campbell

CONTENTS

Obliteration of the
humiliating memories of
1918 and the Versailles
Treaty was one of the first
objectives of Hitler's war.
Here, German troops pose
by the remains of First
World War German
trenches, preserved near
Ypres as a war memorial.

INTRODUCTION
by Laurence F. Orbach

The Treaty of Versailles guaranteed the humiliation of Germany; the Nazi plan to restore German might led Europe into the holocaust of Hitler's war.

GERMAN
FRONT LINE
1917

DANGER
DE FEU

THE GERMAN EMPIRE died with the abdication of Kaiser Wilhelm II on November 9, 1918, two days before the Armistice brought an end to the carnage of the First World War. The Third Reich was born on January 30, 1933, when Adolph Hitler became Chancellor of Germany. Between those two dates Germany was convulsed. Bruised by defeat in war, perplexed by the abrupt move from authoritarianism to democracy, tossed in the seas of misfortune by the economic excesses of boom and slump and bedevilled by a more than usually mythical view of their own past, Germans turned increasingly to the extremes of right and left, both offering a panacea for all the ills of society.

In this the Germans differed only marginally from their neighbours and contemporaries. After all, Russians had made an even more astonishing switch from Tsarism to Bolshevism. By the mid-1920s the Italians seemed to have replaced the governments of musical chairs which had been a feature of the previous few decades with an authoritarian ruler who offered order out of chaos. In the surviving 'democracies' such as the United States, France and Great Britain, governments chopped and changed their strategies in vain attempts to discover the 'right' road. What had happened to disturb that equilibrium which had apparently characterized the years before the First World War? Was the experience of war so shattering that people in the twenties could no longer organize the peace?

The Uneasy Peace

Many people were to ask these questions in the period between the wars. Since the Second World War even more people have wondered why the world seemed to go mad after the Armistice. And it was not only politics and economics that moved like a yo-yo. Prohibition in America, the nightclub scene in Berlin, the idolization of movie stars and the daring of modern artists all symbolized the rejection of pre-war values. But there was no new broom sweeping clean New values, a system of moral, political and economic behaviour more suited to the period did not emerge. For, in truth, the old imperial world which came to an end with

the First World War, had been morally bankrupt for years before its demise.

The industrial world had been a European creation. Until the end of the First World War European affairs had dominated the world, but now things were changing. Unappreciated by many of those playing leading roles in the inter-war period, the center of affairs was moving away from Europe. This is not to say that Europe didn't matter any longer. Far from it: European statesmen and European values still asserted themselves. But, essentially, Europe was no longer the master of the world's destiny. The economics of the post-war world were to be dominated by the emergence of the United States as a world economic power. The politics were to be determined by the successful Bolshevik revolution in Russia. Neither the United States nor the new Soviet Union played significant roles in the politics and diplomacy of the 1920s but, in reality, the importance of these powers cannot be underestimated. Both the United States and the Soviet Union were threats to the dominance that Europe had imposed on the world in the late 19th century.

Culturally, if not economically, this threat was manifest and it flavored the politics of the period. Additionally, in Europe people had the legacy of the First World War to live with. This was not only a legacy of physical destruction but also of moral uncertainty. Both were difficult to assimilate. It was common currency in the 1920s to speak of a 'lost generation' when referring to the dead. The carnage in Europe had been on a previously unparalleled scale. The lengthy war had shattered families and broken ideals and beliefs. It was a war which, so the liberal philosophy of the pre-war period implied, simply should not have happened. Because destruction on this scale could never be 'worthwhile' it was irrational. And because it was irrational, sensible civilized Europeans, conscious of the differences between themselves and the 'savages' they so regularly occupied their lives improving, could not anticipate war.

The shock of realizing that even educated, civilized human beings could descend to such methods of settling their disputes revolutionized post-war Europe. On the one hand there was a

The Allied Delegation pose stiffly in front of the Pullman car in the forest of Compiègne, in which the Armistice ending the First World War was signed. Hitler saw the signing of the Armistice as a symbol of Germany's shame and humiliation at the hands of France, Britain and the United States.

was an unsatisfactory settlement. It was not a compromise between the victor and the vanquished, for the Germans took hardly any part in the deliberations at Versailles. Instead it was a compromise between the partners who had made up the Allied war effort. The French, who had borne the brunt of the fighting in the war and who also wanted to revenge the humiliating defeat they had suffered in the Franco-Prussian war half a century earlier, were in favor of draconian measures that would reduce the German threat for eternity.

Despite the break-up of the Austro-Hungarian Empire the French still counted the Germans as a potential threat and insisted on full reparations for the war from Germany and indefinite occupation of German territory by garrisons from the victorious nations. To the British this seemed both short- sighted and unattractive as a policy. The British had tended to be more anti-French than anti-German over the centuries and, if it were a case of any one power dominating the Continent (a situation which Britain was determined not to allow) they were by no means in favour of France as that power. In the short term, though, the British recalled that their most important trading partner before the war had been Germany and any measures that would impede the recovery of the German economy were against the interests of Britain. In addition, although Zeppelins had managed to bomb English cities and British families had suffered from their own grievous losses in the war, the impact had not been as immediate or long-lasting as in France and the question of forcing huge reparation payments from the Germans was less contentious.

For the Americans, represented in spirit and in person by the ascetic and well-meaning Woodrow Wilson, the war had been a confirmation of the archaic nature of European affairs. Possessed with a messianic purpose to settle Europe anew more on principles suited to America, where institutions were still capable of adaptation and where tradition was something to be discarded rather than applauded, Wilson soon lost patience with the attempt to get his Fourteen Points accepted without amendment. He managed to achieve the establishment of a

strong tendency to try to reassert the primacy of the stable values of the pre-war years, many of which were duly idealized in the process. On the other, there were desperate attempts to reject past values and solutions and instead to look for a 'new' answer. Sometimes these two contradictory tendencies were combined, both philosophically and for the purposes of making common political gains. If Nazism was a 'new' political philosophy, it relied for some of its appeal on its inheritance of traditional German folk values. If the Nazis proposed revolutionary forms of government with one hand, with the other they courted the political support of big businessmen whose own yearnings were for the resurrection of the Germany of Wilhelm II.

The peace that ended the First World War

A great political advance was made by the Nazis in the elections of 1932; here, one of the party's election posters for that year already shows a number of faces which were to become only too familiar to the rest of Germany and the world during the years to follow. As a result of the 1932 elections Hitler was called on to become Chancellor in January 1933.

Hitler's dreams of grandeur also extended to interior decoration. This door to his study in the Reich Chancellery is made of mahogany set in a surround of German marble, surmounted by a plaque bearing the initials 'A.H.'.

signed anyway in 1919) was a continuing feature of German politics.

Italy was one of the first of the World War combatants to undergo post-war political upheaval. The triumph of the Fascist movement under Benito Mussolini in the early 1920s was a portent of things to come. The Russian Tsar had been toppled during the war and the country turned over to revolutionaries. But in Italy this was happening in peacetime. A 'New Order' was being established both with the Bolshevism of the Soviet Union and the Fascism of Italy.

In the political struggles of the 1920s the twin extremes of right and left were confronted by the traditional orthodoxies of conservatism and social democracy. So long as the economies of western Europe prospered, traditionalism prevailed over the novel experiments. There was considerable interest in Communism and Fascism but, at the polls, the old allegiances carried the day.

Collapse and Confrontation

By the end of the decade this confrontation stepped up for two reasons: in the first place, the economic revival made ordinary people seek their own place in the sun and, in the second, that very revival was threatened by its own stupendous success. People came to believe that increasing wealth was a permanent state of affairs and, once having absorbed that idea, they were anxious to benefit permanently from its inevitability. On the stock exchanges of America working people without any reserves of capital traded 'on margin' which was a manifestation of the trend to get rich quick. It was a trend accepted as gospel by manufacturers and farmers alike. Output was rising, investment was increasing, but the market was not expanding fast enough to absorb this output. Agriculture was the first to feel the cold winds of depression. Land had been put under the plow almost regardless of market factors, in the belief that demand for cereals was insatiable. This was to be proven wrong and the toll on farmers and their financiers was heavy. Much the same sequence (which some believed to be a normal cyclical business occurence) infected manufacturing and, with the collapse of the New York

League of Nations, which was to enshrine his faith in a more open relationship between nations.

When the German delegates were summoned to sign the treaty in May 1919 they were appalled at the terms and balked at signing. Since the Allies refused to accept modifications this provoked a government crisis in Berlin which brought into the open all the aspects of the treaty. Germans found themselves unable to accept the implications of the notorious Article 237 'War Guilt' clause which placed all responsibility for the war upon the Germans. Even if Germans were prepared to accept that they bore a major responsibility for the outbreak of the war they regarded themselves as a changed people. The autocratic emperor had given way to a progressive democracy and the Germans in government could not see any way of shouldering the burden of the past and moving into a brighter future. The terms of the Versailles Treaty united the Germans in opposition and this refusal to accept the terms (which had to be

Never forgetful of his Austrian origins, Hitler gazes over a model of his pet project: the development of the town of Linz, where he spent much of his youth, into a huge cultural and administrative metropolis.

Stock Exchange in October 1929 and the failure of the important Credit-Anstalt bank in Vienna in 1931 (whose finances were connected with the old Austro-Hungarian Empire and thus affected most of the newly independent Balkan states), the confidence bubble burst and unemployment soared.

Of the industrial nations of the world Germany and the United States suffered the highest levels of unemployment but Germany's rose earlier and with more dramatic impact. The depression in Germany signalled the collapse of the compromise politics of the democratic Weimar Republic. Still treated as a pariah in Europe, Germany had turned on its own resources, both material and spiritual.

There was no statesman of the stature of Bismarck in Germany to provide Germany with any sense of destiny in the confused period after the War. The great General Ludendorff made a fool of himself by throwing in his lot with an upstart hectoring soap-box orator named Adolf Hitler, who launched an abortive coup, known

as the Beer-Hall Putsch, in Munich in 1923. Marshal Hindenburg, a victor on the Eastern Front early in the war and, with Ludendorff, in charge of operations after 1916, was a limited man of no great charismatic appeal. In any case, although Germans still found it difficult to believe that they had actually *lost* the war (Germany had not been invaded, after all, and they felt that they had been 'tricked' into losing), if anybody was responsible for those defeats, military commanders such as Hindenburg and Ludendorff had to take some of the blame.

In the absence of a Bismarck, the new democratic Weimar Republic had a precarious existence. It was neither able to overcome the problems which the peace treaty imposed on Germany nor able to counter the resentment that was growing over its lack of achievement. Germans were quick to blame the government and the system for the problems that existed. With the arrival of the depression and high unemployment the resentment boiled over and the choice rapidly became one of accepting

traditional political solutions, with all their well-known weaknesses, or experimenting with revolution. Two courses were open for would-be revolutionaries: the Fascism proclaimed by Hitler's Nazi Party or the Communism offered by the admirers of the Soviet Union. Only fifteen years after the Revolution the achievements in Russia were indeed substantial and people in the early 1930s were not aware of all of the horrors to come in the great purges. Indeed, in the 1920s Russia had enjoyed a fairly free atmosphere for a time and German Communists, knowing that their own people were better educated and trained, felt strongly that Communism was a viable alternative to the Weimar Republic.

By the same token, despite the medieval trappings and pageantry of much of the Nazi paraphernalia, it too was a forward-looking movement offering a revolutionary alternative. True, its anti-Semitism was obnoxious to many, but its opposition to capitalism and the aristocracy was almost as pronounced in the years before 1933. What both movements shared in common was a rejection of industrial capitalism and of an aristocratically and professionally controlled government. They also shared a common dependence upon working-class and lower-middle-class support. If the Communists ignored the need for peasant support (and this the Nazis capitalized on), they more than made up for it with the vociferous backing of sections of the intelligentsia. Essentially though, both Communists and Nazis were battling for the same people's allegiance. This goes part of the way towards explaining the extremism of German politics, for had the struggle been between rival classes rather than rival groups within the same classes, the triumph of one side would have led to the extinction of the other. The Nazi-Communist struggles had all of the bitterness of a civil war, of a family struggle.

The German Army in Support

Fortune favored the Nazis. As a result of his popular success, both the industrialists and the military preferred Hitler as an alternative to the Communists. In their ignorance of what was happening to both groups they believed that Hitler and his party could be controlled. But Hitler turned the tables on them. The industrialists needed him more than he needed them and he took advantage of this. The military, whose valiant efforts had created the unified Germany, had been suffering under the constraints of the Treaty of Versailles, which limited the number of soldiers and their equipment. Hitler needed their support but what he offered them in return they found hard to resist: the unilateral abrogation of the Treaty of Versailles.

The German military authorities were by no means entirely seduced by Hitler. Throughout the period of the Third Reich, and sometimes at great personal risk and sacrifice, distinguished military men talked and acted against their nominal commander-in-chief. They did not admire him, neither could they forsake him. After all, an army does not like to be under restrictions and Hitler offered to remove them. Few commanders would prefer to dominate a small army when offered a large one. Again, implicit in Hitler's reliance on the military was the notion that, at some point or other it would be used. And when it came to the time to fight, the German Army wanted to acquit itself nobly, to expunge the humiliation of Versailles.

Peace at any Price

Hitler's Thousand-Year Reich was launched in 1933. It lay in ruins in 1945. In those twelve years were six years of peace, in which Germany was hauled up 'by its bootstraps', its confidence returning with the large-scale armaments and public works expenditures which brought prosperity and an adventurous foreign policy, which not only released Germany from the shackles of Versailles but also showed Hitler to be a profound statesman with an intuitive grasp of the weakness of Germany's former adversaries. This policy also brought six years of war, in which the achievements of the peace were to grow with German victories on land in Europe and North Africa and were to disappear more rapidly as the military balance swung in favor of the Allies.

So long as Hitler's policies and strategies were successful few questioned his direction. In the years of peace and the first years of war his achievements were considerable. Few noticed

The war of action: nowhere was German foresight in planning a fast-moving campaign better demonstrated than in Rommel's tactics in the Desert War. Here, German artillery moves into position for the second, decisive siege of Tobruk, the collapse of which on June 21, 1942 was a hard blow to Allied morale.

The arms factories and
designers of Germany
had made the Wehrmacht
the best-equipped fighting
force in the world by 1939.
This propaganda
photograph of an artillery
workshop is captioned 'In
the workshop of the
giants'.

Huge sums of money were lavished on the tactical bomber force of the new Luftwaffe, which had its first combat experience during the Spanish Civil War. This factory is turning out Heinkel medium bombers, in which Göring was to place great faith for the advance through Europe and the final assault on Britain.

any inherent weaknesses or stopped to ask where these achievements were taking them. There were good reasons for this. Hitler and his close supporters would not tolerate criticism. The flamboyance which was part of everyday life at the court of Nazism covered an essential conformity. Nazism was not a profound philosophy: its thinkers were conspicuous for the shallowness of their ideas. Constructive criticism could not be allowed because it would expose this sham. As for questioning the general direction of Nazi policies, Hitler had given his answer in naming his regime the Thousand-Year Reich. Designed to counter the threat of Bolshevism – a threat as much to racial purity as to political ideas – and to increase the power and influence of the German people, his policy direction was best obscured in rhetoric.

It was in such an atmosphere that the policy of appeasement was born. Never an article of faith, appeasement was adopted by Britain as a practical way of dealing with Germany. Many Britons believed the Versailles Treaty had been harsh and the Germans were right to rail against it. They could not appreciate the French obsession with Germany and considered that to

accept some of Hitler's demands would achieve two objectives: a better balance of power on the continent, where France had been concentrating her energies on encircling Germany with hostile neighbors and a more stable Germany, better able to trade with Britain, more useful as a bastion against Communism and, ultimately, less overtly aggressive when it could gain its just demands by negotiation. Put generously, it was a noble if flawed vision. More unkindly, it was naive and cowardly.

There remained a genuine desire to keep the peace, almost at any cost. The United States had withdrawn from world affairs in disgust at the end of the First World War. In Europe the new generation was convinced that the First World War had not solved any problems, so what likelihood was there that another bout of carnage would settle everything? They were sure the problems were not military and national but economic and social.

While the 'democracies' were speaking with two voices the Third Reich under Adolf Hitler appeared purposeful and formidable. From the occupation of the Rhineland in 1936, in defiance of the demilitarization clauses of the peace

An image of Hitler's new Germany: this propaganda photograph of a young German pilot in his trainer appeared in *Signal*.

treaty, Hitler's policies demonstrated both daring and success. His initiatives were not opposed. The *anschluss* with Austria, which had the effect of wiping out overnight much of the value of the expensive and well-worked out Czech defenses, was greeted with diplomatic notes but no hostile action. When the 'democracies' did force a halt over Czechoslovakia in 1938 they eventually capitulated at Munich to Hitler's hectoring and their consciences were salved by the leaving of a rump Czech state to exist without any means of defending itself. When the rump of Czechoslovakia was unceremoniously absorbed in March 1939 they sighed and agreed that Herr Hitler could not be trusted. By now, having given Germany a virtually free hand in Eastern Europe, they noticed how she had grown and they worried. In a trice, a Poland which they could never assist in war was given written guarantees of her territorial integrity. In September 1939, despite some wriggling and squirming, Britain and France took the bit between the teeth and honored those guarantees by declaring, if not waging, war against Hitler's Germany.

The War of Action

The Second World War was the most dramatic event in modern history. Unlike the First World War, the Second World War really was global and was a war of movement, of action. Unlike the First World War, in which the partners fell against each other rather bewildered by the collapse of rational efforts to maintain the peace, the Second World War was a crusade. For the Allies, the Nazis were a perfect symbol of evil. For the Axis, the Allies were surviving examples of the decadence they had sought to root out and destroy in their own countries. The war had other elements that made it dramatic. The tactics of warfare evolved by the Germans, which brought stunning victories in Poland and in western Europe, challenged all the resources that the Allies could muster. The Allies lost the first round but they learned some lessons. The Germans, gloating over their tremendous achievements, followed the strategy of Hitler as if it were infallible and in this lay the seeds of their defeat. For, while Hitler had the strategic

The battlecruiser *Scharnhorst* and her sister *Gneisenau* (background) at sea. Expansion of the Kriegsmarine was an important part of Hitler's rebuilding of German confidence and prestige, but these ships also had a role to play in his long-term plans.

daring that many of his commanders lacked, he was a poor tactician and could not adapt to minor tactical reverses. This first became very visible in the war against Russia but, with hindsight, we can see that it existed even earlier. Hitler had become so accustomed to achieving rapid results that he either lost patience or nerve when the results did not occur according to his timetable. As early as the Battle for France he was showing a dangerous tendency to wobble uneasily when it came to taking tactical decisions. He did not vacillate during the Battle of Britain: he simply gave up the strategy when the tactics did not appear to work. This was the fatal flaw which, because of the fear he had built up in people who surrounded him, was never corrected. Hitler and his court were infected with a collective paranoia and when success did not come easily, treachery was suspected. If Hitler was unable to deal with a slow moving military campaign he was quite unequipped to accept reverses. His furious insistence that not an inch of territory be relinquished lost him a brave army at Stalingrad. The same insane *idée fixe* condemned thousands to premature death or dismemberment.

Hitler's Military Dream

Hitler was an amateur strategist. So was Winston Churchill. Both men had flashes of intuitition that far surpassed the insight of their military subordinates. Neither man had the intimate knowledge of tactics or the staying power to command the movement of armies effectively. Churchill was a victim of a system of government that constricted his urge to dominate the military scene. Hitler was free of such constraints and he must bear the blame for the strategy pursued.

It is impossible to say how much of Europe the Nazis could have dominated realistically on a long-term basis. Certainly they could have been the dominant power for a long time had Hitler been prepared to compromise. He often proclaimed that he was prepared to discuss peace, but this was believed by very few. In the context of a continuing struggle his realistic ambitions gave way to delusions of grandeur. With Russia, America and Britain fighting

EINSATZ
DER DEUTSCHEN KRIEGSMARINE

Considered by the Germans as one of the most important aircraft in the Luftwaffe's huge bomber arm, the Ju 88 – the so-called 'wonder bomber' – was too lightly armed to withstand British fighter attacks during the Battle of Britain.

JU 88

JUNKERS FLUGZEUG- UND -MOTORENWERKE A.-G. DESSAU

against him the odds were always poor. Need Hitler have fought against America? Would he have been Hitler if he hadn't?

The factories and designers gave Hitler's army the best weapons that money could buy. Even during the days of the Weimar Republic design work had gone on with the help of the Soviet Union and other countries. From 1936 the Spanish Civil War provided the testing ground. By September 1939 the Wehrmacht had confidence in its weapons, tactics and training – it was without doubt the most competent and best-equipped army in the world.

The air force or Luftwaffe had only been created after Hitler's denunciation of the Versailles Treaty but, as with the Wehrmacht, money had been spent lavishly to provide the best aircraft. The Luftwaffe was designed to support the Army and tactical bombing was its main offensive role. Although the latest fighters were as good as anything flying elsewhere the bombers were poorly designed for anything but the tactical role. The flamboyance of the Luftwaffe's commander Herman Göring did not foster a profound approach to these problems, and the fact that the successes in Spain were achieved against practically no opposition was soon forgotten.

U-Boats and First Victories

The Navy, rechristened the Kriegsmarine under Hitler, came a long way behind the other two services. This was partly because Germany's enemies were seen to be the land powers France and Russia, but it was also caused by the unhappy fate of the Navy after the Armistice. Although the High Seas Fleet had served with distinction in 1914-1918 the entire fleet surrendered meekly and had then scuttled itself. The need to erase this memory had much to do with the long-term plans drawn up by the Navy. Admiral Raeder envisaged a powerful surface fleet which would avoid battle with the British Navy and instead prey on shipping. A fleet of U-Boats would be built as well, but they were seen as only part of a grandiose scheme, rather than the major striking force.

The nine campaigns and battles which make up this book have been chosen, not only for their

AUTO UNION

The cult of personality had played a vital part in the organization of the Nazi party, as this National Socialist election poster demonstrates: 'Who is the most important man in the world?' But his tendency to run war-time Germany on the lines of a medieval court led Hitler to make many disastrous military decisions.

Hitler savours initial triumph: taking the salute at the victory parade of the German 8th Army in Warsaw on October 5, 1939.

decisive nature, but also for the way in which they illustrate both the thinking of Hitler and the Nazi war machine and the good and bad qualities of that machine. In each of these areas Hitler's influence can be seen, sometimes as an inspiration but just as often as an evil genius. In some cases the Nazi system was stunningly triumphant initially, as in France and Russia, but ultimately the enemies of the Third Reich proved more dogged, more cunning and more flexible in their responses.

The Reich at Bay

On land the Russians proved to be far tougher and more inventive than Hitler and his fellow ideologues could credit. The 'effete' demo- cracies of the West suffered for their appease- ment and isolation, but proved capable of far greater exertions than the militarized state of Germany. The essential shallowness of Nazi dogma led to such absurdities as the refusal to recruit women factory-workers, and the dis- missal of nuclear physics as 'Jew science'. But even if we disregard the follies of a government run more like a medieval court than a modern corporate state, German scientists and designers failed to use their talents to the greatest benefit. Hitler was fascinated by gadgets, and ordered 100-ton tanks at the expense of the medium types needed to stem the Russian advance. The relatively simple 'electro-U-Boat' was held up to allow designers to try to produce hydrogen- peroxide motors with endurance measured in tens of miles rather than hundreds. In elec- tronic warfare the failures to co-ordinate scientific research with tactical requirements and intelligence reports produced the biggest setbacks of all.

Nevertheless the story of the rise and fall of the Thousand-Year Reich is a fascinating story of achievements against all odds. Despite being hemmed in between enormous Allied armies in the East and West, Germany held out until 1945, and inflicted enormous losses. Despite fearful attacks by British and American bombers, the civilian population continued to work for Hitler, just as his soldiers fought to the end. It was a remarkable testimony to his hypnotic leadership.

First the bombers, then the tanks, and finally the German infantry poured through the Low Countries, where token defences of Holland and Belgium received no effective support from the French or British.

BATTLE FOR FRANCE:
LIGHTNING WAR

Hitler's instinct for detecting his opponent's weaknesses triumphed over his general's caution, and his armies smashed the ill-trained British and French forces.

THE GERMANS CALLED it Blitzkrieg, 'lightning war', and that was just what it was, as Poland had discovered in September 1939. First came the Junkers 87s in waves – the notorious 'Stuka' dive bombers – with their alarming and demoralizing wail, the so called 'Jericho trombone' effect. Then came the Panzer tank divisions, rolling fast, hitting hard, flattening pockets of opposition, and close in their tracks came the artillery regiments and infantry brigades, 'mopping up' and consolidating the newly-taken positions.

Blitzkrieg was a new and terrifying concept of warfare, a body blow to all who stood in its way. Colonel-General Heinz Guderian, one of its greatest exponents, had a favourite phrase to express its philosophy: 'Klotzen, nicht Kleckern', a slang term roughly meaning 'boot 'em, don't spatter 'em'. And it was Guderian and his Panzer colleagues who between May and June 1940 swept through France in a devastating Blitzkrieg and literally booted the Allies into the English Channel.

Nine months previously Hitler, delighted with the smashing success in Poland, had ordered his generals to prepare a similar offensive on the West. The Germany Army High Command had come up with a rather half hearted plan which they titled *Fall Gelb* – 'Plan Yellow'. It bore a strong resemblance to the Schlieffen Plan of 1914, so that it was not new, and its object was not primarily to destroy Allied resistance. It was intended principally to cut through Belgium towards Ghent and Bruges, establishing bases from which to strike at Britain and at the same time protecting the Ruhr against enemy attack through Belgium.

Hitler was impatient to fight an autumn/winter campaign, and he began to tinker with 'Plan Yellow' himself. Besides the Belgian strike, he decided, he would deploy his forces to take the line of the Meuse to the north and south of Liège and push on towards Rheims and Amiens. By the end of October he had issued a directive that the army should 'destroy the Allied forces in the sector north of the Somme and break through to the Channel coast'.

The Belgian offensive was to fall on the shoulders of General von Bock, commanding the Germany Army Group 'B'. Operations on the southern sector, facing the Ardennes and Luxembourg, would be left to Army Group 'A', commanded by General Gerd von Rundstedt. Elaborating further on 'Plan Yellow' Hitler conceived what he called his 'new idea'; this would involve von Rundstedt in driving through a gap in the Belgian Ardennes which was guarded only by neutral Luxembourg, and carrying on to take the French frontier town of Sedan, which lay on the upper Meuse. He would then break through the Maginot Line in that area and split the whole French front.

General von Rundstedt and his brilliant Chief-of-Staff General von Manstein were far from happy with 'Plan Yellow' from its conception, and simultaneously with Hitler's 'new idea' were making new plans of their own. They wanted Army Group 'A' to be reinforced until it was strong enough to make a sweeping movement right through France, crossing the Meuse south of Namur and continuing in the direction of Arras and Boulogne; thus they would contain the Allied armies, forcing them up into Belgium and onto the coast.

Manstein's Memorandum

In November, Manstein called in Guderian and outlined the idea to him. Guderian, who had commanded the XIX Panzer Corps in Poland, was at that time principally concerned in planning future operations in the West, and listened eagerly to what Manstein proposed. After a lengthy study of maps in the light of his memories of the terrain from the First World War Guderian told Manstein that his operation could in fact be carried out.

'The only condition I attached' he said in his memoirs, 'was that a sufficient number of armored and motorized divisions must be employed, if possible all of them'.

As a result of this meeting, Manstein wrote a memorandum to High Command which was approved and counter-signed by General von Rundstedt. It was received on December 4, 1939 but as Guderian puts it 'by no means joyfully'.

To begin with, High Command wanted to

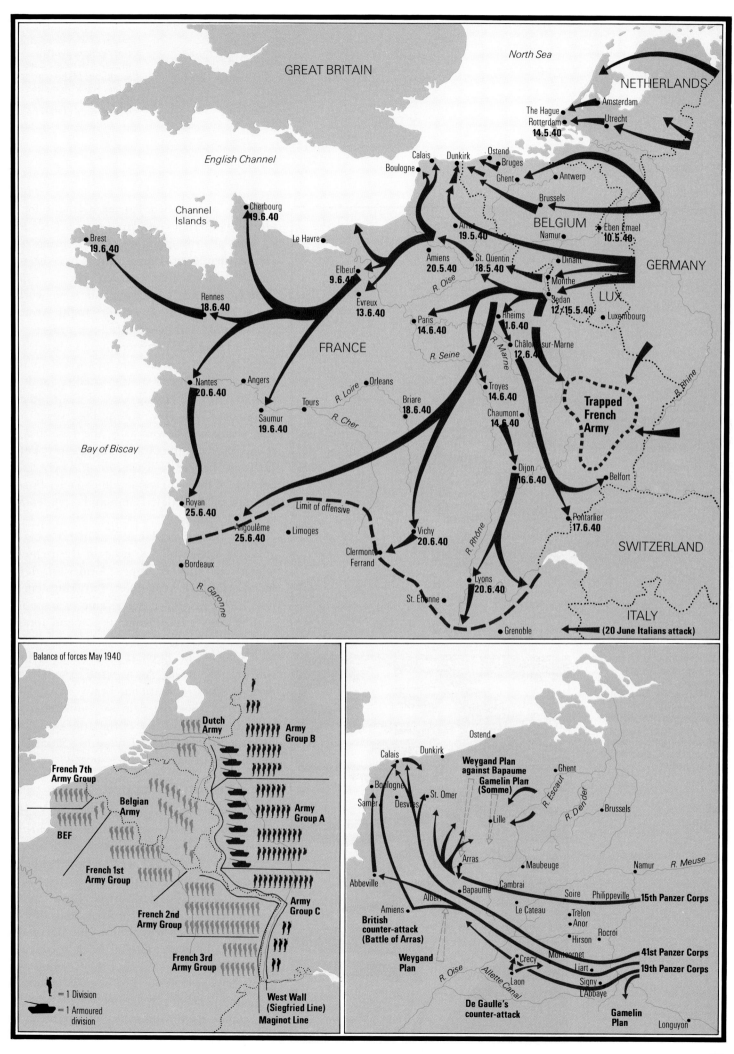

GREAT BRITAIN

North Sea

NETHERLANDS

Amsterdam

The Hague
Rotterdam
14.5.40
Utrecht

English Channel

Calais
Dunkirk
Ostend
Bruges
Boulogne
Ghent
Antwerp

Brussels

BELGIUM
Eben Emael
10.5.40

Channel
Islands

Cherbourg
19.6.40

Le Havre

Arras
19.5.40
Namur

Brest
19.6.40

Elbeuf
9.6.40

Amiens
20.5.40
St. Quentin
18.5.40

Dinant
Monthe

GERMANY

LUX

Sedan
12./15.5.40
Luxembourg

R. Oise

Evreux
13.6.40

Rennes
18.6.40

Rheims
1.6.40

FRANCE

Paris
14.6.40

R. Seine

R. Marne

Châlons-sur-Marne
12.6.4

R. Rhine

**Trapped
French
Army**

Nantes
20.6.40

Angers

R. Loire

Orleans

Briare
18.6.40

Troyes
14.6.40

Tours

R. Cher

Saumur
19.6.40

Chaumont
14.6.40

Belfort

Bay of Biscay

Dijon
16.6.40

Pontarlier
17.6.40

Royan
25.6.40

Limit of offensive

Angoulême
25.6.40

Limoges

Clermont
Ferrand

Vichy
20.6.40

R. Rhône

SWITZERLAND

Bordeaux

R. Garonne

St. Etienne

Lyons
20.6.40

ITALY

Grenoble

(20 June Italians attack)

Balance of forces May 1940

Dutch Army

Army Group B

**French 7th
Army Group**

**Belgian
Army**

BEF

Army Group A

**French 1st
Army Group**

**French 2nd
Army Group**

**Army
Group C**

**French 3rd
Army Group**

**West Wall
(Siegfried Line)**

Maginot Line

👤 = 1 Division

🚂 = 1 Armoured
division

Ostend

Calais
Dunkirk

**Weygand Plan
against Bapaume**

**Gamelin Plan
(Somme)**

Ghent

R. Escaut

R. Den der

Boulogne
St. Omer

Lille

Brussels

Samer
Desvies

Abbeville

Arras

Maubeuge

Namur

R. Meuse

Cambrai

15th Panzer Corps

Albert
Bapaume
Soire
Philippeville

**British
counter-attack
(Battle of Arras)**

Amiens

Le Cateau

Trelon

**Weygand
Plan**

R. Oise

Crecy

Montcornet

Anor

Rocroi

Hirson

41st Panzer Corps

Laon

Liart

Signy

19th Panzer Corps

**De Gaulle's
counter-attack**

L'Abbaye

**Gamelin
Plan**

Longuyon

33

PzKpw Panzer 1A (above) proved itself in the Spanish Civil War. Then in 1940, backed by German artillery (right), it spearheaded the drive which in a few days cut down French defences and swept the Allies into the Channel.

use only one or two Panzer divisions for the attack; Guderian considered such a force to be so weak as to be pointless. Any splitting of his already slender tank forces would have been the 'greatest mistake that we could make'.

Since Poland, Guderian had been working for a re-organization of the Light Armored Divisions. It had eventually been ordered that they be changed to Panzer divisions bearing the numbers 6 to 9, while the motorized infantry divisions had been made smaller and less unwieldy by removing one of their infantry regiments. This new, streamlined strike force was hampered however by the fact that the re-equipping of the tank regiments with Panzer III's and Panzer IV's was going slowly, partly because of limited production capacity but also because of the High Command's tendency to hoard new tanks.

Now, it seemed, High Command were not going to make full use even of the regiments which were fully equipped. Guderian, despite his disapproval, kept quiet, but Manstein did not. In his insistence he became so unpopular that he was removed from his post and appointed commanding general of an Infantry Corps – his request to be given at least a Panzer Corps was turned down. As a result, the German Army's 'finest operational brain' as Guderian called him, took the field as commander of a corps in the third wave of the attack, although in the end it was largely due to his initiative that the operation was such a success.

Plan Yellow Scrapped

By a stroke of fate and the flouting of strict orders not to fly by night over enemy territory, a Luftwaffe officer-courier brought about the scrapping of the 'Plan Yellow' 'Schlieffen' scheme. Carrying important papers referring to 'Plan Yellow', he was forced down in mid-winter near the Belgian frontier, and although he managed to destroy most of the documents, enough intelligence filtered back to convince Allied High Command that the Germans were going to repeat their 1914 strategy and strike through the north of Belgium.

German High Command naturally had to assume that the French and the British knew

all about their plans, so that the deposed General Manstein, reporting to Hitler in person before taking over his Infantry Corps, was surprised when the Führer asked him to repeat his previous proposition and took it seriously. It appeared that the German Commander-in-Chief, Field Marshal von Brauchitsch, and his Chief-of-Staff General Halder had been playing war-games and had realised that Guderian was right in his 'all out force' policy. Army Group 'A' would have to be strengthened. On February 7, 1940, Guderian demonstrated his points during a war game held at Coblenz.

'One Smashing, Decisive Blow'

During the course of this he proposed that on the fifth day of the campaign a strong armored and motorized attack be made to force a crossing of the Meuse near Sedan with the object of achieving a breakthrough which would then be continued towards Amiens. General Halder denounced these ideas as 'senseless'. He was worried about Guderian's theories on 'single handed' tank warfare; while he could envisage tanks taking the Meuse crossings and perhaps securing bridgeheads, he felt that they should then wait for the infantry forces to catch up so that *einen rangierten Gesamtangriff* – 'a properly marshalled attack in mass' – could be launched on perhaps the ninth or tenth day of the campaign.

Guderian 'contradicted him strongly'. He argued that all the available power of the German armor, though limited, should be used in one smashing blow at one decisive point, 'to drive a wedge so deep and wide that we need not worry about our flanks; and then immediately to exploit any successes gained without bothering to wait for the infantry corps'.

For the tank expert was fully aware that the French High Command was wedded to outmoded ideas, and felt that he could safely gamble on French defense being based almost solely on fortification in the shape of the Maginot Line – which to a large extent it was. The Generals polished the new strike plan: they would use Manstein's suggestion of a southward swing to trap the Allies in Belgium or on the north coast, coupled with Hitler's proposed exploitation of the Ardennes gap and the taking of Sedan to establish a crucial bridgehead across the Meuse, plus heavy Luftwaffe air-cover for particular objectives.

By February 24, the new operation was ready. Brauchitsch had decided that seven of the Wehrmacht's ten Panzer divisions should force crossings on the Meuse between Dinant and Sedan, while he altered the ratio of force between Army Groups 'A' and 'B' drastically. Rundstedt's Group 'A' had grown from 22 to $45\frac{1}{2}$ divisions. The final plan was given the ominous code name 'Sichelschnitt' – 'the sweep of a scythe'.

During the winter months in which Hitler and his generals had debated the attack on France, France herself had shivered, wondering which way the blow would fall. As the German High Command had predicted, the French commander in Chief, General Gamelin, had kept most of the troops under his command, including the nine divisions of the British Expeditionary Force under its general, Viscount Gort – along the Maginot line. There they mixed concrete to shore up the fortifications which in any case guarded nothing but Alsace and Lorraine in the east. The line ended opposite the south east corner of Belgium and the British and French spent a great deal of useless effort in trying to extend it to afford some cover north-westwards to the Channel.

German Armor on the Loose

On paper the French army was powerful with more tanks than the Germans but neither Gamelin nor his four immediate aides, Generals Bineau, Georges, Weygand and Billotte had much idea of armored strategy and their forces were scattered in small pockets in an effort to plug holes in the national defenses.

French air support was negligible for aircraft production had been held up by strikes and nationalization, and the British were holding their precious Spitfires back for the impending defense of Britain; only a few Hurricane squadrons operated in the north. The Germans on the other hand had learned to use air power as an integral part of their

Crack troops of the Waffen SS Regiment *Gross Deutschland* dropped behind Allied lines to harry the Belgians and Dutch, drawing attention away from the German armored thrust to the south.
Rare film footage (left) shows a paratrooper leaping from his Junkers 52 aircraft.

blitzkrieg forces, Heinkel III's bombing behind the enemy lines while the Stuka dive bombers supported the attacking armor directly.

By the end of the first week in May the Germans were on battle alert and ready to move. General Guderian had resumed command of the XIX Panzer Corps which was to form the southward wing of the German armored group under the overall command of General von Kleist and drew up his three divisions of the Corps in line for the thrust through Luxembourg and south Belgium. In the center was the 1st Panzer Division commanded by General Kirchner and behind it the corps artillery headquarters and main bulk of the corps anti-aircraft artillery. To start with the 1st Panzer Division was to be in the van. On the right of the 1st Panzer was the 2nd Panzer Division, commanded by General Veiel, and on its left the 10th Panzer Division and the *Gross-Deutschland* Infantry Regiment, under the command of General Schaal.

Guderian knew his subordinates well: 'They shared my belief', he said, 'that once armored formations are out on the loose they must be given the green light to the very end of the road. In our case this was – the Channel! That was a very clear inspiration to every one of our soldiers, and he could follow it even though he might receive no orders for long periods of time once the attack was launched'.

Paratroop Ploy

The first sign of the German attack came at dawn on the morning of May 10. A battalion of Waffen S.S. Infantry Regiment *Gross Deutschland* was dropped from 'Storch' aircraft to land behind the Belgians at Witry, west of Martelange. Some landed on the actual roof of Fort Eben-Emael, a key Belgian fortification on the Meuse. Glider born paratroops landed around Rotterdam and the Hague, while others were unloaded from military aircraft at the besieged airfield of Waalhaven. And all through the early morning Heinkel bombers rained their daily loads on railway junctions and air bases in north eastern France.

The paratroops were relatively few in number, and their main purpose was to draw the

French and British forces' attention away from the Ardennes gap. The plot worked beautifully; General Gamelin immediately sent his crack regiments, along with Lord Gort's British Expeditionary Force under the overall command of General Billotte, to meet what he thought would be the spearhead of the German attack in Belgium. General Giraud, commanding the French 7th Army, raced up through Belgium into southern Holland taking with him the best of France's armored units and most of the available Allied air-cover.

Guderian's Breakthrough

It was said that when Hitler heard the news he almost 'wept for joy'. At 0530 hours on May 10, meanwhile, Guderian and the 1st Panzer Division had crossed the Luxembourg border near Wallendorf and headed for Martelange, crashing through the flimsy Belgian border defenses and joining up with the air-borne Infantry Regiment 'G.D.' troops who had dropped there earlier. The only thing hampering a deep thrust into Belgium was the state of the roads, some of which had been mined and partly demolished by the fleeing Belgians, and mountainous terrain made the craters hard to by-pass. The roads were repaired during the night, however, and towards noon on May 11 the 1st Panzers, headed by their tanks, were able to roll forward. The 2nd Panzer Division was already fighting near Strainchamps, while the 10th Panzer Division had swept through Habay-la-Neuve and Etalle to hit the French 2nd Cavalry Division and the 3rd Colonial Infantry Division. Amazingly, some of the French cavalry units were actually mounted on horseback, and when the modern German armor met them it was hard to tell which side was the more startled.

During the rest of the day the three Panzer Divisions drove on almost exactly as planned, taking Neufchateau from its defending Belgian Chasseurs Ardennais without trouble, taking Bertrix, and attacking Bouillon as dusk was falling, although the French managed to hold the town throughout the night; the 2nd Panzer Division had taken Libramount. On May 12, Whit Sunday, Guderian's XIX Corps had

The French Char B tank (left and below) was well-armored and robust, but the one-man turret and the fixed forward gun reduced its tactical effectiveness.

Right: German 105mm howitzer advancing over a pontoon bridge. This was the standard divisional support artillery piece and remained in service until 1945. Despite the emphasis on mechaniza-tion this gun is being towed by a horse team.

bridged the Semois near Bouillon despite Allied air attacks, and by the evening the 1st and 10th Panzer Divisions had occupied the northern bank of the Meuse and had captured the historic fortress city of Sedan. After brisk fighting the French defenders feared a German outflanking movement to isolate them and evacuated the town, and following this with-drawal there was a general retreat by the Allies from the east bank of the Meuse as far north as Dinant in Belgium.

On May 13, after establishing his corps head-quarters in La Chapelle, Guderian watched the Luftwaffe blast the last remnants of defense along the Meuse, and later that day crossed in the first assault craft. There he saw the attack by the 1st Rifle Regiment and by the Infantry Regiment 'G.D.' 'developing as though it were being carried out on maneuvers'. In two days, through the capture of Sedan and the routing of the French General Huntziger's 2nd Army's left wing, Guderian had made the all important breakthrough planned by Hitler back in December.

Meanwhile to the north the Allies were moving slowly through Belgium along the line of the river Dyle. The advance guard was

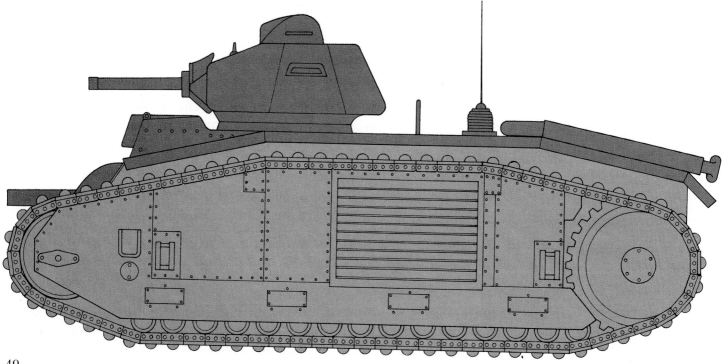

France's crack armored cavalry corps under General Prioux, followed by General Blanchard's 1st Army. Blanchard had planned to take up positions on the Dyle, but on May 13, Prioux's Cavalry Corps clashed headlong with the German XVI Panzer Corps and the superior training of the Germans, plus heavy support from Stukas, carried the day.

On 1st Army's right flank, General Corap's 9th Army was ranged along the Meuse west bank southwards from Namur, but despite this the Germans were able to establish bridgeheads across the Meuse north of Dinant on May 13 and 14, largely due to the skill and judgement of the commander of 7th Panzer Division, the young and relatively untried General Erwin Rommel.

In the south, 1st Panzer Division had fought their way up the Meuse's southern escarpment and had taken Marfée Wood, although 10th Panzer Division had established little more than a foothold and 2nd Panzer Division had been dispersed and was busy reassembling. The 1st Panzers now had a bridgehead on the south bank stretching for three miles along the Meuse.
The French 7th Tank Battalion made a feeble effort to counter attack, along with the mis-managed 3rd Armored Division whose commander, a raw young officer, panicked and

strung the force out in a series of weak pecking jabs at the superior German forces.

In a last frantic effort to destroy the bridgehead established by 1st Panzer Division, the Allies despatched almost every available tactical bomber; but the planes were nearly all obsolete and the German anti-aircraft defenses were uncannily deadly. Allied air losses were enormous – 150 aircraft lost – so that in a few hours all effective Allied air offensive power in France was destroyed. The anti-aircraft commander, Colonel von Hippel, was rewarded with the Knight's Cross.

By the afternoon of May 15, Guderian was eager to be off to his great objective – the Channel ports to the west. Leaving 10th Panzer Division momentarily behind to guard

The 21cm gun formed part of the Corps Artillery. An elderly design, it was slow to emplace and remove and was soon overtaken by events.

A French super-heavy railroad gun opens fire at dawn. Guns of this type had a maximum range of some 25 miles but were to be of little use in the mobile warfare of 1940.

the Meuse bridgeheads until relief arrived, he headed 1st and 2nd Panzer Divisions directly west, and the following day reached Marle and Dercy – 55 miles west of Sedan. Driving to what appeared to be the deserted market place of Dercy, Guderian ordered his men to go through the houses surrounding the square. Within a few minutes they had rounded up several hundred French prisoners from a number of units, all of whom were obviously amazed at the speed with which the Germans had pushed forward. Even better, a tank company from Colonel Charles De Gaulle's division – which had been reported in the area north of Laon – drove unsuspectingly into the town later in the day and was captured almost without incident. Guderian's shock tactics were paying off.

To the north, Rommel's 7th Panzer Division had crossed the Meuse at dawn on May 14, while Stukas demolished all hope of counter attack. He lacerated the French 9th Army, destroying its supply and disrupting communications, so that by nightfall Rommel's entire force was four miles west of the river and the 5th Panzer Division hard on his heels. Corap informed his group commander, General Billotte, that he could not hold 9th Army together, and by dusk the French force was straggling backwards before

the advancing German might. The French 1st Armored Division made an attempt to cover the rear of the retreat, but was caught by a detachment of Rommel's Panzers near Flavion. Joined by 5th Panzer Division, the Germans pounded the French force until only seventeen of their tanks were left intact.

On the night of May 15, General Giraud, arriving at French 9th Army headquarters at Vervins to take over command from Corap, discovered to his horror that there was virtually no army left; General Reinhardt's XLI Panzer Corps had ripped through what remained of the defenses and was a mere 11 miles away at Montcornet. Guderian had caught up with XLI Panzer Corps in the town before going on to his bloodless victory at Dercy'.

Ironic Setback

And now came the first set back in the five-day sweep into Allied territory, ironically not from any action on the part of the Allies but from the German High Command itself. On arrival at Montcornet, Guderian had heard that an order for a general halt had been received from his immediate superior General von Kleist, but had in any case decided to push on to Dercy to 'use up the last drop of his gasoline.

On the morning of May 17 he received a terse message from Panzer Group headquarters; von Kleist would meet him promptly at 0700 hours. When von Kleist arrived his face was black with rage. Without even wishing Guderian a good morning he immediately tore into him for disobeying orders, totally neglecting to mention the success of XIX Panzer Corps so far. When von Kleist paused for breath, Guderian snapped crisply to attention and asked to be relieved of his command. Equally crisply, though somewhat taken aback, von Kleist agreed, and Guderian returned to his quarters and summoned General Veiel in order to hand over to him. He then sent a radio message to Commander-in-Chief von Rundstedt telling him what had happened, only to receive an immediate reply telling him to stay where he was.

Later that day Colonel-General List, head

The Mauser Gewehr 98 rifle, in 7.92mm caliber, was the standard rifle of the German Army from 1898 to 1945.

Panzergefreiter France 1940. The special black uniform designed for the new tank arm was also a practical garment for the crews. By 1940 the beret was being replaced by a black forage cap. The death's head collar patches were distinctions for armored formations, with pink piping (*waffenfarbe*) for tank crews.

of the German 12th Army, arrived and told Guderian that his resignation would not be accepted, and that the orders to stop the advance had come from Hitler himself and therefore must be obeyed. But he had a let-out for Guderian: 'reconnaissance in force' would continue to be carried out by Guderian's Panzers, though 'corps headquarters must in all circumstances remain where it is, so that it may easily be reached'.

It was an almost overt invitation to the Panzer commander to carry on his advance, and Guderian was not slow to interpret it liberally.

Hitler had, in fact, been swayed by the same views as General Halder in his original interpretation of the Manstein plan – he was worried that the infantry was not able to keep up and that the armored units might therefore be caught by a sudden surprise attack from the French. He need not have worried. On May 15 General Gamelin had had to admit to Defense Minister Daladier that he had no reserves left, and that the French army was virtually finished. Four days later he was replaced as supreme commander by the 73 year-old General Weygand, though the appointment achieved nothing but delay in re-organizing the scattered French troops. And on May 16 the Prime Minister Paul Reynaud had summoned Winston Churchill to Paris for a panic conference – Churchill having become Prime Minister of Britain on May 10. Apart from promises to send RAF fighter squadrons as soon as possible, Churchill too had achieved nothing.

Before the order to halt had been received, 1st Panzer Division had reached and taken Ribémont on the Oise and Crécy on the Serre, while 10th Panzer Division, catching up rapidly, had reached Saulces-Monclin, and on the evening of May 17 a bridgehead had been thrown across the Oise near Moy, some 70 miles from Sedan. On the move again, Guderian's 1st and 2nd Panzers now reached St Quentin and crossed the Oise and the Somme near Peronne and on May 19 drove across the First World War Somme battlefield. There they skirmished briefly with Colonel De Gaulle's 4th Armored Division, which succeeded in reaching within a mile of Guderian's advanced headquarters in Holnon Wood, before being beaten off.

Apart from de Gaulle's attempt, no real effort had been made by the Allies to strike at the rapidly rolling German armor. Billotte had withdrawn what were left of his troops from Belgium in an attempt to flank the Germans to the north, while Weygand's main force lined the Somme on the south side, but the moves were vain.

The British Hit Back

On May 20 the Allied forces were completely cut in two, for 1st Panzer Division had taken Amiens by noon, while 2nd Panzer captured Abbeville in the evening and at dusk reached Noyelles on the Atlantic coast after a lightning drive of 60 miles that day.

Resistance had been sporadic, and Guderian met real personal danger only once, at Amiens, when his artillery was attacked mistakenly by German aircraft.

'It was perhaps an unfriendly action on our part' he wrote later, 'but our flank opened fire and brought down one of the careless machines. The crew of two floated down by parachute and were unpleasantly surprised to find me waiting for them on the ground. When the more disagreeable part of our conversation was over I fortified the two young men with a glass of champagne.'

Rommel's 7th Panzer Division, meanwhile, had reached Cambrai on the evening of May 18, and here the young general paused to rest his men and bring up supplies, before travelling on during the following night towards Arras, where the British rear headquarters was being hastily evacuated. The position of the British Expeditionary Force was perilous in the extreme, a fact only too clearly realised by Lord Gort, at his headquarters at Wahagnies.

Seven of his nine divisions were arrayed along the Scheldt, and even if they could be moved their withdrawal would leave a further gap through which the enemy could penetrate. Strong enemy forces were moving round the British right flank between Arras and the Somme, and Gort had a total of only four days'

The Young Lion. Erwin Rommel was a junior General in the Battle for France. But the flair and determination which later distinguished him in the Western Desert showed through – particularly in the battle for Arras. Here, in peaked cap, he consults with General Hoth, later thwarted at Stalingrad.

supplies and enough ammunition for one more battle. Then, on May 19, Gort was visited by General Sir Edmund Ironside, Chief of the Imperial General Staff. Ironside told Gort that only a concerted attack in the direction of Amiens, supported if possible by the French, would prevent the British Expeditionary Force from being surrounded and either captured or wiped out.

Gort had two divisions in hand, the 50th and the 5th, and if he could get co-operation from General Weygand in attacking from the south he might at least keep open a corridor to the coast. Ironside himself went in search of General Billotte and found him at Lens with General Blanchard, commander of the French 1st Army. Both men were shattered, physically and emotionally, and in a state of acute nervous depression. General Ironside, a large and irascible man, was in no mood to tolerate such dithering. Grabbing Billotte by the collar of his tunic he shook him and told him: 'You must make a plan! Attack at once to the south with all your forces on Amiens'.

Early on the morning of May 20, the British 1st Army Tank Brigade and the 5th Division were ordered to Vimy, to the north of Arras, to join up with the 50th Northumbrian Division for an attack in order to aid the garrison at Arras and attempt to hold the German advance. The group was to come under the command of Major General Harold Franklyn, commander-in-chief of the 5th Division, and was code named 'Frankforce'. The 1st Army Tank Brigade had had little time for re-equipping since moving down from Belgium, and when it reached Vimy at dawn on May 21 it boasted only 58 Mark I infantry tanks and 16 Mark II 'Matildas'. Of the 50th Northumbrian Division only the 151st Brigade, consisting of three Durham Light Infantry territorial battalions, were to support the attacking tank force in its first sweep towards Arras. It would then be joined by the 13th Brigade of the 5th Division. The French 3rd Division of the Cavalry Corps was to support the British right flank with its battered Somua S35 medium tanks.

The attacking force, under the command of

Major General Martel, an expert on armored warfare, consisted of 74 tanks and fewer than 3,500 men.

Rommel's intelligence had informed him that British and French tank movement was brisk in the Vimy area, and on May 21 he began to move his 7th Panzer division around the west flank of Arras, while the 5th Panzer Division deployed itself to the east. They were still to the south of the town when shortly after noon Rommel heard the sound of gunfire and noted that one of his howitzer batteries in the village of Wailly was 'firing rapid' at enemy tanks attacking southward from Arras.

Martel, at first unsupported by infantry, which had been slow in catching up his tank force, had driven across the Scarpe and had taken the German-held village of Duisans. Then, joined by several companies of the 8th Durham Light Infantry, he went on to take Warlus and Berneville, in the face of opposition by Rommel's 7th Rifle Regiment and part of SS Division *Totenkopf*. At Berneville, however, the Germans, at first taken aback by the boldness of the British thrust, began to rally. Machine gun and mortar fire cut down almost 50 per cent of the Durham Light Infantry, and a 20 minute Stuka support raid made the rest take cover. Only the amazingly robust Matildas seemed impervious to everything – one took 14 hits from 37mm shells without its 10-60mm armor being dented.

Battle for Arras

At one point, German artillerymen began to desert their howitzers around the village of Wailly as the Matildas trundled towards them, spraying .5 Vickers machine gun bullets as they came. Allied tanks had crossed the Arras-Doullens road and were knocking out German vehicles which had jammed the road in panic, escaping from the onslaught. At one point Rommel himself dashed from gun to gun, giving specific targets to the layers. He reported afterwards that morale was suddenly very low indeed.

The British force pounded its way deep into the German lines, capturing four villages, destroying a motor transport column and an anti-tank battery, and then the tide turned. Rommel managed to build up a line of guns from Neuville to Wailly which sealed off the Matildas. Pounded by these and harried by Stuka dive bombing, the British beat a fighting retreat.

It had been the first British tank attack of the war, penetrating Rommel's lines to a depth of ten miles, and had been a limited tactical success. The Germans suffered casualties of 300, with a further 400 being taken prisoner, plus the loss of about 20 tanks and several anti-tank guns and transport units. On the other hand 46 British tanks were lost during the nine hour battle, though the fight at Arras was in fact well worth such loss in terms of strategic and psychological advantages gained.

As Arras was being fought, Guderian and the XIX Panzer Corps were moving up the coast. On May 22 they had cut off Boulogne and by the next day Calais, while forward units were pushing on to the Aa canal, only 10 miles from Dunkirk. The British forces in and around Arras – including staff officers and commanders who would later play a vital part in bringing about final victory – were 46 miles away, and it seemed merely a matter of hours or at the most days before they were forced to capitulate, cut off as they were.

But then came a sudden 'Führer Order': any further advance beyond the Aa was forbidden. After the war, Field Marshal von Rundstedt explained to Sir Basil Liddell Hart: 'A critical moment in the drive came just as my forces had reached the Channel. It was caused by a British counter-stroke southward from Arras on May 21. For a short time it was feared that the Panzer divisions would be cut off before the infantry divisions could come up to support them. None of the French counter-attacks caused any serious threat such as this one did.'

'Fight Like Bloody Hell!'

Rommel had become convinced during the Arras battle that he was being attacked by vastly superior forces, numerically speaking, and when he reported this information General von Kleist became nervous. He ordered 6th Panzer Division to take up a defensive stand west of Arras, and held back Guderian's 10th Panzer Division in reserve. Hitler had issued his order to halt on May 24, and it was not until

The victors encountered scenes of desolation at Dunkirk, with thousands of derelict vehicles.

The French destroyer *Bourrasque* was one of several French and British warships sunk by bombing during the evacuation.

two days later that the true situation began to become clear and the order was rescinded, but by then the British Expeditionary Force had reached Dunkirk and was beginning to evacuate across the Channel.

Between May 22 and May 26, Guderian was experiencing surprisingly stiff opposition from the defenders of Calais, under cavalry Brigadier Claude Nicholson. When asked to surrender, Nicholson told the Germans: 'The answer is "no" as it is the British Army's duty to fight as well as it is the Germans'.

Calais was fortified on much of its perimeter by its vastly thick walls, erected in the 17th century. These proved too much for the German armor, though infantry defenders on the walls could do little against the Panzers below. Nevertheless Nicholson had told the defenders – two crack Rifle Brigade battalions and Territorials of the Queen Victoria's Rifles – 'Get into the houses and fire from the windows. You must fight like bloody hell'. It was a gallant, bloody, and in the end pointless defense,

and it ended in the afternoon of May 26. The Germans took 20,000 prisoners, including between 3-4,000 British, among them Brigadier Nicholson. The remainder were French, Belgian and Dutch, 'of whom', wrote Guderian, 'the majority had not wanted to go on fighting and whom the English had therefore locked up in cellars'.

It was outside the walls of Calais after the surrender that Guderian finally patched up his differences with General von Kleist, whom he had not seen since tendering his resignation nine days earlier. Now von Kleist was in a sunny mood, and heartily congratulated his subordinate on the splendid work done by XIX Panzer Corps.

British High Command in London had hoped, even at this late date, that the French might remass and counter attack to avert total disaster, but the hope quickly died. The French armies in the north had been further disorganized by the death in a motor accident of General Billotte, who unfortunately had been carrying what plans he had made with General Weygand to the south in his own head, for security reasons.

Weygand, for his part, had dug in his troops along the Somme and the Aisne in a vain attempt to prevent the Germans taking Paris. And in London, Ironside was writing in his diary: 'We have lost faith in the French power of attack. Whether it will come once again it is impossible for a foreigner to say. Only a Frenchman can incite them to advance'.

As it turned out, Weygand's troops fought with greater morale in the defense of Paris than they had during the initial stages on the Meuse, but by now it was far too late. All the Germans really needed to do was to move and keep moving, and they did so. General Hoth's armor took Rouen, von Kleist's occupied Burgundy, and on June 17 Guderian reached his final objective, the Swiss frontier. Three days previously Paris had fallen without a fight, and on June 22 the 84-year old Marshal Pétain was forced to agree to a humiliating armistice, signed in the same railway carriage in which Marshal Foch, accompanied among others by

General Weygand, had accepted the German surrender in 1918. Hitler triumphantly sat in Foch's chair for the occasion.

Gamelin had apparently told Ironside before the war that he felt too much time and money was being spent on the Maginot line; if he had had his way he would have strengthened, among other things, France's air defenses. Certainly fixed fortifications for defense were an outmoded idea even in 1939, and Britain, for one, had learned the lesson. While the Germans celebrated their triumph among the bright lights of captured Paris, across the Channel the RAF were making use of the brief respite to marshal their own fighter squadrons for the forthcoming Battle of Britain.

Meanwhile, the German 'blitzkrieg' concept was triumphant once more. In less than six weeks France had been utterly routed by the bold, fast-moving armored divisions. The size of the achievement was measured in a corps order issued by its commander to the XIX Panzer Corps in late May. 'We have covered a good 400 miles since crossing the German border: we have reached the Channel coast and

A rare photograph of Gen. Erwin Rommel's command tank on the North French coast – taken by the General himself.

A TOUS LES FRANÇAIS

La France a perdu une bataille!
Mais la France n'a pas perdu la guerre!

Des gouvernants de rencontre ont pu capituler, cédant à la panique, oubliant l'honneur, livrant le pays à la servitude. Cependant, rien n'est perdu!

Rien n'est perdu, parce que cette guerre est une guerre mondiale. Dans l'univers libre, des forces immenses n'ont pas encore donné. Un jour, ces forces écraseront l'ennemi. Il faut que la France, ce jour-là, soit présente à la victoire. Alors, elle retrouvera sa liberté et sa grandeur. Tel est mon but, mon seul but!

Voilà pourquoi je convie tous les Français, où qu'ils se trouvent, à s'unir à moi dans l'action, dans le sacrifice et dans l'espérance.

Notre patrie est en péril de mort.
Luttons tous pour la sauver!

VIVE LA FRANCE !

18 JUIN 1940

C. de Gaulle.

GÉNÉRAL DE GAULLE

"To all the French! France has lost a battle! But France has not lost the war!" As a tank corps Colonel, de Gaulle harried the German invaders. As a General, his strategy and his propaganda posters boosted Free French morale.

the Atlantic Ocean. You have thrust through the Belgian fortifications, forced a passage of the Meuse, broken the Maginot Line extension in the memorable Battle of Sedan, captured the important heights at Stonne and then, without a halt, fought your way through St Quentin and Péronne to the lower Somme at Amiens and Abbeville. You have set the crown on your achievements by the capture of the Channel Coast and of the sea fortresses at Boulogne and Calais.

'I asked you to go without sleep for 48 hours. You have gone for 17 days. I compelled you to accept risks to your flanks and rear. You never faltered. With masterly self-confidence and belief in your mission, you carried out every order with devotion.

'Germany is proud of her Panzer Divisions and I am happy to be your commander. We remember our fallen comrades with honor and respect, sure in the knowledge that their sacrifice was not in vain. Now we shall arm ourselves for new deeds.

For Germany and our leader, Adolf Hitler!
signed, Guderian'.

RAF pilots run to their
Spitfire fighters, alerted by
the order to 'Scramble'.

THE BATTLE OF BRITAIN:
THE EAGLES ATTACK

Hitler's aim of destroying the RAF over the skies of
Britain was defeated, not so much by technical superiority of men
and machines as by meticulous pre-war planning.

When Germany's new air force was announced in 1935 it was given uniforms different in cut and fabric to anything in the German military tradition. The buttoning tunic with lapels and collar were complemented by a fly-fronted 'flying blouse'. The diving eagle breast badge differed from the Army, Navy and SS patterns and the system of rank insignia was quite separate. This Leutnant wears a collar patch edged in aluminium wire with oak leaves and a single set of wings against the yellow indicating arm of service.

FROM THE CLASSIC point of view, the Battle of Britain was a particularly untidy affair. No one doubts that it was one of World War II's most decisive battles, and probably one of the most decisive in English history, outranking in importance Agincourt, Trafalgar, Waterloo and virtually everything else since the Battle of the Spanish Armada. Yet for the analyst, it has its problems.

We cannot say precisely when the Battle of Britain began, and still less when it ended. We cannot pinpoint the moment when victory was achieved or tell exactly what caused it. None of the lesser battles that composed the battle was in itself decisive and, indeed, the defenders were not sure they had won until well after the battle was over. According to some military historians (eg. Hanson Baldwin), it cannot even be said that the British 'won' the Battle, merely that they prevented the Germans from winning it. And of course we cannot be certain what would have happened if the Germans *had* won.

Yet this formlessness is more apparent than real. In the first place, as a battle of successful defense, the Battle of Britain could not possibly have been as clear-cut as those set-piece actions in which two forces meet in the field and one soundly thrashes the other.

The second thing to remember about the battle is its singularity. It was history's first great air battle. There had never been anything quite like it before, and, as it happens, there has not been anything like it since. Thus one must be cautious about trying to understand the battle in conventional military terms. These may all too easily suggest that the battle lacked coherence, whereas all that is really lacking is apt analogies. The Battle of Britain is better viewed in its own terms.

And viewed in its own terms, it bids fair to rank as a military masterpiece. The victorious commander foresaw and prepared for the

A fighter pilot's routine was much the same, whether in the Luftwaffe or the RAF: periods of intense activity punctuated by boredom and idleness.

contest with an insight not far removed from genius. During the battle he exercised over his forces a degree of control that was unprecedented both in precision and speed. At every stage his decisions were marked by the highest order of intelligence and moral courage, and he may have been responsible for saving England. One could not say more of a Wellington or a Nelson.

Disillusionment

The story of how Sir Hugh Dowding achieved so much for so many with so little is considerably more edifying than its squalid aftermath, in which a few vindictive individuals and an ungrateful nation contrived to consign a hero's name to near oblivion. The story begins – to the extent that one can ever set a date to the origins of a major historical event – in the early 1930s.

The illusions of the post-World War I era were rapidly distintegrating. Adolf Hitler's new German government had withdrawn from the League of Nations amidst vitrolic denunciations of the Versailles Treaty and had accelerated the pace of German rearmament, so that what had for years been going forward in secret now became plain for all the world to see. By mid-1935 the protracted Geneva international disarmament talks had finally collapsed and everywhere in Europe men began to face the unnerving possibility that a new war was in the making.

Particularly alarming to the air-minded was the phenomenal speed with which the new German air force – now, since March 1933, an acknowledged branch of the German armed forces – was taking shape. In July 1934, the Member of Parliament for Epping, Mr. Winston S. Churchill, warned the House of Commons that the Germans already had two-thirds as many warplanes as the RAF and were producing them at a very much faster rate. Equally disturbing to some progressives within the RAF and the British aircraft industry was the presentiment that German aircraft procurement would almost certainly move in the direction of modern designs which emphasized power, speed and heavy armament at the expense, if need be, of such old-fashioned virtues as

maneuverability and even range. In the RAF as a whole there was as yet no such consensus about future warplane design requirements.

The official British response to the looming threat of German airpower may have been tardy. and inadequate, but considering that ten years earlier the British had nearly disbanded the RAF entirely, it was welcome. Late in the summer of 1934 the Government authorized a gradual expansion of the RAF by 41 squadrons, so as to bring the home defense force to a total of 75 squadrons of all types of aircraft by mid-1939. And within the RAF itself, as the debate about future aircraft design requirements intensified, the 'modernists' began to make significant headway against the 'traditionalists.'

Bombers or Fighters?

No one was more concerned with the outcome of this debate than the tall gruff officer who, as the Air Council's Member for Research and Development, presided over the department responsible for the RAF's technical progress. Air Vice Marshal Sir Hugh Dowding was one of those odd, difficult men destined to be admired by his subordinates and disliked by his superiors – a phenomenon not, alas, unconnected with the fact that he was usually right. Because he had a relentlessly original mind, Dowding was unimpressed by the prevailing orthodoxies in military thinking. And because his unbending nature made it difficult for him to compromise, he often disputed those orthodoxies in the most impolitic ways. One of the reasons he had been passed over for the post of Chief of Air Staff may have been because he had had the temerity to argue with General Hugh Trenchard, then the most powerful man in the RAF, about the latter's obsession with bombing planes. What good were offensive bombers, asked Dowding, if their bases could not be made secure by defensive fighters? Either despite or because of the question's logic, Trenchard was annoyed.

It was lucky for England that the Air Member for Research and Development had such decided views on the importance of fighter planes, because the debate between the modern-

The Hawker Hurricane was the most numerous British fighter during the Battle of Britain. Easier and cheaper to build than the Spitfire, it was slower but still deadly against bombers.

The two opponents of the Battle of Britain

The Supermarine Spitfire IIA was slightly slower than the Bf109 but more maneuvrable. This aircraft was flown by 41 Squadron.

SPITFIRE
Max Speed: 365 mph
Engine: Rolls-Royce
Merlin 1224 hp
First ordered: 1936

The Messerschmitt Bf109E-3 was almost as good as the Spitfire but faulty tactics nullified its advantages. This machine was flown by II/JG77.

Bf109E
Max Speed: 354 mph
Engine: Daimler-Benz DB601A 1100 hp
First ordered: 1938

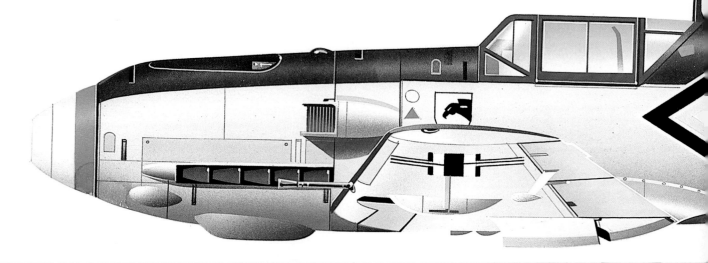

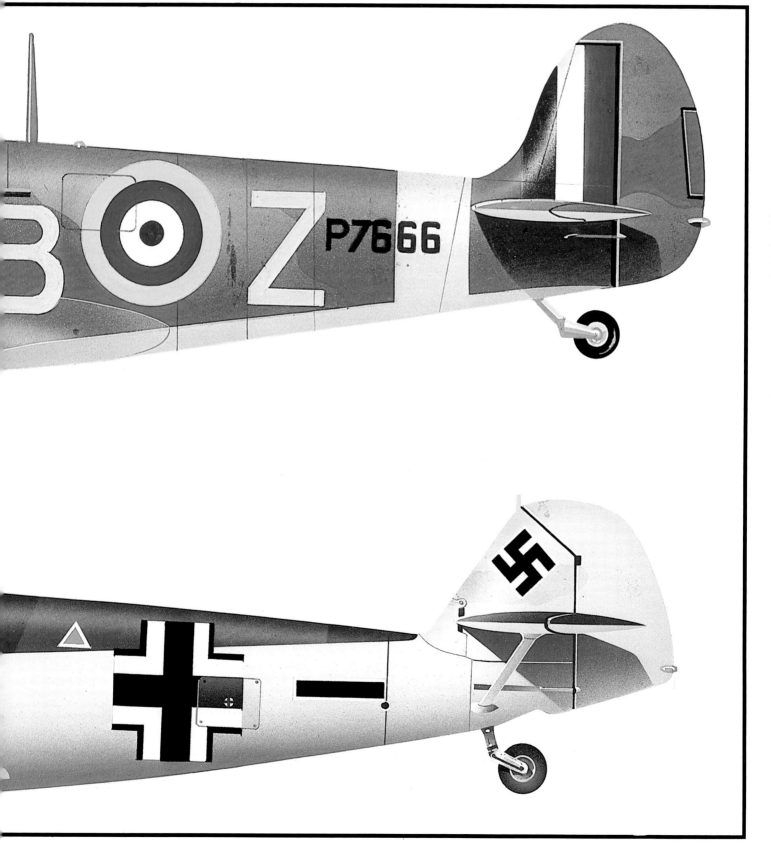

ists and the traditionalists had come to focus on the matter of fighter design. Dowding had become a partisan of the modernist faction and was therefore crucial to the 1934 modernist triumph known as Air Ministry Specification F5/34. This was, in effect, an official invitation to the British aircraft industry to develop a fighter of the most advanced kind then envisaged: a low-winged monoplane with an enclosed cockpit, retractable landing gear, a speed of at least 275 mph at 15,000 feet and eight .303 inch machine-guns ('Eight guns is going a bit far,' one traditionalist had objected).

But it was one thing to ask for modern fighters and another to get them. The problem was not lack of creativity; Sidney Camm of Hawker, R. J. Mitchell of Vickers-Supermarine and several other exceptionally talented designers had been working on ideas for modern fighters since the early 1930s. Rather, the trouble was that there was no aircraft engine sufficiently powerful to accommodate the requirements of these designs and no official plan to create one. But once again, England was lucky. Long before the RAF expansion program or the issuing of F5/34, Rolls-Royce had foreseen the need for such a new engine. On their own initiative, without any official support and using their own funds, Rolls-Royce had set to work on what was known as Private Venture No. 12, the creation of a completely new, super-powerful in-line aircraft engine. By the end of 1934 Rolls had succeeded and the PV-12 was ready. It was christened 'Merlin.'

Thanks to the availability of the Merlin, the exacting requirements of F5/34 could now be met. Drawing on the huge reservoir of resources and experience represented by Hawker Aircraft Ltd., England's leading manufacturer of military aircraft, Sidney Camm raced ahead with his design. Before the end of 1935 the Hawker Hurricane was ready for testing. An ingenious compromise between conventional engineering (to facilitate ease of production) and advanced concepts, the Hurricane was obviously a world-class machine. Dowding and other RAF progressives were overjoyed.

Yet the Hurricane would need every virtue it possessed. Unknown to the British, at approxi-mately the same time that the Hurricane was being readied for test, Professor Willi Messerschmitt of the small Bayerische Flugzeugwerke had presented to the Luftwaffe his new fighter, the Bf-109. The 1935 Bf-109 was probably inferior to the Hurricane, but it was one of those happy designs that permitted great evolutionary improvement. By 1940 it would be the Hurricane's superior.

Reginald Joseph Mitchell had neither Sidney Camm's physical resources nor his experience in designing fighter planes. But he had one important advantage: genius. On May 5, 1936 Mitchell's response to F5/34 was first test flown at Eastleigh Airfield near Southampton. Unlike the Hurricane, the Supermarine Spitfire made few concessions to the past. Its engineering innovations would create production problems for the aircraft industry (and teach it valuable lessons, as well), but no one could fail to be impressed with the plane's incredible performance, which clearly surpassed that of any other military aircraft in 1936 and would continue to do so in 1940.

Radar Provides the Key

While the Spitfire and Hurricane were being hastened into production, another equally important weapon was coming into being. Since early 1935 Dowding had been encouraging the development of the extraordinary new long-range electronic detection device that would later be known as radar. Experiments with similar devices were being conducted in other countries as well, but there they were regarded as little more than scientific curiosities. Only Dowding and a handful of other far-sighted RAF officers realized that radar might provide the key to the problem of successful air defense, that around it might be built an entire new system of fighter control. Dr. Robert Watson-Watt's invention had hardly completed its first official test before the RAF initiated a request for the construction of a chain of 20 radar stations covering the coast from the Tyne to Southampton.

Thus the essential technical foundations of Britain's future air defense were set down during the period between 1930 and 1936 when

Bf109 airframes on the assembly line. Despite extravagant claims the production of fighters in 1940 was only half that of the British. Below: the director of the statistical office at the Messerschmitt works explains the single-spar wing of the Bf109, pioneered by Willi Messerschmitt.

Dowding was responsible for the RAF's research and development program. But this was only a beginning. What remained to be done was to *apply* all the burgeoning technology, to infuse both men and machines with purpose and organize them into an effective fighting force. That is why July 6, 1936, was another lucky day for England. On that date the RAF created a new, independent command, Fighter Command, with Air Marshal Sir Hugh Dowding as its first Commander-in-Chief.

For Dowding the remaining years of peace were a desperate race against time. The direst forebodings in 1934 about the future of German airpower hardly compassed the reality. The German aircraft industry poured forth a torrent of formidable new warplanes – the big bent-nosed Heinkel He-111 bomber, the series of sleek Dornier medium bombers, the splendid Junkers Ju-88 all-purpose bomber, the sinister-looking Junkers Ju-87 Stuka, the twin-engined Messerschmitt Bf-110 escort fighter, and, of course, the supremely deadly single-engined Messerschmitt Bf-109.

In addition, between 1937 and 1939, the

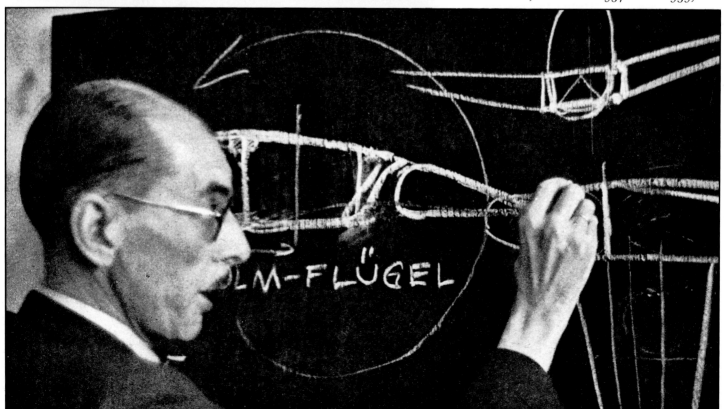

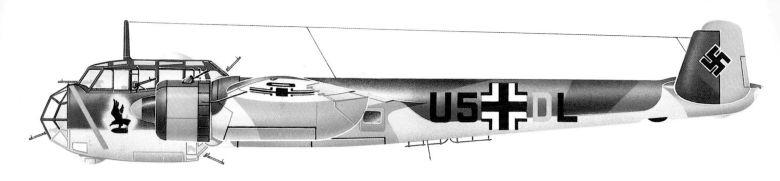

Luftwaffe was able to exercise both its men and machines under live combat conditions in Spain. The practical lesson learned by the German 'volunteers' who made up the Condor Legion produced a stream of technical modifications in Luftwaffe aircraft and invaluable improvements in the skills of their aircrews. The Bf-109, for example, underwent three major modifications during the period of the Spanish Civil War, emerging in 1939 as the Bf-109E, the configuration in which it would enter World War II and challenge the Spitfire in the Battle of Britain. By the same token, when Condor Legion veterans returned to Germany, they would be rewarded, depending on their ranks, with the command of squadrons, groups or wings (Geschwader). It was against such experienced professionals that the young pilots of RAF Fighter Command would soon have to fly.

The Germans were less than shy about advertising their growing strength on the land and in the air. Hitler was convinced that by boasting of his military might he could demoralize his potential enemies. Doubtless he was right in one sense, but perhaps not in the most important sense. The RAF, for example, tended to believe most of the exaggerated claims Dr. Goebbels made on behalf of the Luftwaffe during the late 1930s. As a result, however dismayed they may have been, the RAF leaders were stimulated to ever greater activity in trying to counter the mounting German air threat. The original 1934 target of 75 home defense squadrons gradually crept upwards until by 1939 it stood at 145 squadrons. The energetic Lord Swinton, who became Secretary of State for Air in 1935, worked tirelessly to expand the productive capacity of the aircraft industry. Similarly, Henry Tizard's Scientific Committee at the Air Ministry labored to perfect radar, direction-finding equipment, high-frequency radios and other electronic gadgets deemed crucial for the future. And at the heart of all the activity was Dowding, trying to assemble the strands and weave them into the fabric of a truly effective air-defense system.

By the beginning of World War II, this system had evolved to a level of sophistication beyond the dreams of any other air force in the world. At its core was the hierarchy of Operations Rooms – the master Room at Dowding's headquarters in Bentley Priory near Stanmore; a second echelon of four Rooms, one for each of the four Groups into which Fighter Command was divided; and a tertiary level of Rooms, one for each of the several Sectors that composed the Groups.

All Operations Rooms were similarly constructed, had similar functions and were interconnected by an elaborate communications network. Typically, an Operations Room looked like a small amphitheater, the center of which contained a large horizontal map of the geographic area for which the Room was responsible and on which WAAFs moved colored counters representing plots of hostile and friendly air activity in the area. In a gallery above, looking down on the map, sat the Controller and his aides. On the wall opposite the Controller were panels carrying up-to-the-minute information on the readiness status of all fighter squadrons under the Controller's direction, as well as local weather and direction-finder information (for pinpointing the precise location of airborne friendly aircraft).

The Chain of Command

Radar information on incoming raids would be filtered downwards from Stanmore to Group and Sector Controllers, and, later on, would be amplified by visual sighting reports from the Ground Observer Corps. Groups would allocate responsibility for intercepting specific raids to Sector Controllers who, in turn, would order individual fighter units into the air and vector them to interception points. Meantime, Stanmore would pass along relevant information to anti-aircraft and searchlight batteries, to barrage balloon commands, to the Royal Navy, and so on.

For all its extreme modernity and flexibility, the system was none-the-less chain-like in form, its effectiveness dependent on the soundness of each link. It made the most severe demands on all who were part of it, from the radar operators along the coast to the pilots in the cockpits of the fighters. Split-second timing, absolute accuracy, sound judgment and iron nerves were merely minimum requirements. Especially in the later stages of the Battle of Britain, when British resources were stretched thinnest and when the navigators in the German bombers had taken to making razzle-dazzle course changes so as to disguise their objectives until the last possible moment, it became clear that the most important feature of the system lay in the extraordinary competence of its human components.

Dowding's Foresight

For Dowding, of course, the creation and elaboration of this efficient fighting machine was only the first step. The real test of his skill as a commander would be in how well he deployed and used it. In retrospect, his decisions about deployment seem almost uncanny. Originally Fighter Command had consisted of two Groups, one bearing responsibility for the defense of the northern half of England and the other for the south. But by 1939, as the contours of the approaching war began to take shape in Dowding's imagination, he realized that something much more sophisticated was needed. He therefore increased the number of Groups in Fighter Command, first to three and then to four: No. 10 Group, responsible for the extreme south and Wales; No. 11 Group, responsible for London and a fan-shaped wedge of south-eastern counties close to the French coast; No. 12 Group, responsible for all of central England; and No. 13 Group, responsible for the north and Scotland. He no longer believed, as earlier theorists had, that the most likely avenue of German air attack would be across the North Sea. It would come, he was convinced, from France, even though this implied forecasting France's eventual defeat. Accordingly, he crammed approximately half his available forces into the relatively small geographic area opposite the French coast and appointed his most trusted lieutenant, Air Vice Marshal Sir Keith Park, to the command of No. 11 Group.

Since Dowding had in effect bet that the coming Battle of Britain would be fought in the sky over No. 11 Group, one might suppose the No. 13 Group in the north, farthest from the predicted scene of action, would be allocated the fewest squadrons. On the contary, Dowding gave to No. 13 Group nearly one quarter of Fighter Command's total strength: No. 13 Group was to be his strategic reserve. In his mind's eye, Dowding imagined the scenario: the main struggle – a gruelling battle of attrition – would be fought in No. 11 Group's area. No. 10 and No. 12 Groups would serve as flanks, bearing some of the action and feeding replacement squadrons into No. 11 Group. When these forces had been depleted, as a last throw of the dice, the fresh squadrons from No. 13 Group would be brought south to fight. It would require great self-control and the soundest judgment to withhold these squadrons until the last possible moment. Once they had been committed, there would be nothing left.

On September 1, 1939, Germany invaded Poland and World War II began. The long years of waiting and speculation were at an end. All Dowding's plans and preparations, like those of every other European military leader, would shortly be put to the test. Whatever inadequacies remained – technical weaknesses, failure of vision, lack of fortitude or intelligence – would not now be forgiven by history.

The Luftwaffe Supreme

The Luftwaffe's conquest of the Polish air was accomplished even more quickly than the Wehrmacht's conquest of the land. It could not have been otherwise: nearly 2000 (about two-thirds of the total available) modern German warplanes, with every advantage of surprise, against an airforce composed of less than 400 obsolescent first-line aircraft. Nor was the conquest of Norway any less rapid or complete: the Norwegians were incapable of offering any significant resistance and the British and French were incapable of offering any significant help.

In contrast to these lightning victories, the first nine months of the war on the western front appeared to be stalemated in what the French soon began to call the *drole de guerre*. Air activity during this period was limited to patrol actions, punctuated by occasional small night bombing raids. On paper, the French *Armée de l'Air* was almost as large as the Luftwaffe; but,

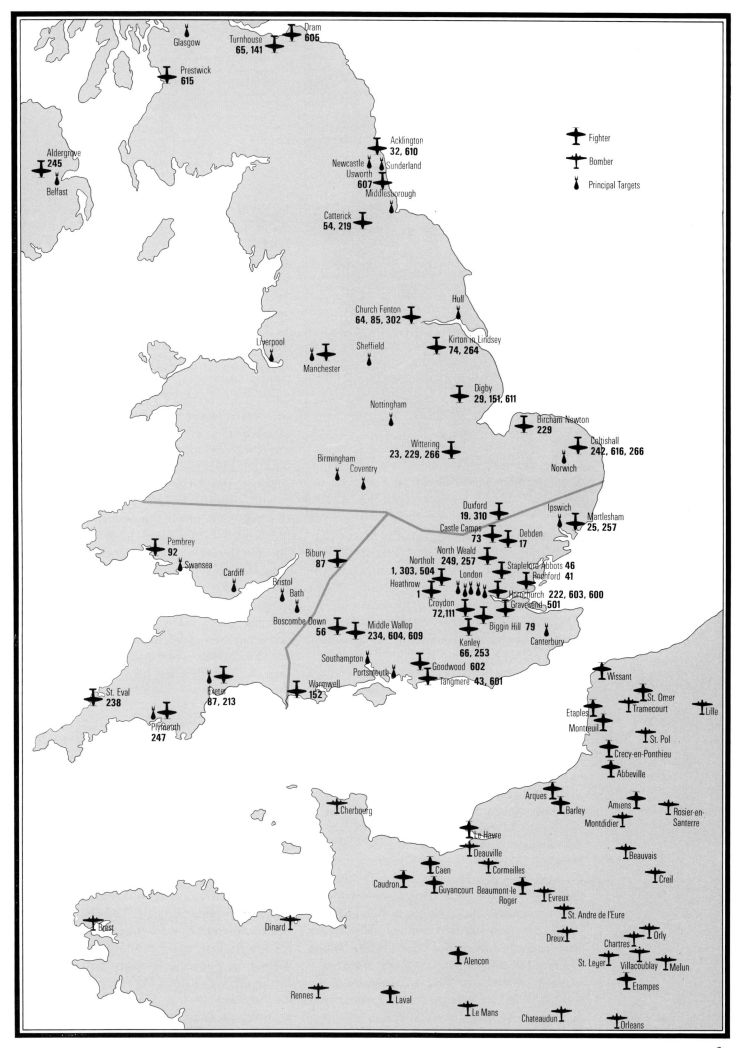

Glasgow

Turnhouse
65, 141

Dram
605

Prestwick
615

Aldergrove
245
Belfast

Acklington
32, 610

Newcastle
Usworth
607

Sunderland

Middlesborough

Catterick
54, 219

Hull

Church Fenton
64, 85, 302

Liverpool

Manchester

Sheffield

Kirton in Lindsey
74, 264

Nottingham

Digby
29, 151, 611

Bircham Newton
229

Coltishall
242, 616, 266

Norwich

Birmingham

Coventry

Wittering
23, 229, 266

Duxford
19, 310

Ipswich

Martlesham
25, 257

Castle Camps
73

Debden
17

Pembrey
92

Swansea

Cardiff

Bibury
87

North Weald
249, 257

Northolt
1, 303, 504

Stapleford Abbots **46**

Rochford **41**

London

Heathrow
1

Hornchurch **222, 603, 600**

Gravesend **501**

Bristol

Bath

Croydon
72, 111

Boscombe Down

Biggin Hill **79**

Middle Wallop
234, 604, 609

Kenley
66, 253

Canterbury

Boscombe Down
56

Southampton

Goodwood **602**

Portsmouth

St. Eval
238

Exeter
87, 213

Warmwell
152

Tangmere **43, 601**

Plymouth
247

Wissant

St. Omer

Etaples

Tramecourt

Lille

Montreuil

St. Pol

Crecy-en-Ponthieu

Abbeville

Cherbourg

Arques

Barley

Amiens

Rosier-en-Santerre

Montdidier

Le Havre

Deauville

Beauvais

Caen

Cormeilles

Creil

Caudron

Guyancourt
Beaumont-le Roger

Evreux

Brest

Dinard

St. Andre de l'Eure

Dreux

Orly

Chartres

St. Leger

Villacoublay

Melun

Alencon

Etampes

Rennes

Laval

Le Mans

Chateaudun

Orleans

Fighter

Bomber

Principal Targets

67

The British had left most of their anti-aircraft weapons in France, and in many cases airfield defense was limited to rifle-caliber machine guns. This is a .303in Bren gun on its anti-aircraft tripod.

with minor exceptions, the quality of its equipment was markedly inferior, and it suffered from a chronic lack of organization and competent command. The enormity of the difference between the two airforces did not, however, become fully apparent until the Germans unleashed their Blitzkrieg against France on May 10, 1940.

Dowding had steadfastly opposed sending a large Air Expeditionary Force to supplement the *Armée de l'Air*'s fighter defenses. His entire strategy was based on what Fighter Command would do in the event of a French defeat. Ruthlessly logical, he knew that the RAF could not win – but could all too easily lose – the Battle of Britain in France. Thus on May 10, he had only six Hurricane squadrons on French soil. In the following days, under pressure from the French and the new Prime Minister, Winston Churchill, who had rashly promised Premier Paul Reynaud heavy fighter support, Dowding sent ten more Hurricane squadrons into battle. But there he drew the line. He obstinately refused to commit any more Hurricanes, or any Spitfires at all. When Churchill remonstrated, Dowding threatened to resign. Already, by May 21, a quarter of the total RAF fighter strength had been destroyed in France. At that rate of attrition, Dowding argued, there would be no Fighter Command

left by the end of July. 'If the Home Defence Force is drained away in desperate attempts to remedy the situation in France, defeat in France will involve the final, complete and irremediable defeat of this country.' There was no refuting the figures. Chagrined, Churchill was compelled by the force of Dowding's logic to break his word to Reynaud. But like Trenchard before him, he was annoyed.

Yet however much Dowding wished to avoid further attrition in France, events forced his hand. The German Blitzkrieg, following on the breakthrough at Sedan, had caught the allied armies in northern France in a huge armored vice, driving them relentlessly back onto the beaches at Dunkirk. For all its shortcomings, the *Armée de l'Air* was putting up a valiant and increasingly effective fight against the Luftwaffe, but it was beyond the power of the French fighter forces to provide air cover for the troops on the beaches. Once again, Dowding had to commit Fighter Command. Between May 26 and June 4 all but three RAF fighter squadrons participated in the vast running air battle over Dunkirk, and when it was over, 100 more British fighters had been lost. England now had only 331 first-line Spitfires and Hurricanes left, with only 36 in reserve.

Operation 'Sealion'

If the Germans had been able to attack England in June, when the British ground forces were in disarray and Fighter Command was at the nadir of its strength, Hitler might have won the war. But the Germans were without a plan. The collapse of the French armies had come sooner than the Germans had foretold, and the Germans had simply not given much serious thought to what they would do next. They delayed nearly a month before starting air operations against England and another month before mounting their main attack – vital months for England. Yet attack they would. In early July, Supreme Headquarters announced to the German armed forces that 'The Führer has decided that a landing in England is possible, provided that air superiority can be obtained. . . . The preparations for the entire

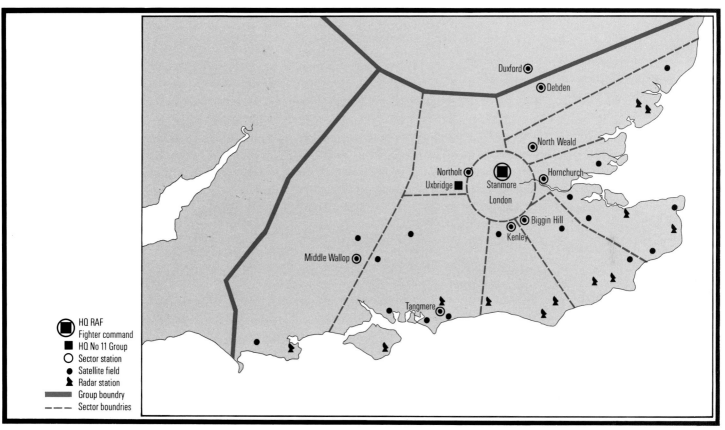

HQ RAF
Fighter command
■ HQ No 11 Group
○ Sector station
● Satellite field
♟ Radar station
▬▬ Group boundry
- - - Sector boundries

operation must be completed by mid-August.' The planned invasion of England was code-named Operation 'Sealion'.

Behind these announcements lay some rapid and not altogether confident calculations. The Wehrmacht had said that if it could get ten divisions safely across the Channel and onto British soil, it could conquer England. The Kriegsmarine had promised to do what it could – ie, in effect, to commit suicide – to prevent the Royal Navy from interfering with the fleet of invasion barges. But both services insisted that none of this would be possible unless the Luftwaffe had first wrested control of the air from the RAF. The fate of 'Sealion', then, lay squarely on the shoulders of the Luftwaffe's C-in-C, Hermann Göring.

Göring's Confidence

Göring, as always, was supremely confident; the destruction of the RAF, he said, would take no more than four days of full-scale air battle. In the month's grace period between the battle over Dunkirk and the beginning of July Fighter

Command had rebuilt its strength to just under 600 aircraft. But the Luftwaffe had also made good a large fraction of the nearly 1000 air-craft lost to the French before the June 23 armistice. When Luftflotten 2 and 3 finally got into position, they anticipated a 4:1 numerical superiority over Dowding's force.

Meantime, while the two Luftflotten were getting ready for their main blow against England, they decided to flex their muscles in the air over the English Channel. Throughout the month of July the Luftwaffe made both incessant small-scale attacks on Channel shipping and night raids on British seaports. Dowding's fighter control system was not up to this kind of challenge. There was no way he could get his fighters in position in time to intercept a raid on a mid-Channel convoy, and night fighting was a still-undeveloped art. Indeed, Dowding was probably wrong in permitting himself to be drawn into trying to defend the Channel at all; yet for the first three weeks of July he regularly sent his fighters out to attack the German raiders, usually after they had

The Heinkel HeIII twin-engined bomber was the Luftwaffe's most numerous bomber from 1937 to 1945.

already struck their objectives. By July 20 the Luftwaffe had all but swept the Channel of British shipping and thenceforth Atlantic convoys were diverted to ports on the English west coast. At about the same time, Dowding, recognizing his error, began to pull his fighters back from the Channel fight. To the Germans, the battle for the Channel seemed a clear-cut victory and a promise of good things to come. Few appeared to wonder how it was that the British fighters even though usually too late, had always managed to locate the raiding aircraft with such astounding accuracy.

By the first week in August the Germans were ready to launch their full-scale air assault. Fighter Command's strength now stood at 708

fighters; Luftflotten 2 and 3, along with the supporting Luftflotte 5 based in Norway, disposed of about 2500 warplanes, of which approximately 1000 were fighters. In addition, the Luftwaffe had 1000 more warplanes in reserve.

Goring had fixed the day for the opening of the great assault – *Adler Tag* he called it – for August 10. But bad weather spoiled the Reichsmarshall's plans and, instead, the main phase of the Battle of Britain got off to a rather desultory start on the 11th. It quickly rose in ferocity, however, coming to a crescendo on August 15, the heaviest single day's fighting of the battle. On that day all three Luftflotten launched 1,786 sorties

Curious sightseers cluster around a crashed HeIII bomber in an English field.

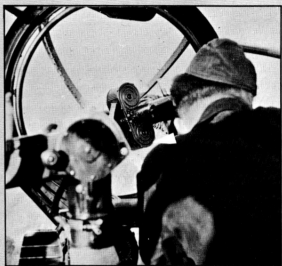

Two views of the cockpit and forward gunner's position in a German bomber.

The 'Eagle' Squadron of the RAF consisted of US volunteers. While some were imbued with a desire to fight Nazism others admit that they enlisted for adventure.

against England. All four of Fighter Command's Groups were engaged in the riposte, mounting a total of 947 sorties. At the end of the day the Luftwaffe's losses stood at 75, the RAF's at 34. The following two days saw fighting on a somewhat reduced scale, but the 18th was another big day, the Germans losing 71 planes against the RAF's 27.

The main battle had now been raging for a week, and during the brief comparative lull that followed the big fight on the 18th, both sides tried to take stock. For the RAF the most obvious facts were that Dowding's scenario was proving to be absolutely accurate and that his radar-based fighter control system was performing brilliantly. Except for the all-out attack on the 15th, German raids had concentrated almost exclusively in No. 11 Group's area, and even on the 15th the British defense system, stretched to its limit, had functioned without a breakdown.

Plane-for-plane, the British fighters were doing very well. The Spitfire was probably superior to the Bf-109E, although their virtues were so different that comparisons are difficult.

At the least, the two planes met on an equal footing. The Hurricane was somewhat inferior to the 109, but it was murderously effective against all other German types. In so far as was possible, Keith Park, No. 11 Group's commander, tried to direct his Hurricane squadrons against the German bomber formations, while sending the Spitfires to cope with the escorting 109s. Unfortunately, this reasonable precept often had to be honored in the breach, since at this time only six of Park's 21 squadrons were equipped with Spitfires.

Two German types proved to be disappointments. The twin-engined Messerschmitt Bf-110 escort fighter was markedly inferior to both Hurricane and Spitfire and was therefore relatively useless in the battle. And the Ju-87 Stuka, so effective in the Polish and French campaigns, was found to be so vulnerable to the British fighters that after the 18th it had to be withdrawn from the conflict.

With respect to tactics, Dowding was perfectly satisfied with Park's bulldog doctrine of trying to intercept every enemy raid that crossed the English coast. On the occasions

A German pilot prepares to take off, like a medieval knight putting on his armor.

when there were many simultaneous raids (most of the time), this meant spreading the defending forces very thin, often requiring small teams of British fighters to attack large German formations. But despite the disadvantages – dissipating his strength, forcing his pilots to fight at long odds, and perhaps accepting a lower rate of kills – Park knew that even a few fighters could often break up a raid and divert it from its target; and that, he believed, was by far the most important objective.

History has thoroughly vindicated this tactical doctrine of Park and Dowding, but at the time it had some bitter critics. Chief among them was Sir Trafford Leigh-Mallory, the Commander of No. 12 Group. Leigh-Mallory believed in concentrating the defending fighters into large formations – "big wings" – and directing them against single raids. Never mind how many other raids got through to their targets unopposed, he argued, the big wings would do such demoralizing damage to the raiders they did intercept that the enemy would eventually give up. Not only was Leigh-

Mallory's thesis about the psychological effect of big-wing attacks never demonstrated, on the occasions when No. 12 Group tried to mount such attacks, it took so long to assemble the big wings that they often missed their interceptions entirely. More basically, Leigh-Mallory was wrong in dismissing the importance of unintercepted raids, especially if their targets happened to be Fighter Command airfields.

It is probably fortunate that the misguided theories of Leigh-Mallory and his lieutenants were seldom put into practice during the Battle of Britain. It is profoundly unfortunate that he nevertheless saw fit to continue to advocate his theories after the Battle had ended, serving no useful purpose, but causing Dowding and Park much injury.

The Germans, too, were divided about tactics. The bomber crews complained that the Messerschmitts were not staying close enough to the bombers to give them adequate protection. The Messerschmitt pilots argued that if they had to stick too close to the bombers, both their speed and their field of manoeuver would be seriously restricted. The bomber faction won the argument, but the fighter pilots were right. Thereafter the effectiveness of the Messerschmitts was diminished.

A Switch of Targets

But on another important matter, the Germans made a correct decision. In the early stages of the Battle the Luftwaffe bombers had attacked a broad variety of targets – ports, factories, military facilities of all sorts. Göring assumed that the category of target didn't make much difference so long as the British fighters were lured into the air and annihilated. The trouble was that they were being lured into the air but they weren't being annihilated – or at any rate, not nearly fast enough.

So the Germans now decided to concentrate their raids on the British airfields. The men and machines of Fighter Command would thenceforth be destroyed not only in the air but on the ground as well. The British were doubtless lucky that Göring's arrogance had prevented him from doing this sooner, for the new German tactic considerably hastened the coming of the

'One of our aircraft is missing'

A A crippled Messerschmitt Bf110 fighter trails smoke.

B Although the English coast is far behind, the fighter loses height and will not make base.

C The pilot keeps the nose of the aircraft up as he prepares to 'ditch'.

D With propellers already bent by the impact the aircraft churns up a cloud of spray as it lands.

E The aircraft vanishes in a cloud of spray.

F As the aircraft tips up one of the crew works his way out of the cockpit.

G The second crew-member forces open the cockpit canopy and climbs out as the aircraft begins to sink.

H The two crew-members swim clear just in time to get clear from the sinking aircraft.

J The inflatable Mae West lifejackets keep the men afloat as the wingtip disappears.

K The two survivors can only hope that a British ship or a German rescue aircraft will pick them up.

A

B

C

D

E

F

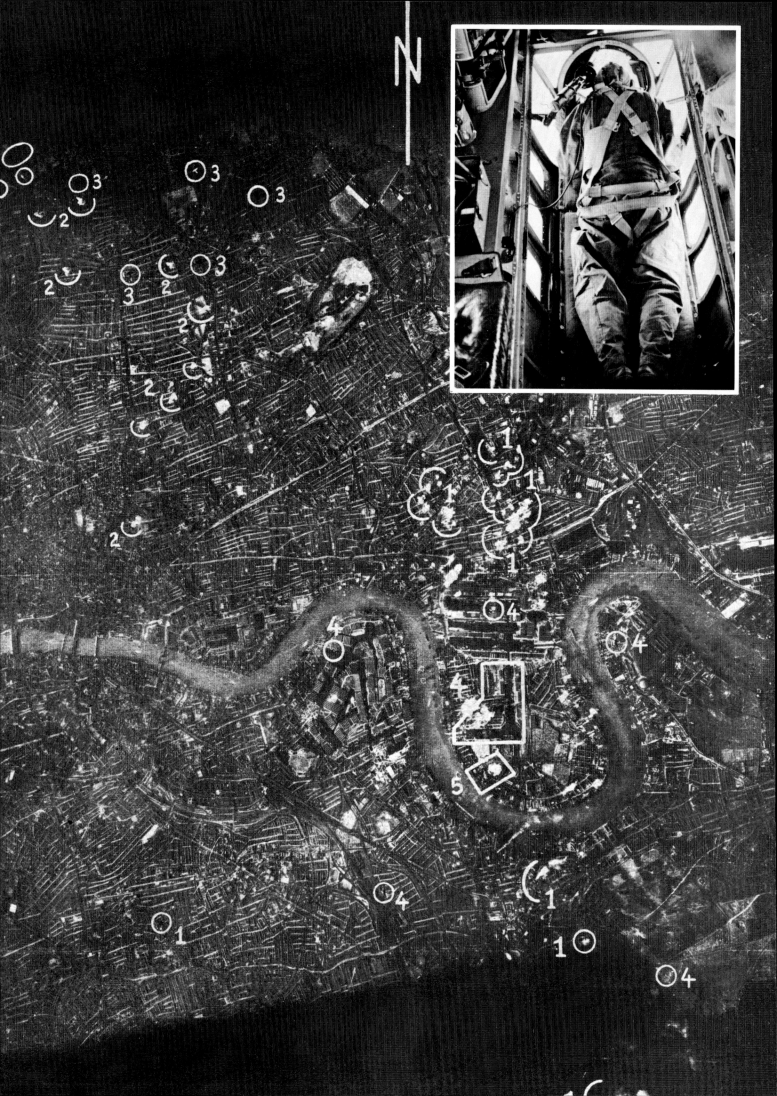

An aerial reconnaissance photograph of London taken from a German bomber at a height of 30,000 feet.
1 Bomb-bursts
2 Anti-aircraft fire
3 German aircraft
4 Docks
5 Grain elevators
6 Flour mills
7 Oil depot

Inset: a Luftwaffe bomb-aimer lying prone during the final run-in, ready to release his deadly load.

crisis that Dowding had always known was inevitable.

The spell of bad weather that had lasted from the 19th to the 23rd at last lifted and air fighting resumed with a vengeance on August 24. Pursuing their new tactics, the Germans heavily bombed the No. 11 Group Sector Stations at North Weald and Hornchurch and so badly damaged the airfield at Manston (a satellite field of Hornchurch) that it had to be abandoned. In all, during the day the Germans lost 36 aircraft and the RAF 22.

That night, some German bombers made a costly error. Hitler, unsure of the reaction of the British public, had so far forbidden raids on London. But in the darkness of the night of the 24th a group of Heinkels missed their targets at Rochester and Thameshaven and inadvertently dropped their bombs on the city of London itself. Churchill's reply was instantaneous. The following night a mixed force of Hampton, Whitley and Wellington bombers attacked Berlin. Hitler, in his turn, was furious. In time his fury would provoke a fatal change in German tactics. But first, Fighter Command would have to endure its Calvary.

The raids on the airfields continued with mounting ferocity. On the 26th the Sector Stations at Kenley, Biggin Hill, Hornchurch and North Weald were attacked, and in the following days virtually every No. 11 Group airfield was repeatedly bombed. Fighter Command losses began to soar. By September 1 the RAF had lost a total of 426 aircraft, with another 222 badly damaged. More important, 181 pilots had been killed and another 145 were injured.

Dowding watched these figures with dismay. Although aircraft production was barely managing to keep pace with fighterplane losses, the losses in pilots could not be made good. Nearly 40 per cent of Fighter Command's original complement of pilots had been lost by September 1, and the attrition was particularly high among experienced Squadron and Flight leaders. Moreover, the surviving No. 11 Group pilots were fatigued almost beyond endurance. On days of heavy action it was not uncommon for pilots to make as many as six sorties a day,

staying on the ground only long enough to refuel and rearm. Many had had enough harrowing experiences for several lifetimes. For example, Flight Lieutenant Alan Deere of No. 54 Squadron, the highest-scoring ace of No. 11 Group's highest-scoring unit, had been shot down over Dunkirk, had had a mid-air collision with a Bf-109 during the Channel fighting, had been shot down in flames during the big battle of August 15, was shot down again on the 28th, and was blown 100 feet into the air by an exploding bomb while trying to take off in the midst of an air raid on the 31st. That men like Deere lived through such experiences is perhaps no more remarkable than that they were always ready to return to the battle afterwards. But will-power alone was not enough. Inevitably their efficiency was being eroded and their vulnerability was rising to critical levels. It was time to bring in the reserves.

The changeover did not, of course, happen all at once. Dowding fed in his reserve squadrons piecemeal and always as a last resort. It was between August 27 and September 9 that the major shift occurred. During that period eight squadrons from No. 13 Group, five from No. 12 Group and two from No. 10 Group were sent to replace the shattered squadrons of the original No. 11 Group.

Thus by the end of the first week in September, Dowding had played his final hand. If the reconstituted No. 11 Group could hold out until October, there was a slim chance that the rains and mists of autumn might slow down the German air assault and that Fighter Command might survive. If not, the RAF would be unable to prevent the threatened invasion. Had Dowding known the German timetable for the invasion, he might have been even more anxious. The final decision was to be made on September 14, and if it were favorable, the invasion itself would take place on September 27.

Dowding's replacement squadrons were fresh, but they were also green. Most had come from comparatively tranquil sectors; now they were abruptly hurled into an inferno. The price of their inexperience was very high. No. 222 Squadron, lately of No. 12 Group, was scram-

Both sides suffered heavy losses. This doomed Hurricane has been hit by tracer bullets which set its gasoline tank ablaze. Within seconds the whole plane is obscured by flames.

bled 35 minutes after reaching its new base at Hornchurch and lost seven aircraft. No. 72 Squadron, flying south from No. 13 Group to Biggin Hill, was engaged in an air battle even before it had a chance to land. No. 253 Squadron and No. 203 Squadron both lost 13 aircraft in their first week in No. 11 Group. No. 79 Squadron, which arrived in No. 11 Group on August 27, lost all but six of its Spitfires in the first four days of battle and itself had to be replaced on September 9. And so it went.

On the Brink of Defeat

For one ghastly week, from August 31 to September 7, it looked as though Dowding – and England – had lost. The replacement squadrons were being torn to pieces and No. 11 Group was melting away before Dowding's eyes. In those seven days the RAF lost 161 planes – more than the Luftwaffe – and by the end of the week Fighter Command had only 125 fighters left in the front line. If the current loss rate persisted, Fighter Command would have less than two more weeks to live. Meanwhile, in London, the Joint Intelligence Committee was predicting that the invasion would occur sometime before the 10th. Not since 1066 had England been so close to total disaster.

Yet in that darkest, finest hour – call it September 7 – salvation was at hand. It was composed of three decisive elements: British competence, German error and German failure of will. On the British side, it can only be described as a rally. The green replacement squadrons had nearly been destroyed, but not quite. The surviving pilots had learned the harsh lessons of combat; now they qualified as veterans. Gradually, during the week of September 8-14, the kill ratios began to tilt once again in the RAF's favor while total British losses significantly declined. In itself, this remarkable British recovery might not have been enough to turn the tide, but it was powerfully assisted by a serious German blunder.

Ever since the British Berlin raid of August 24, Hitler had been pressing the Luftwaffe to retaliate in kind and re-direct its bombers to London. Göring and Sperrle were dubious at first – the raids on the British airfields *seemed* to be effective, even though it was difficult to be sure. But Kesselring tended towards the Führer's view, not because he felt strongly about the need for vengeance, but because he still mistakenly believed that Fighter Command could only be destroyed in the air and that if London were attacked, the British fighters would have to rise *en masse* to defend it. On September 3, Göring finally capitulated and announced *Zielwechsel* – a change of objective – to his bomber forces: beginning September 7, the major thrust of German air raids would shift to the British capital. Thus London's long ordeal began: with only one exception, London would be bombed every night, and many days as well, between September 7 and November 13.

But the beginning of London's trial by fire also marked the end of Fighter Command's desolation. In its new-found strength, and as the unbearable pressure of daily air raids on its airfields receded, No. 11 Group began to re-establish itself as a formidable fighting force. By the 11th Park realized that not only were the raids on London something more than a temporary aberration in German targeting, the attacks were beginning to fall into identifiable patterns of timing, routing and composition. If these patterns held good Park would be able to concentrate his airborne interceptors to a degree never before possible – in effect, to do what Leigh-Mallory had always wanted to do when it was not possible. Accordingly, Park issued to his Sector Controllers a set of new tactical instructions which were to pay off very handsomely indeed in the days to come.

The third element that contributed to Fighter Command's salvation is difficult to quantify. The Luftwaffe had been fighting as long and as hard as Fighter Command, and its total losses were considerably higher. Granted, the Luftwaffe was in a much better position to sustain such losses, and granted, too, that its air crews were quite as capable of enduring the harrowing rigors of daily combat as were the pilots of Fighter Command. But there was an important difference in expectations. The Germans had begun by anticipating a quick victory. As the

days multiplied into weeks and then into months, the Germans tried to console themselves, ever less persuasively, with a succession of incorrect estimates that the collapse of Fighter Command was only a matter of hours away. By early September these estimates were actually beginning to assume some validity, but the Germans were not only unaware of the effectiveness of their offensive, they had begun to lose faith in it. From pilots' messes, through to the highest levels of command, to Hitler himself, the daily Luftwaffe Intelligence summaries of the RAF's losses and the latest assessments of declining British strength were greeted with mounting cynicism. From the German point of view, it was beginning to look as though the Battle of Britain would never end.

On September 14 Hitler announced to his commanders that he would postpone his promised decision on the invasion of Britain until the 17th. In the interim, it was hoped, there would be one final day of all-out air battle which would at last accomplish what had for so long eluded the Germans. According to the weather report September 15 promised to be that day.

'The Few'

On the morning of September 15, alerted to the impending battle by the top-secret Ultra code-breaking device, Churchill went down to No. 11 Group headquarters at Uxbridge to sit beside Keith Park in the Operations Room gallery and watch the course of the day's events. All told, from 11 a.m. to dusk, Wing Commander Eric Douglas-Jones, the No. 11 Group Controller, plotted three enormous raids comprising a total of nearly 1200 attacking aircraft. Rising in waves to meet them was every available fighter plane in England (at one point, when Churchill asked, 'What other reserves have we?' Park could only reply grimly, 'There are none'). So furious was this day-long air battle that both sides were later misled into inflating the other's losses – in fact the RAF lost only 27 aircraft and the Germans 52.

But the psychological impact of the battle of September 15 was far greater than anything

suggested by its statistics. For the disheartened Germans, it was a kind of last straw. It broke their will to continue by setting the final seal on their pessimism about the Luftwaffe's chances of ever destroying Fighter Command. It convinced Hitler and his commanders that the invasion could not be undertaken in 1940 and prompted him to postpone *Sealion* indefinitely. It was probably the moment, if not by any means the sole cause, of Britain's deliverance.

In the days that followed, as the German daylight raids gradually tapered off and Fighter Command's strength grew, it began to dawn on the defenders that they had succeeded, that England had been saved. Many long years of war still lay ahead, but England's survival would not again be seriously called into question.

Today we can see that the British victory in the Battle of Britain was a decade in the making, that it was, in a sense, won at many points in time: in 1934, when F5/34 was authorized; in 1936, when Dowding became Chief of Fighter Command; in 1937, when the first Spitfire entered squadron service; in May, 1940, when Dowding refused to send any more fighters to France; and at hundreds of other crucial moments both before and during the Battle itself. Nor could it have been won without the historic contributions of such men as Mitchell, Camm, Swinton, Watson-Watt, Park and many more. Certainly it could not have been won without the skill and sacrifice of 'The Few', of 'Dowding's boys', the heroic young pilots of Fighter Command. Yet above all, Hugh Dowding was its author and its architect. If any one man had saved England, it was he.

It would be pleasant to record that Dowding was honored for his achievement. Instead, a group of his long-time enemies on and off the Air Staff, soon raised a chorus of criticisms about his conduct of the Battle – criticisms that in retrospect seem at best wrong-headed and at worst malicious – and by November he was replaced. His brilliant chief lieutenant, Keith Park, was likewise shunted off to the relative obscurity of Flying Training Command. The man who replaced Park as Commander of No. 11 Group was Leigh-Mallory.

A British convoy under the watchful eye of a destroyer.

THE U-BOAT WAR:
THE WOLFPACKS UNLEASHED

With too few U-Boats in 1939 the German Navy was not able to overwhelm the British convoy-system, and both sides built up their strength for the bitter struggle to come.

THE BATTLE OF the Atlantic was unlike any other battle of the Second World War. It was in one sense not even a battle but rather a campaign lasting five years, and yet it was a very real confrontation between the armed forces of the two belligerents with a precise moment of decision which can be identified. It was also the most important battle of the Second World War for the Allies, for until it was decided in their favor their strategic plans could not be put into operation. Had it not gone in their favor there can be no doubt that Hitler's armed forces would have been left in control of Western Europe and the Mediterranean.

The German submarine offensive of 1916–17 had nearly defeated the combined maritime resources of the British Empire, France and the United States, and when in September 1935 Kapitän zur See Karl Dönitz was appointed to command the Kriegsmarine's new submarine force he began to plan a new submarine strategy. Dönitz and other senior military men knew that an eventual clash of interests would occur between Britain and Germany, and his brief was to train his U-Boat Arm to operate against British merchant shipping. It was known that the British would adopt convoy, the sailing of merchant ships in groups protected by warships, the counter-measure which had robbed the U-Boats of victory in 1917. It was also known that the British had developed a potent underwater detection device, and Dönitz and his commanders worked hard on countermeasures. But one of the biggest problems was the U-Boat Arm's relations with the rest of the Kriegsmarine and the other two Services. The majority of senior naval officers were obsessed with the need to wipe out the 'stain of Scapa Flow', the bitter memory of the scuttling of the High Seas Fleet in 1919 and this put them at a disadvantage when talking to Army and Air Force officers, who could boast that they had never done more than sign an Armistice after being 'stabbed in the back'. In their zeal to reverse the verdict of World War I Admiral Raeder and his colleagues hankered after a big surface victory over the British and planned giant battleships, while the bombast of Her-

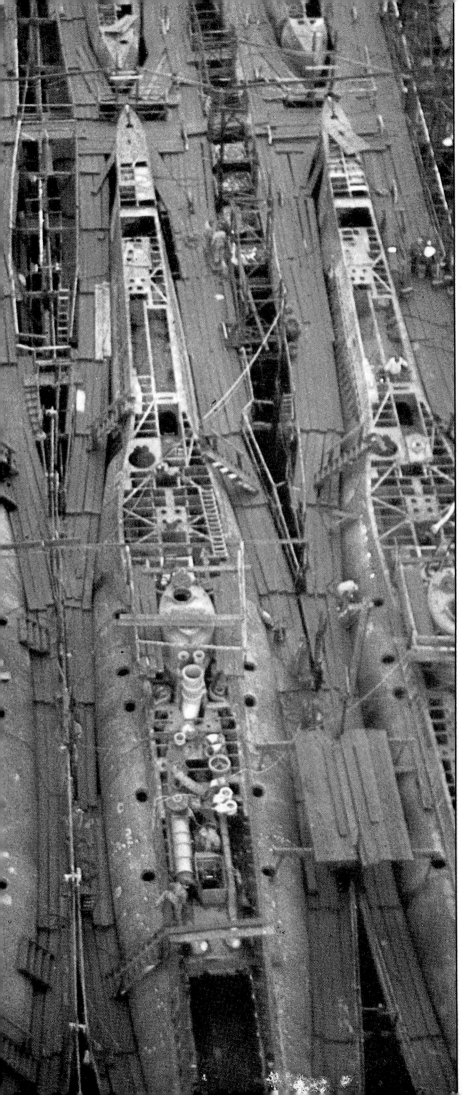

The key to the struggle in the Atlantic was U-Boat production. If U-Boats could be built faster than they were being sunk the losses of Allied shipping would make victory certain. In the photograph Type VIIC U-Boats are being mass-produced at Krupp's Kiel shipyard.

mann Göring ensured that 'his' Luftwaffe kept control of all air operations. Lip service was paid to the need for U-Boats, and optimistic plans were drawn up to use the surface fleet (when it was completed) to destroy the British convoy system so as to allow the U-Boats a free hand, but in practice only 57 U-Boats had been commissioned when war broke out. Another reason for this meager total was Great Britain's timely insistence on the Anglo-German Naval Treaty of 1936, which limited the German Navy's tonnage of submarines to the same total as the Royal Navy. Although the 'Z-Plan' of 1938 proposed a further 250 U-Boats the production facilities did not exist, so long as Germany wished to be strong in surface ships as well as in land and air forces.

The British and their French allies viewed the obvious preparations for a campaign against their shipping with growing alarm. Fortunately both navies still had a large preponderance of numbers over the new German Navy. Even if Hitler's swaggering junior partner Mussolini came into the war (and after Munich there was little doubt that war was coming) the modern and efficient French Navy would be able to contain the Italians. The combined French and British navies would be able to contain the German Navy in its North Sea bases, and coastal escorts and shore-based aircraft would hunt the U-Boats. To this end both navies expanded their anti-submarine forces, and the British in particular were relying on their superior ship-building capacity. In short, time appeared to be on the side of the Allies.

Too Few U-Boats

The first months of World War II seemed to confirm the correctness of the Allied planning. Dönitz had too few U-Boats and not enough of them were large boats, while the coastal patrols were able to afford a fair measure of protection to shipping. Hitler was very anxious to avoid antagonizing neutral opinion, and ordered his U-Boat commanders to honor the Prize Ordinance in the opening weeks. As World War I had proved, U-Boats could not wage effective war if they had to surface, warn the target to heave to, and then examine her

The USS *Tenacity* (PG-71) was a British 'Flower' Class corvette transferred to the US Navy during the early part of 1942. The rapid build-up of the USN in 1940-41 had not included anti-submarine escorts, and 25 corvettes had to be acquired under 'Reverse Lend-Lease'.

cargo and papers to ascertain whether or not she was a legitimate prize, and the U-Boats scored relatively few successes. But *U.30* exceeded her orders and sank the liner *Athenia* without warning, so the Admiralty put into effect its contingency plans for unrestricted warfare. But in spite of a gradual escalation the U-Boats were nowhere near cutting off British supplies, and the British were slowly but surely building up their armed strength after years of neglect. In the first nine months only 242 ships totalling 850,000 tons had been sunk, while 24 U-Boats had been sunk.

It is difficult to predict how long the sea war would have gone on in that form, but in April 1940 the scene changed rapidly when first Norway· and then the Low Countries were invaded by Germany. By the middle of June

German troops were on the Atlantic coast, what was left of the French Navy was neutralized and the Italian Navy was ready to challenge British control of the Mediterranean. The U-Boat Arm wasted no time in moving its base facilities to the Biscay ports of France. From Lorient, La Rochelle, La Pallice, St Nazaire, Brest and Bordeaux the U-Boats completely outflanked the British and lay much closer to the convoy routes. This meant that they could operate further to the West out of range of shore-based aircraft, and immediately losses of shipping began to rise. Thus the fall of France marks the beginning of the Battle of the Atlantic. What had been a clash between two powerful adversaries was now for the British a fight for survival. For the Germans it was at first nothing more than a long-drawn out struggle to finish off a stubborn opponent, but by early 1941 it was obvious that German bombers would not be able to subdue Britain, and that the U-Boats would have to achieve this alone, before the United States could be drawn into the War.

The U-Boat Aces

As the U-Boats moved steadily westwards into the Atlantic the British escorts had to follow, but the shore-based aircraft could not. Even the escorts found it difficult to operate satisfactorily at extreme range, for they could not pursue at high speed, zig-zag or wait to finish off a U-Boat which had been detected. The detection device suspected by the Germans lived up to expectations and proved able to detect submerged U-Boats; known to the British as ASDIC (in the US Sonar), it used ultrasonic beams and provided escorts with an accurate range and bearing of an underwater target. But there were too few escorts and too many U-Boats, for the German shipyards were turning out U-Boats faster than the hard-pressed escorts could sink them. Worse, the U-Boats were sinking ships as fast as they could be built. The first phase of the Battle of the Atlantic, June 1940 – March 1941, was the heyday of the 'aces', the highly skilled U-Boat commanders who could inflict unbearable casualties on a convoy. Men like Otto Kretsch-mer sank over 200,000 tons of shipping each, and were often able to attack on the surface at night. If a U-Boat could penetrate the columns of merchantmen she was practically immune from discovery, for the escorts usually assumed that the attack had come from outside. The hard-pressed convoy and its slender escort had no respite until the U-Boats had expended their torpedoes.

The surface fleet also played its part in harrassing British shipping. The first of the 'pocket battleships' the *Admiral Graf Spee* had been hunted down early in the war but her sister *Admiral Scheer* and the big battlecruisers *Scharnhorst* and *Gneisenau* all operated against the Atlantic convoys. Fortunately for the British, the German high command showed such timidity that inferior forces were often

able to deter an attack; orders from Hitler were hedged about by so many restrictions that his captains and admirals frequently did nothing rather than risk breaking the rules. The 'auxiliary cruisers', or fast merchant ships armed with hidden guns, operated well away from the convoy routes; by varying their disguises they were able to trick solitary merchant ships into coming within range, and their presence tied down scores of cruisers. But the Royal Navy never relaxed its vigilance, and it became harder and harder for German surface raiders to slip out into the Atlantic and even harder to slip back unseen by the patrols.

In May 1941, just after the end of the first phase of the Battle of the Atlantic, the Kriegs-marine mounted its last great sortie against the convoys by sending out the new battleship *Bismarck* and the heavy cruiser *Prinz Eugen*. Here at last was a ship which could fight the British on equal terms, for she was large, fast and well-protected. Her first encounter with the Home Fleet vindicated Admiral Raeder's hopes, for she destroyed the elderly British battlecruiser *Hood*, apparently drove off the new *Prince of Wales* and then vanished from sight. For three agonizing days the Royal Navy threw every ship it could spare into the search, and finally on May 27, 1941 the battleships *King George V* and *Rodney* pounded the *Bismarck* into a wreck. It was the last opportunity for the German Fleet to intervene decisively in the Battle of the Atlantic. By the time *Bismarck*'s sistership *Tirpitz* was ready the situation had changed beyond recognition, and all she could do was lie menacingly in Norwegian fjords, the target for numerous attacks.

Aircraft in the Atlantic

The Luftwaffe also did what it could to harass shipping. Long-range Condor bombers inflicted heavy casualties on ships in the South-Western approaches to the British Isles and scouted for the U-Boats further afield, but their range did not permit them to operate far out into the Atlantic.

The British answer to the Condors was to fit merchant ships with a fighter aircraft launched by catapult; although the fighter

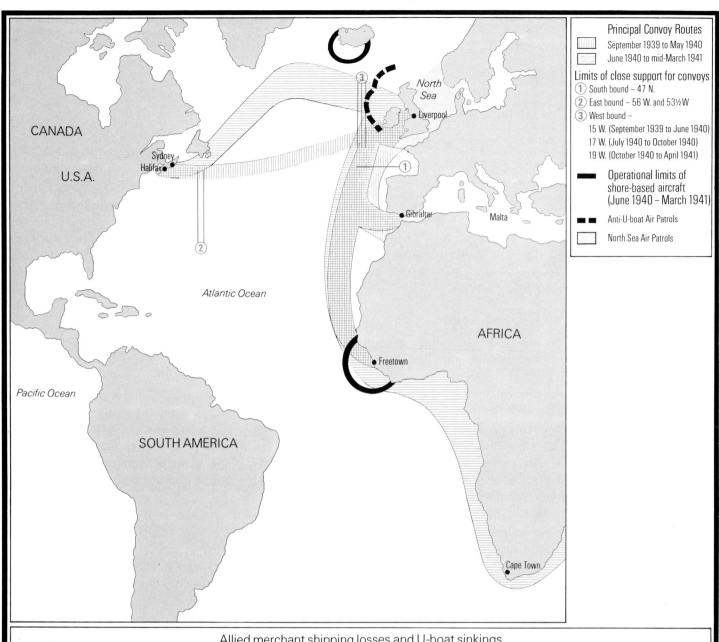

Allied merchant shipping losses and U-boat sinkings

1942 Tonnage	Ships sunk	U-boats sunk		1943 Tonnage	Ships sunk	U-boats sunk
419,907	106	3	January	261,359	50	6
679,632	154	2	February	403,062	73	19
834,164	273	6	March	693,389	120	15
674,457	132	3	April	344,680	64	15
705,050	151	4	May	299,428	58	41
834,196	173	3	June	123,825	28	17
618,113	128	11	July	365,398	61	37
661,133	123	10	August	119,801	25	25
567,327	114	11	September	156,419	29	9
637,833	101	16	October	139,861	29	26
807,754	134	13	November	144,391	29	19
348,902	73	5	December	168,524	31	8
7,790,697	1,664	87	Totals	3,220,137	597	237

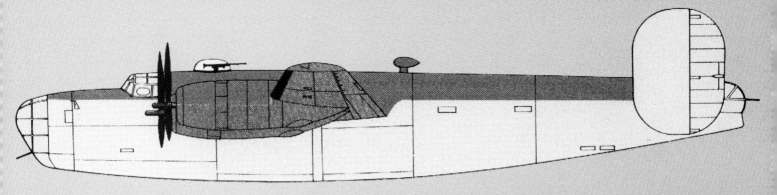

A 'very long-range' (VLR) version of the Consolidated B-24 Liberator bomber was produced. Defensive machine guns and armor plate were stripped to allow more gasoline to be carried. In this version Liberators could spend three hours with a convoy.

Long-range maritime patrol aircraft proved to be the U-Boat's worst enemy. The Consolidated PBY Catalina flying boat (right) was first used in May 1941 and had a range of 3,000 miles. Even this phenomenal endurance was not enough to cover the 'Black Gap' in mid-Atlantic, where U-Boats scored their greatest successes.

was forced to 'ditch' in the sea it usually shot down the aircraft that was shadowing the convoy, and thus robbed the U-Boats of the reconnaissance that they needed so badly. The limited field of vision from U-Boats' bridges meant that they could do very little without information about the positions of likely targets. To overcome this lack of precision Dönitz planned the *Rüdeltaktik* or 'Wolf Pack' tactics. Using his own experience in World War I, Dönitz believed that a massed attack by U-Boats could swamp a convoy's defenses and accomplish its destruction. But to achieve such a concentrated attack meant that the U-Boats had to be centrally controlled and 'homed' onto a convoy. By siting patrol lines in the path of a convoy it was possible for at least one U-Boat to locate a convoy, and if that U-Boat refrained from attacking, but instead sent out a stream of signals about speed, track, position and composition of the convoy, the U-Boat HQ at Lorient could then lay on a concentrated attack. Every U-Boat within range would be ordered to join the shadower, and when each boat was in position a massive onslaught would begin at nightfall.

The 'wolf pack' was first used in September 1940, but only as a temporary measure to offset a change in Admiralty cyphers which had robbed the U-Boats of much useful intelligence. In March 1941, however, the British scored a remarkable series of successes against the aces, which brought the first phase of the

Battle of the Atlantic to an end. On the night of 15–16 March *U.*99 and *U.*100, commanded by the aces Kretschmer and Schepke, were sunk while attacking a convoy. The device which had defeated them was Radar, which was now becoming available in escorts, and it was to put an end to the surface attacks at night. The loss of these two aces and other successful U-Boat commanders robbed the U-Boat Arm of its front-line. More than ever Dönitz had to rely on wolf pack methods, if only because the less-skilled commanders were finding it too hard to take on a well-defended convoy single-handed. Something else happened in March 1941; the United States put the Lend-Lease Act into operation, and in effect undertook to supply the British with whatever war material they needed.

New Counter Measures

The second phase of the Battle of the Atlantic was ushered in with several important changes. First, the British were able to set up bases for escorts and aircraft in Iceland, with the result that they could now extend air cover to convoys out to 35° West. In May 1941 the first Catalina long-range flying boats arrived from the United States, followed by a specially adapted maritime version of the Liberator bomber. Known as the VLR (Very Long Range), this aircraft sacrificed defensive armament and armor plate in favor of fuel stowage for extended endurance. Very few

of these aircraft were available at first, because of the over-riding requirements of RAF Bomber Command, but even the ten aircraft operational by September 1941 were invaluable. The problem of ships' endurance was also tackled vigorously, and in July the first of a large class of high-endurance escorts was laid down. Known as the 'River' Class frigates, these well-designed and powerfully armed ships could travel across the Atlantic without refuelling, and proved far better suited to the North Atlantic than the original 'Flower' Class corvettes. Large numbers were built in British and Canadian yards but the first were not ready until 1942. As a stopgap 22 destroyers were converted to 'Long Range Escorts' by replacing one boiler with an extra fuel tank; their speed was still sufficient for a high-speed dash after a U-Boat, but like the frigates they could now stay with a convoy.

Although neutral the United States made no secret of its true allegiance, and from April 1941 US Navy warships escorted American ships loaded with war material bound for the United Kingdom, and in addition the extension of the Pan-American Security Zone allowed US warships to patrol the convoy routes. This was a sore provocation to the Germans, and it was only a matter of time before one side fired on the other, but for the moment they behaved with restraint.

In 1941 the battle for technical superiority began to dominate the scene. Radar had already proved its usefulness, but in May a much more advanced set, the Type 271 came into service; it enabled U-Boats and even their periscopes to be picked up at considerable range, and did much to redress the balance in favor of the escorts. In the same month the British captured not only code-books but the vital Enigma coding machine from *U.110*. This 'pinch', which the British concealed for 25 years, was probably the greatest intelligence prize of the War, for it gave the British all that they needed to fill the gaps in their knowledge of the U-Boats' information service. From now on the British could intercept the constant stream of signals which went back and forth be-

The 'Flower' Class corvette was the standard escort built for the Royal Navy. Although small and slow it was seaworthy and well-armed with Sonar and depth-charges. To speed construction the hull was adapted from a pre-war whalecatcher design and over 300 were built in Britain and Canada. When the USA entered World War II 25 corvettes were handed over to the USN as an emergency measure.

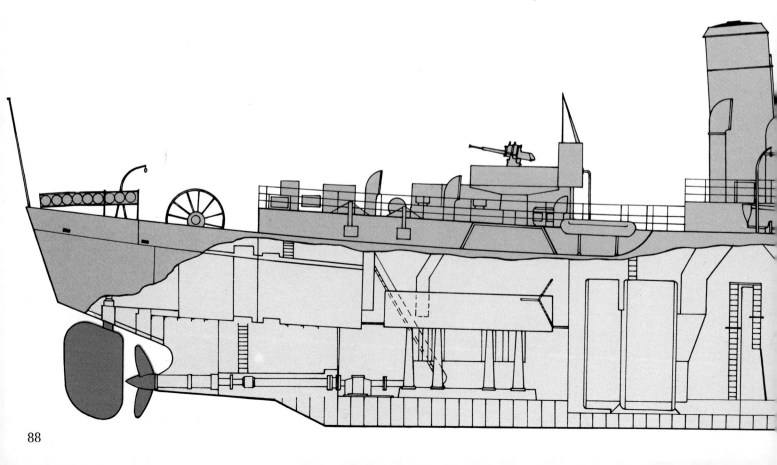

The depth-charge was the standard weapon against U-Boats in the war. An escort could lay a pattern of 14 charges primed to explode at a pre-set depth. Here a duffle-coated crewman prepares to fire a corvette's starboard thrower, capable of hurling a 300lb charge a distance of 70 yards.

tween the wolf packs and U-Boat HQ at Lorient. The first tangible result was the sinking of the five supply ships sent out to refuel the *Bismarck* and *Prinz Eugen*.

But the 'Black Gap' remained in mid-Atlantic. It was now imperative that convoys had not only constant surface escort all the way across the Atlantic but also constant air escort. The answer was the escort carrier, a merchant ship given a flight deck to allow her to operate half-a-dozen aircraft. The first was HMS *Audacity*, a former German banana boat captured in 1940; she sailed with her first convoy in September 1941, and although she lasted only three months her outstanding success resulted in

a further 11 being ordered. With wooden flight decks and very few of the refinements of big fleet carriers, the escort carriers were nonetheless robust and more than adequate for the Atlantic. They operated a variety of aircraft, such as the obsolescent Swordfish biplane, but the presence of an aircraft was usually sufficient to force a U-Boat to submerge. Here lay an important weakness in the wolf pack system, for if the shadowing U-Boat submerged the convoy could be re-routed away from the pack before it reached its rendezvous.

Another weakness of the wolf pack system was the volume of radio-traffic between the U-Boats and their base. It was recognized by Dönitz that shore-based direction-finding stations could get a cross-bearing on a transmission, but it was known that these medium-frequency stations could never get a preicse position. But British scientists developed a high-frequency direction-finder which was small enough to be fitted in a warship. Once the device, nicknamed 'Huff-Duff', was at sea two escorts could pin-point a U-Boat to within a

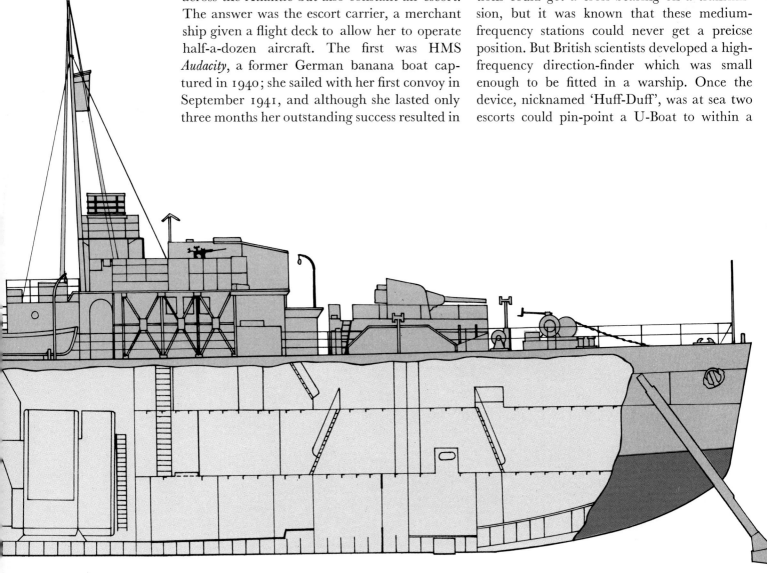

quarter of a mile, and even a single escort could track a transmitting U-Boat. 'Huff-Duff' proved a potent countermeasure against the 'shadower', which could be forced to submerge repeatedly, even if there was no time to mount a full-scale attack.

In September 1941 the inevitable happened – a US Navy destroyer was fired on by a U-Boat, which mistakenly believed that she had been attacked. The USS *Greer* was not hit, but the incident caused great ill-feeling between the US and Germany. This was aggravated when the destroyer *Kearny* was torpedoed off Iceland with many casualties. The *Kearny* limped into an Icelandic anchorage, but when the *Reuben James* was torpedoed two weeks later she sank with only 45 survivors. But still the United States was not politically ready for war against

Towards the end of 1941 the convoys began to carry their own aircraft to fight off the U-Boats. The MAC-ship was a bulk cargo-carrier fitted with a wooden flight deck and an elevator to allow her to operate six anti-submarine aircraft while still carrying her vital cargo of oil or wheat.

The escort carrier or CVE differed from the MAC-ship in being converted from a freighter into a fully-equipped carrier with up to 30 aircraft. The old Swordfish biplane torpedo-bomber proved to be one of the most useful types for operating from these small carriers when armed with rockets and search radar.

Germany, although indignation was expressed and the US Navy moved to a war footing. Finally it was Germany which declared war on the USA, in a quixotic response to the Japanese attack on Pearl Harbor.

America's entry into the War heralded the beginning of the third phase of the Battle of the Atlantic. In theory the vast resources of the United States and its large navy should have quickly tilted the balance against the U-Boats, but in fact the opposite happened. Admiral Dönitz had shrewdly transferred U-Boats to the eastern seaboard of the USA and the Caribbean. These first boats, only five in number, found a submariner's killing ground, ships sailing unescorted, reporting their positions 'in clear'. The escort techniques were crude, for the US Navy had not

developed a detection system comparable in performance to the British ASDIC and had failed to develop a suitable tactical doctrine. Against these green and untried sailors and airmen Dönitz' veterans had no trouble in running up enormous scores of shipping sunk, some 675,000 tons in the first three months of 1942. The countermeasures were desperate but ultimately successful; all shipping was convoyed, the British and Canadians handed over 95 escort vessels under 'Reverse Lend-Lease', and a gigantic program of 1,000 escort ships was started.

The British introduced several new counter-measures early in 1942. The 'Hedgehog' was a multiple mortar which enabled escorts to make better use of their ASDICs by permitting an attack earlier. The Leigh Light was a powerful searchlight used by aircraft in conjunction with radar and, like the Hedgehog, its introduction resulted in many more effective attacks on U-Boats. Throughout this time German shipyards were keeping up with the losses and U-Boats were deployed over a much wider area than before. Supply U-Boats and long-range types made it possible to operate in areas where the escorts were few or non-existent, such as the Caribbean or the coast of Brazil. The Allies were forced to move their aircraft and ships, and to organize

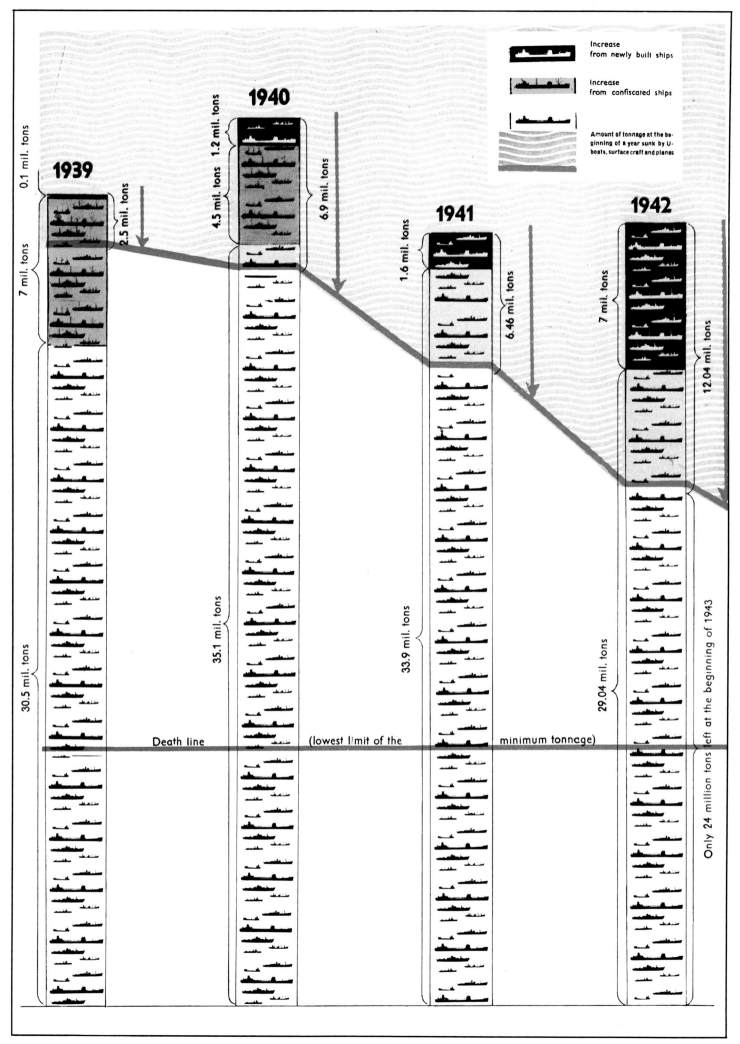

1939
0.1 mil. tons
7 mil. tons
2.5 mil. tons
30.5 mil. tons

1940
1.2 mil. tons
4.5 mil. tons
6.9 mil. tons
35.1 mil. tons

1941
1.6 mil. tons
6.46 mil. tons
33.9 mil. tons

1942
7 mil. tons
12.04 mil. tons
29.04 mil. tons

Only 24 million tons left at the beginning of 1943

Increase from newly built ships

Increase from confiscated ships

Amount of tonnage at the beginning of a year sunk by U-boats, surface craft and planes

Death line   (lowest limit of the   minimum tonnage)

The German propaganda magazine *Signal* had its own view of Allied shipping losses (left and above), but even the official estimates were too optimistic.

island supplied, and these two commitments drew off large numbers of escorts. The U-Boats, however, were not as effective in these theaters as they were in the Atlantic. In the Mediterranean there were too few and the clarity of water made detection by aircraft easier; in the Arctic the extreme cold and appalling weather also made submarine operations difficult and dangerous. In the Mediterranean, too, the success of the British at the Battle of El Alamein began the process of clearing German and Italian air bases from the coast of North Africa, which eased the problems of running convoys eastwards. In August 1948 the massive 'Pedestal' convoy battle finally secured Malta's safety and effectively restored Allied control over the central Mediterranean.

Operation 'Torch'

The other great distraction was the proposed amphibious landing in North Africa. For pressing political reasons rather than military necessity the Americans were anxious to establish an Allied bridgehead in French North Africa, and it was proposed to run convoys directly from the USA to Morocco. Such a daring venture needed a large number of escorts, and in addition there were convoys from the British Isles to be guarded. Operation 'Torch' in November 1942 was highly successful but it drew off from the Battle of the Atlantic an enormous number of escorts, the newly-formed 20th Escort Group (the first of the support groups) and seven of the desperately few escort carriers. The 'Torch' convoys reached their destination without loss but the same could not be said for the Atlantic convoys. Sensing the slackening of pressure the U-Boats fought even harder and shipping losses rose once more.

The U-Boats fought back in the scientific war as well. In September 1942 they received the first radar search receiver, the Metox, which gave warning of an aircraft using radar. This simple device helped to reduce the losses of U-Boats, but of course did not help them to sink more merchant ships. The Allies had to counter this by introducing centimetric waveband radar. This took time and at a crucial stage the

shipping to an unforeseen extent, and all this imposed a nearly intolerable strain on their war effort. The third phase of the Battle of the Atlantic was the period of balance, in one sense a race by both sides to build up their strength for the showdown. By the fall of 1942 this had been achieved.

The fourth phase, the most crucial, opened in August 1942. At last the Allies had sufficient escorts to form support groups. These were well-trained teams of escorts which operated independently of the convoys, coming to their rescue if needed, but free to remain behind and hunt U-Boats to destruction. This was the first effective example of escorts being able to take offensive action against the U-Boats, but it could not be put into practice until such time as the convoys were adequately escorted.

It must be borne in mind that the Allied navies were under heavy strain at this time. Since 1941 convoys of war material had been going to North Russia, running the gauntlet of German aircraft and U-Boat attacks from Northern Norway. The parlous state of Malta necessitated massive operations to keep the

U-Boats had a valuable respite. The 'B-Dienst' or cryptanalysis service also had a stroke of luck in breaking into the convoy cypher early in 1943; this countered to a certain extent the British ULTRA operation using their knowledge of the Enigma coding machine, and enabled the U-Boat Command to plot the courses of many convoys.

The shipping losses in the Atlantic during the fall of 1942 and the first months of 1943 were a grave setback to the Allies' plans. It slowly dawned on the Americans and British that they had been pursuing long-term objectives at the cost of neglecting the Battle of the Atlantic. It was all very well to achieve a brilliant success in North Africa and to mount 'round-the-clock' bombing raids against Germany, but if the U-Boats sank too many oil tankers there would come a time when the bombers could not take off and the expeditionary forces could not set sail for lack of fuel. In January 1943 at the strategic conference at Casablanca the conflicting aims were to some extent resolved, and defeat of the U-Boats was made the first priority. Unfortunately this was used as an excuse for extending strategic bombing to include U-Boat bases and building yards. Unfortunate because the apostles of strategic bombing then tried to prevent the allocation of four-engined bombers to anti-submarine operations, and because bombing proved singularly useless as a means of hampering the U-Boat offensive. Between January and May 1943 over a hundred heavy bombers were lost over Germany without destroying a single U-Boat. The new ASV III centimetric radar set was desperately needed, but the strategic bombers' ground-mapping radar (of basically the same design) had priority.

The Crunch

Eventually the objections of the RAF were overcome, and some bombers were transferred from Bomber Command to Coastal Command, but in March 1943 the margin between victory for the U-Boats and survival for the Allies could be qualified as no more than two squadrons of VLR Liberator bombers. In January 1943 there was an average of 116 U-Boats at sea *each day*, and with these numbers it was possible to swamp the defenses of a convoy. As an example, in five days in February a wolf pack sank 14 ships totalling 85,000 tons and lost only one U-Boat. In January U-Boats sank 37 ships of 203,000 tons, but in February as the weather improved the total rose to 63 ships of 359,000 tons, while in March the massive total of 108 ships of 627,000 tons was sunk. The Allies were stunned by this resurgence of the U-Boats; nothing seemed to be able to stem the tide. It seemed that Dönitz was to be proved right in his forecast that the U-Boat would win the War. Even the convoy system, which had been the cornerstone of Allied anti-submarine measures, seemed to be crumbling, and at one time during the worst moments in March the Admiralty

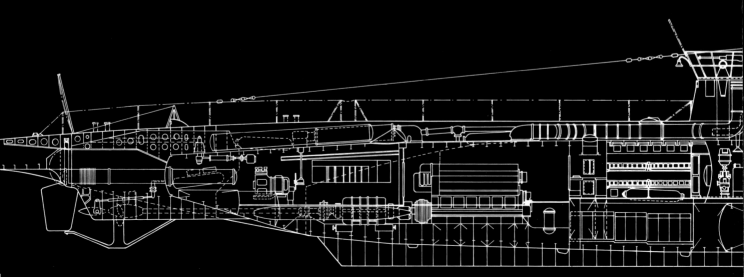

In August 1941 the Royal Navy captured a Type VIIC U-Boat intact when *U.570* surrendered to a pair of Hudson bombers south of Iceland. Below: the inboard profile of *U.570* showing the cramped accommodation. Above: after a lengthy series of trials *U.570* was commissioned as HMS *Graph*.

for themselves. In April the losses from U-Boats dropped to 56 ships of 328,000 tons, and in May to 50 ships of 264,000 tons.

The U-Boats paid a fearful price, and in May 41 were sunk, 30 per cent of the total at sea. Losses on this scale were more than flesh and blood could bear, and on May 24, 1942 Admiral Dönitz reluctantly gave the order for a 'temporary' withdrawal from the North Atlantic. It was the turning point of the naval war, and indeed the point at which the Germans lost their last chance of victory. But, like other great strategic victories, it did not conclude the War, and the Battle of the Atlantic was to go on for another two long years. There were still many U-Boats at large, and although they never reached the peak of success that they had in March 1943 they remained dangerous to the end.

The Defeat of the U-Boat

The fifth phase of the Atlantic battle started in June 1943, with a massive offensive against the U-Boats. Four US escort carriers were sent to the Azores, where they accounted for 13 U-Boats in three months, many of them victims of a new homing torpedo called 'Fido'. In the Bay of Biscay the RAF organised heavy offensive patrols, which led to the phenomenon of the 'flak-trap' U-Boats. Because of the early success of the Metox radar search receiver in detecting airborne radar pulses the U-Boat Command falsely assumed that U-Boats would

thought of abandoning the convoy system altogether.

Unfortunately for Dönitz and his devoted U-Boat Arm they were on the brink of defeat. First, the escorts and aircraft diverted to cover the 'Torch' landings were at last returned to Western Approaches Command. Second, improved cryptanalysis enabled convoys to be routed away from U-Boat patrol lines, and third, the Canadians, British and Americans had finally decided to pool their anti-submarine forces, which enabled a much more economical use of the total strength available. The increased number of escorts also enabled Western Approaches Command to form five new support groups, while US Navy escort carrier groups were sent to the mid-Atlantic to put down the supply U-Boats which had been a most important factor in extending the danger areas. Another factor which was not so obvious was the return of the Allies' most talented U-Boat hunter, Captain F J Walker, whose new tactics were now becoming standard among the escorts. But whatever the cause the figures speak

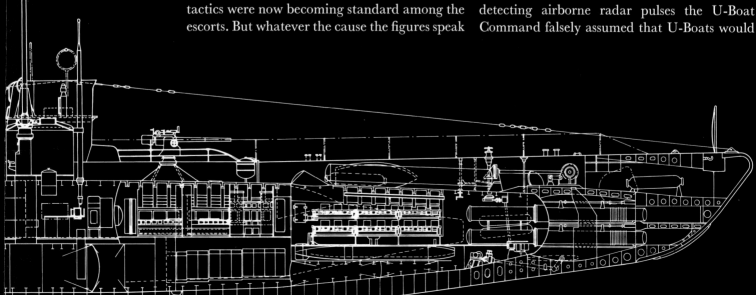

have a better chance of survival if they stayed on the surface, using their deck-guns to fight off the clumsy bombers. Some bombers were caught by U-Boats in this way, but the Allies' use of centimetric radar went undetected for a time, and this concealed the fact that a very large number of aircraft were constantly operating over the Bay. The U-Boats were badly hammered for their temerity, and it was soon realised that they were as vulnerable as ever, no matter what anti-aircraft armament was provided.

The next phase was a remarkable game of tit-for-tat, as the two sides rapidly switched tactics in an attempt to gain dominance. First the Luftwaffe sent Ju88 fighters to attack the anti-submarine aircraft, so the RAF retaliated by sending out Beaufighters and Mosquitoes to protect the patrols. Then the Royal Navy sent in support groups to make it harder for U-Boats to stay on the surface when attacked by aircraft. The German reply to this was to use glider-bombs in high-altitude attacks on the warships, and as a result the support groups were withdrawn out of range until such time as jamming equipment became available. The ruthless slugging match went on throughout 1943, and in all 40 U-Boats were sunk during the year in the Bay of Biscay.

The U-Boat Command was down but not out, and it used its withdrawal from the Atlantic as a chance to re-equip and re-train. A new and potent weapon was available, the 'Zaunkönig' T5 acoustic homing torpedo. Know to the Allies as the GNAT (German Naval Acoustic Torpedo), this slow-running torpedo 'homed' onto the propeller-noises of a surface ship running at speeds of 5 to 25 knots. It proved particularly deadly against escorts, which often had to accelerate suddenly in response to tactical needs. Convoys ON202 and ONS18 were the first to encounter the new tactics in September 1943. First the frigate *Lagan*, one of ON202's escorts, was hit in the stern and two merchantmen were sunk. Two more attacks on escorts were unsuccessful, but as the attacks seemed unusually heavy ON202 was ordered to unite with the slow convoy ONS18, now only 30 miles away. Despite the arrival of a support group and the presence of an escort carrier the

U-Boats sank three escorts and another four merchant ships. In this fierce six-day battle 20 U-Boats had taken on a total of 65 ships and 22 escorts, and had sunk six ships of 36,000 tons and three escorts with only 24 GNATs. But three U-Boats had been sunk, and the results were disappointing.

Escorts were given 'foxers', noisemakers which could be towed astern to decoy the GNATs, and it was soon clear that at certain speeds the acoustic homing device was not effective. Another countermeasure was to drop depth-charge patterns in the path of approaching GNATs, which then homed on the disturbed water or were detonated by the noise. The GNAT was a nuisance which increased the strain on escort crews, but it tempted the U-Boats to go for the escorts and thus tended to reduce merchant shipping losses. As a result of the generally disappointing performance of the new weapon U-Boats were withdrawn from the outer convoy routes to allow them to be refitted. The 'schnorchel' was an air-mast which allowed a U-Boat to recharge its batteries while running submerged, and it did reduce losses from air attack. But using the schnorchel was a nerve-wracking business, and it tended to foster a less aggressive attitude among the U-Boats.

The Last Chance

The only promising development in sight was the fast submarine. This project was first mooted in 1943, although ideas for closed-cycle motors had been under development since 1940. Briefly, there were two ways of producing high speed, to fit a closed-cycle (ie not using atmospheric oxygen) hydrogen peroxide Walther engine or to expand the battery-capacity and reduce hull-resistance. The German Navy pushed ahead with both, but with hindsight it is clear that the 'electro-submarine' or Type XXI, with its sound and workable principles was a better bet than the dangerous and unreliable Walther Type XVII. But, as with tanks, Hitler and his advisers showed a fatal affection for advanced weapons which over-extended the already inefficient German war industry. However fast the Walther U-Boats could travel, a

1. The U-Boat Commander's stopwatch times the run of his torpedoes. 2. At the end of the run, one torpedo hits a tanker. 3. During the counter-attack, crewmen count the depth charges. 4. On rare occasions a U-Boat might surface to finish off her target with gunfire, but this propaganda view was most unlikely in the Atlantic.

theoretical maximum of 20 knots, they carried fuel for only 114 miles; the fuel was unbelievably expensive and difficult to make. The U-Boat building program was already absorbing vast quantities of steel and other raw materials, but above all it used up manpower. To make matters worse the obsolescent Type VIIC U-Boats were still being built by skilled labor, whereas the complex, prefabricated Type XXIs, on which all Dönitiz' hopes rested, were assembled by 'diluted' labor made up largely of semi-skilled workers.

In the series of conferences on naval strategy known as the Führer Conferences on Naval Affairs, which were started early in 1943, the true state of affairs was revealed. It was hoped to increase production of standard U-Boats (VIICs) to 27 per month by the second half of 1943, but the program was already using 4,500 tons of steel per month for hulls and a further 1,500 tons for torpedo-casings. It was hoped to

increase production to 30 U-Boats per month, and Dönitiz was forced to admit that even if this could be raised to 40, where would the men to man them come from? In June 1943 the U-Boat Arm totalled about 103,000 men, but by the beginning of 1945 the requirement would be for 438,000 men. If the planned number of 634 U-Boats were commissioned they would require crews totalling 62,000 men. The Kriegsmarine was already short of 200,000 men because the Army had the lion's share of manpower. The extra U-Boat crews could be found but they would have to come from the surface fleet, which included such effective units as E-Boats, as well as useless capital ships.

The Allies were aware of the race against time, and early in 1944 several bombing raids disrupted production of electric motors for the Type XXI boats, while raids on canals slowed down the delivery of prefabricated sections. The tempo of the fighting in the Atlantic, on the

4

other hand, was easing. The US Navy 'hunter-killer' groups in mid-Atlantic had growing success in 1944, and once again Dönitz had to give up his plans to operate in distant waters. The build-up before D-Day and the actual invasion in June 1944 resulted in all U-Boats being diverted to the English Channel in an attempt to attack the enormous concentration of shipping. To counter this the Allies deployed no fewer than ten support groups and an escort carrier. These proved highly effective in preventing the U-Boats from achieving any results at all.

The last phase of the Battle of the Atlantic coincided with the Normandy Invasion, as the first of a smaller and simplified version of the Type XXI U-Boat, known as Type XXIII came into service at this time. Being small and maneuverable they proved unusually hard to detect, especially as they operated in coastal waters. The change from deep waters found

many experienced ASDIC operators unprepared, and as the schnorchel was hard to detect with existing airborne radar sets, even the most successful aircrew had to fall back on visual sightings. Right up to the end the U-Boats achieved sinkings around British coastal waters, and the last phase proved in many ways to be the most irksome and frustrating to the hard-worked Allied anti-submarine forces.

The success of the Allied landings in Normandy soon made a very important contribution to the Battle of the Atlantic, when land forces occupied first Brest and then the Britanny coast. Even those bases that were not captured were subjected to merciless bombing and became untenable. The crews made their way back to Germany if their boats were knocked out, and when this became impossible they took passage in U-Boats to Norway or Germany, the last U-Boat leaving Brest in August 1944. But the Norwegian bases were also under attack, and the growing concentration of Allied warships made patrols very difficult. In Germany the situation was even more chaotic, with shipyards and dockyards increasingly paralysed by bombing and shortages of material.

Despite all these tribulations the U-Boat Arm retained its cohesion to the end. There was no refusal to carry out orders, despite the discomfort and danger which was an inescapable part of a submariner's life. Out of a total of about 39,000 U-Boat officers and men, 28,000 were killed and 5,000 were captured, a casualty rate of 85 per cent. This was easily the worst casualty rate suffered by any arm of the fighting forces of any of the belligerents, and gives some idea of the devotion with which the U-Boat Arm

served Adolf Hitler and his lieutenant Karl Dönitz.

The last act in the Battle of the Atlantic came on May 1, 1945 when Germany surrendered. All U-Boats in harbor were ordered to be surrendered, and all those at sea were to surface, hoist a black flag and make for designated ports. And so the 'sea-wolves', as the German press liked to call them, came in to surrender; very few disobeyed orders and scuttled themselves, although one solitary U-Boat chose internment in South America rather than surrender.

The statistics of the Battle of the Atlantic are almost unbelievable. Convoyed ships covered 200 million miles, and 2,282 ships totalling 14.4 million gross tons were sunk. Another 1.9

Grand Admiral Raeder distributes decorations to the crew of a U-Boat at Kiel.

Despite heavy losses the morale of the U-Boat Arm remained high, but the other services tended to siphon off recruits, and so an energetic recruiting campaign was mounted.

Freiwillig zur

KRIEGSMARINE

million tons of shipping was damaged by submarine attack. The German Navy commissioned 1,150 U-Boats, of which 807 were sunk, 251 of them by surface vessels, 282 by aircraft and 46 by aircraft and ships in collaboration. A further 37 were mined, 25 sunk by allied submarines, 96 by strategic bombing (83 of them *after* June 1944) and 60 lost by various means such as accident, stranding etc. No fewer than 587 were sunk in the North Atlantic and the waters around Britain and Germany.

British Lessons

The important lessons of the Battle of the Atlantic were two. First, that a maritime nation like the United States or Great Britain dared not neglect sea communications, and second, that an all-out onslaught on those sea communications could in the long run only be overcome by a combination of all arms, land, sea and air. The two principal Allies drew up grandiose schemes for the prosecution of the war against the Axis in 1942, but their overconcentration on taking the offensive, however pressing the reasons, at the expense of the Battle of the Atlantic nearly brought about their defeat. True, the United States could not have been defeated outright in 1942 or 1943, but the loss of Great Britain as an ally through starvation would have made it impossible for the United States to intervene in the European theater or anywhere else in the Atlantic and Mediterranean. Not only would this have left Europe totally under the control of Nazi Germany but in the long run it would have cut the USA off from its markets, which was the underlying preoccupation of President Roosevelt when he first took a hand in the Battle of the Atlantic.

As for the second lesson, it is significant that the defeat of the U-Boats was finally accomplished when not only the air and sea elements combined, but the land forces made their contribution. Strategic bombing proved a very expensive and relatively ineffectual way of cutting back U-Boat production, and ultimately it was the capture and neutralization of U-Boat bases and building facilities by Allied ground troops that brought the five-year old agony to

Survivors of a sunken
U-Boat are helped aboard
a British escort in the
Atlantic.

an end. It is fitting that the principle of tri-service operations should have proved so valid in winning this vital battle.

The other lessons taught by the Battle of the Atlantic were more mundane. Clearly the British Admiralty was guilty of complacency regarding the Royal Navy's ability to defend shipping. To some extent this can be blamed on the RN's concentration on the screening of warships, which reached a high pitch of efficiency between 1919 and 1939. The grinding economies of the 1920s and early 1930s meant that no fuel could be spared for additional exercises in mercantile convoying, and in any case the Navy's political masters would point out that unrestricted submarine warfare against merchant shipping was banned by international treaty. Only when it was clear that the British would be facing the Germans once more, and a German Navy under the direction of Adolf Hitler, did the Admiralty plan on the assumption that shipping would be sunk at sight. As soon as that contingency was established the Admiralty began the construction of a series of convoy escorts; their design proved to be excellent, and they later formed the core of the Atlantic support groups, but too few were ready in 1939.

Final Victory: the Reasons

The US Navy, which had fought with the British in 1917-18, had not developed anti-submarine tactics to the same extent, largely because it was looking to the Pacific, and thought in terms of fleet actions against the Japanese. In one respect, however, the USN showed great foresight. Thanks to the keen interest in naval air power the subject of air cover for convoys was investigated, although as happened with the British, lack of funds prevented any further progress. The worst mistake was the failure to provide any worthwhile anti-submarine doctrine, which took the form of a reluctance to accept convoy as the automatic defense against submarines. Great faith was placed in 'offensive patrols', despite the fact that the British had lost millions of tons of shipping in 1916-17 by following just that course. One very serious failure was in the

German Navy Matrosen gefreiter 1941. This leading seaman aboard a surface raider is wearing a fur-lined reed-green anorak over his dark blue uniform; the ear flaps on the boarding cap are worn down. By 1942 U-Boat crews were being issued with more specialized protective clothing.

Watch keepers on the conning tower of a U-Boat wear oilskins and sou'westers against the driving spray.

supply of weapons. RAF Coastal Command aircraft wasted many of their early opportunities because the design of anti-submarine bombs was faulty. In one notorious case in September 1939, two of the carrier *Ark Royal's* aircraft managed to shoot themselves down while attacking a U-Boat! A hastily adapted naval depth-charge had to be used until a proper aerial depth-charge could be designed.

So much for Allied shortcomings. The most serious failure on the German side was the comparative failure to make the best use of scientific advice and knowledge. During the crucial months of 1942 and year 1943 the U-Boat Arm was unable to match the Allies' technical skill in producing new devices and countermeasures. The long time taken to realise that high-frequency direction-finding was in use and the misunderstanding about centimetric radar can be blamed on the organization rather than the abilities of the people involved. Possibly one of the best features of the British setup was the close liaison between the escort commanders, senior officers and the scientific side. Complaints about equipment and practical points could be made direct to senior scientists from time to time, and the new concept of Operational Research threw up a succession of remarkable ideas for weapons and tactics.

Beating the U-Boats called for the mobilization of the resources of two powerful nations, and it must be remembered that the Battle of the Atlantic nearly over-stretched the resources of even the United States. This was a remarkable achievement for a force which had numbered only 56 U-Boats on the outbreak of war. But the Battle of the Atlantic also claimed the lives of some 30,000 merchant seamen. Untrained for war and yet fighting on an almost equal footing with naval seamen, these men were ultimately the obstacle which foiled the U-Boats. Had the morale of British, American or any other nationality of seamen cracked, had merchant ships been unable to sail because their crews refused to face the U-Boats, then nothing could have stopped the U-Boats from winning. As in other campaigns, the human element could never be ruled out.

Hitler's War may well have been lost on the Eastern Front, German troops and equipment all proved inadequate in their advance over the boundless Russian hinterland.

BARBAROSSA:
THE NAPOLEONIC DREAM

In 1941 Hitler attempted to do what Napoleon had failed to do, in the biggest military operation in history, but once again the vast Russian hinterland proved unconquerable.

Oberschutz, summer 1941.
He is wearing a uniform
identical to that worn in
1939, before the needs of
the Russian winter made
themselves felt.
Equipment includes gas
mask, canister, gas cape,
water bottle, canteen,
rolled *zeltbahn* (waterproof
camouflage cape); he is
carrying a MG34 machine
gun.

SOON AFTER 3 O'CLOCK on the morning of Sunday, June 22, 1941 a concentrated artillery barrage was directed on the Soviet frontier areas over the entire German-Russian front from the Baltic to the Black Sea, while three German Air Fleets spread chaos and confusion deep into the back areas, destroying air fields and many hundreds of Soviet aircraft on the ground. In the wake of this opening three German Army Groups comprising approximately 3,500,000 men, advanced behind four Panzer Armies, swiftly to envelop hundreds of thousands of Soviet troops manning the Soviet frontier and taken unawares.

Thus on that morning Field Marshal von Brauchitsch, Commander-in-Chief of the German armies, launched the greatest and most tragic land battle in the history of warfare. But Adolf Hitler, the Nazi Führer, was the real power and directing force. The 'object' of this immense operation was the destruction of Soviet military power and of the Soviet Union by a lightning assault. The very essence was speed. Such an object is not an aim in strict military terms; it was a highly emotional desire conceived in the peculiar type of racial obsession that dominated the 'thinking' of the Führer. As early as July 1940 he had voiced his intention of 'dealing with the Soviet Union', and soon afterwards planning began, finally hardening into Operation 'Barbarossa' in December of that year. The reasonable aims were many and sensible: the elimination of any possible Soviet threat, the gaining of the vast wheatlands of the Ukraine, the envelopment of areas yielding mineral wealth vital to Germany's ability to wage war, the safeguarding of oil supplies in the South, and much else. Such an aim clearly defined, together with clear objectives embracing these areas from the Baltic ports and Leningrad in the North, Moscow in the center, to Kiev and the Donetz Basin, to Rostov and the Caucasian oil fields in the South, might well have been possible. But there was, even in such aims, a fatal flaw: Hitler referred to the Slav peoples as vermin to be destroyed. Thus the appalling barbarity of the battle was pre-ordained, and immense populations, many of which might well have welcomed the Germans,

were either brutally exterminated or enslaved. At the same time Soviet unity and power were consolidated.

Moreover, German ignorance of the topography of Soviet Russia was profound except in the vaguest terms. There had been very slight appreciation of the absence of hard roads, even of the existence of considerable towns grown from villages in the years of 'peace' since 1917; even less appreciation of the immensity of the Soviet territory east of Moscow and the almost inexhaustible reserves which were training and would become available. In short the operation was doomed, and even its initial successes were prejudiced. What might have been is pure hypothesis; what was, resulted in the destruction of German military power over a period of three years, and the slaughter of probably 50 million men, women and children, while Soviet hegemony was established over the Slav States on her Western frontiers.

Allied Support for the Soviets

But in the first hours and in the first months none of this was evident, and German successes seemed ominous to many observers in the West. Boldly, Winston Churchill, Prime Minister of beleaguered Britain, swiftly assured Stalin of his full support. The United States would soon follow.

Whether the great weight of material contributed over the years to the Soviet struggles played any decisive part in the Russian victory must remain debatable. It certainly had little or no effect on the outcome of 'Barbarossa'. It was accepted sourly and without thanks. The cost, not simply in the materials of war, but also in ships and men, especially to Britain at a time when she needed everything for her own defenses, was very heavy.

Meanwhile German Army Group North commanded by Field Marshal von Leeb, comprising 26 divisions spearheaded by the Panzer Army of Col. General Hoepner, made rapid progress. Advancing out of East Prussia, the Northern thrust under Col. General Hoth made rapid gains, consolidated by 18th Army and 16th Army. Lithuania was swiftly overrun

The swastika replaces the hammer and sickle in a captured Russian town.

and by the morning of June 23 the Germans had entered Latvia and were marching on in intense heat.

At the same time on von Leeb's right flank General von Manstein's armored corps had established a bridgehead at Daugavpils over the River Dvina. Soviet resistance had been mainly sporadic but far from negligible. Major General Sobennikov's 8th (Soviet) Army, in spite of heavy losses of material, withdrew from Riga. General Morozov's 11th Army, also suffering heavily, had been forced to retreat, rapidly opening up a gap between the 8th and 3rd Armies. While many thousands were in flight, others made sporadic attacks, established themselves in small groups, and in the first week only 6,000 prisoners had been taken by von Leeb's Army Group.

On von Leeb's right flank Field Marshal von Bock's Army Group Center, designed to be the main attack on Moscow with 51 divisions, including two Panzer Armies, advanced across the Bug on Bialystok and Brest-Litovsk, to open the main road to Smolensk and thence to Moscow. Whatever the vacillations soon to develop in Hitler's mind, Moscow was and remained von Bock's objective. Success in the advance and the assault on Moscow was his overwhelming ambition. It was also that of General Guderian, Commander of the Panzer Group racing towards Minsk, who had his eyes on Smolensk. The road to Moscow would then be opened.

The Move towards Minsk

While infantry fought hard against determined opposition in Brest-Litovsk von Bock's left flanking Armored Group under Col. General Hoth pressed on in a wide encircling movement towards Minsk. At the same time infantry of the 3rd and 4th Armies were engaged in an encircling movement to attempt to destroy the Soviet armies in the Bialystok pocket.

On von Bock's right flank, separating Army Group Center from Field Marshal von Rundstedt's Army Group South, lay the Pripet Marshes, an area of swamp and scrub, sluggish streams, few roads or tracks, causeways through forest and swamp, all of which would turn swiftly into quagmires of black mud, like glue. Only tracked vehicles could be relied upon in such an area, and similar conditions were repeated over many areas of the entire battlefield. Overwhelmingly the German armies relied on wheeled vehicles, and this was one of the causes of their undoing.

Stalin's Knowledge of the Attack

The Pripet Marshes, approximately 150 miles ride from North to South and 400 miles deep from West to East, formed a natural boundary and barrier inpenetrable to the Germans, between Army Group Centre and Army Group South. It was also an area in which Soviet troops were able to survive, and to emerge to harry the flanks of the advancing enemy. Yet the Pripet Marshes did not represent any serious threat to the advancing Germans, and in the event complete tactical surprise was achieved by them.

It seems strange that the Soviet High Command and the Kremlin itself should have been taken by surprise by the German attack. It had been the subject of much talk in diplomatic circles in Moscow for months, but somehow it seems to have escaped the ears of Stalin. In any case it did not impress him. Moreover, German preparations were very evident and massive troop movements, however well disguised as maneuvres, should have given grounds at least for grave suspicion that attack was imminent. Yet it was several days after the assault before Stalin knew and began to appreciate what was happening.

The West was in a rather different way equally ignorant. Neither the Germans nor anyone else knew of the rapid Soviet training of their manpower and the creation of immense reserves in their Eastern territories. The 'liquidation' of senior Soviet officers in the drastic purge of 1937 and the extensive inroads made into the command structure of the Soviet armies was thought to have gravely weakened Soviet military power.

In fact, Stalin had no illusions about German ambitions, nor was he misled by the Soviet-German Pact. The German need of Soviet raw

A PzKpw III command tank (note the radio aerial at the rear) advances into Russia.

The PzKpw III Ausf.F, armed with a 75mm gun, was the backbone of the panzer attack.

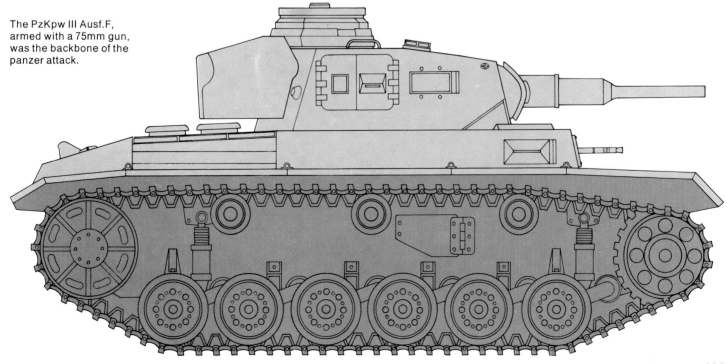

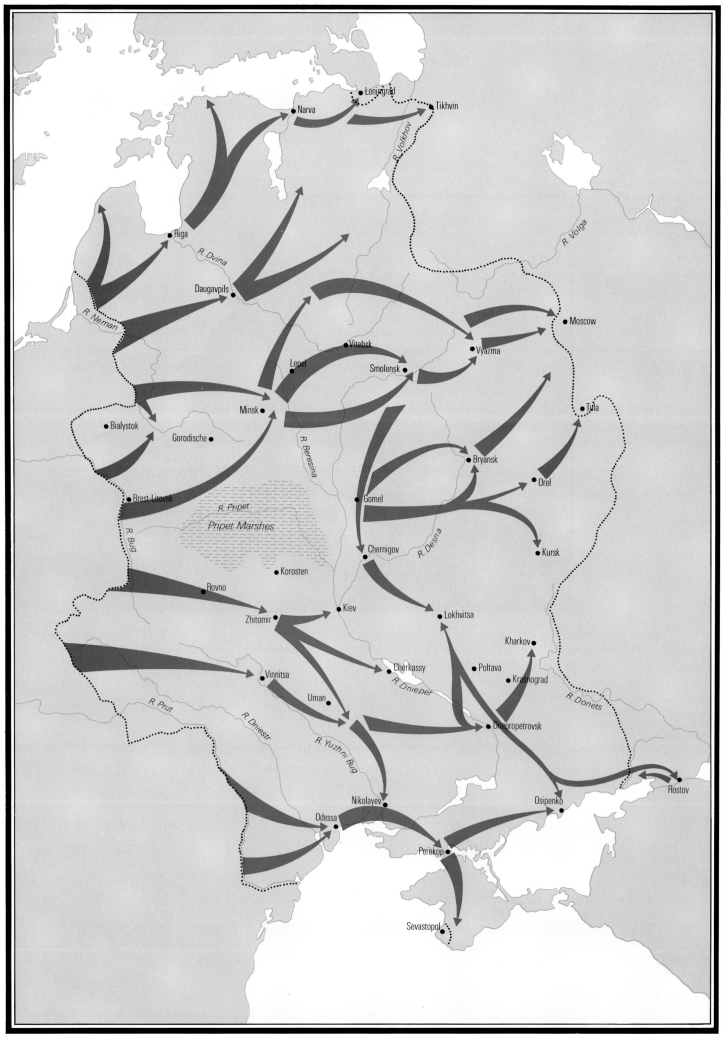

Riga

R. Dvina

R. Neman

Daugavpils

Narva

Leningrad

Tikhvin

R. Volkhov

R. Volga

Vitebsk

Lepel

Smolensk

Vyazma

Moscow

Minsk

R. Beresina

Bialystok

Gorodische

Brest-Litovsk

R. Pripet

Pripet Marshes

R. Bug

R. Pripet

Korosten

Rovno

Zhitomir

Kiev

Cherkassy

R. Dnieper

Vinnitsa

Uman

Odessa

R. Prut

R. Dniestr

R. Yuzhni Bug

Nikolayev

Gomel

Chernigov

R. Desna

Bryansk

Orel

Kursk

Tula

Lokhvitsa

Kharkov

Poltava

Krasnograd

R. Donets

Dnepropetrovsk

Osipenko

Rostov

Perekop

Sevastopol

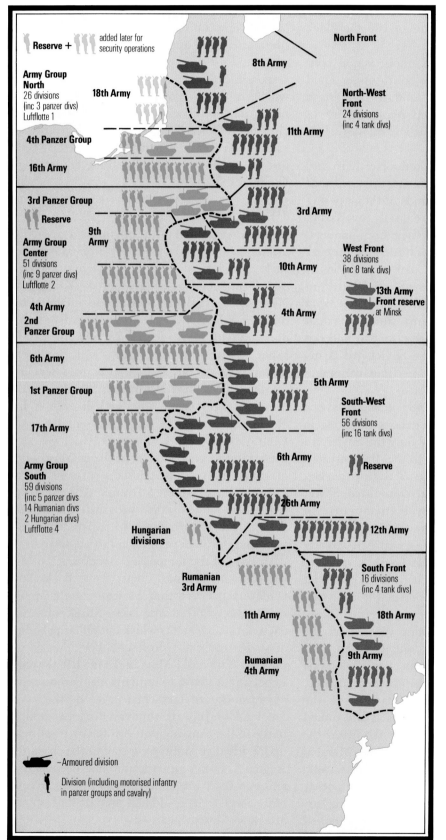

Reserve + added later for security operations

Army Group North
26 divisions
(inc 3 panzer divs)
Luftflotte 1

18th Army
4th Panzer Group
16th Army

3rd Panzer Group
Reserve
9th Army
Army Group Center
51 divisions
(inc 9 panzer divs)
Luftflotte 2
4th Army
2nd Panzer Group

6th Army
1st Panzer Group
17th Army

Army Group South
59 divisions
(inc 5 panzer divs
14 Rumanian divs
2 Hungarian divs)
Luftflotte 4

Hungarian divisions

Rumanian 3rd Army
11th Army
Rumanian 4th Army

North Front
8th Army
North-West Front
24 divisions
(inc 4 tank divs)
11th Army

3rd Army
West Front
38 divisions
(inc 8 tank divs)
10th Army
13th Army Front reserve at Minsk
4th Army

5th Army
South-West Front
56 divisions
(inc 16 tank divs)
6th Army
Reserve
26th Army
12th Army

South Front
16 divisions
(inc 4 tank divs)
18th Army
9th Army

— Armoured division

Division (including motorised infantry in panzer groups and cavalry)

materials was very great and the Russians had observed their commitments under their treaty meticulously. While the rapid success of the German lightning defeat of France had surprised Stalin he still could not believe that Germany would turn against him while Great Britain remained undefeated. Trying to understand Hitler's mind in terms of his own he had found it impossible to believe what should have been obvious. Yet his assessment of the German targets if an attack should come was correct.

Early warnings from Britain and the United States of the impending attack were discounted by Stalin because his suspicious mind, well aware that a war between Germany and the Soviet Union could save Britain, could not understand that her warnings might be genuine and were not some devious trick to make war.

On June 13 the warnings of Marshal Timoshenko, Commander-in-Chief of the Soviet Armies, were disregarded. Nevertheless Stalin was becoming uneasy, and summoned Marshals Timoshenko and Zhukov and General Vatutin to the Kremlin, while on June 21 the Politburo met with the Soviet Marshals present to discuss the possibility of war.

Even in the first days, although almost completely deprived of accurate news from the front by the breakdown of communications due to the heavy enemy artillery barrage and the devastation wrought by the German air fleets, Stalin asked Japan to mediate. Nevertheless the news from Col. General Kirponos commanding the Soviet front from the Pripet Marshes to the Rumanian frontier was reasonably accurate. He alone of the forward generals had not been surprised. He had been in his battle headquarters and had reported the immediate likelihood of attack on June 21 but his fears were not accepted. Yet the Ukraine and Kiev with all the wealth of wheat and minerals which this vast area yielded, must be, Stalin believed, the major target of the Germans. Donetz coal and iron and all the armament industries in the area were obvious targets as was Caucasian oil. Thus Stalin had his greatest concentrations of troops on the South West front under Field Marshal Budyenny, 56 Soviet divisions including 16 tank divisions under Col. General Kirponos and 16 divisions including 4 tank divisions under General Tyulenev from Rumania to the Black Sea.

The Germans also had their major concentrations in Army Group South under Field Marshal von Rundstedt, a total of 59 divisions including 5 Panzer divisions reinforced by 14 Rumanian and 2 Hungarian divisions, all supported by an air fleet.

But it was development on the Northern and Central fronts in the opening phases that seemed to dominate the minds of the opposing dictators, both of whom were totally involved in directing the war in spite of their Commanders-in-Chief and their Chiefs of Staff. On June 22 Field Marshal Zhukov, Chief of the Soviet General Staff, was sent to the South West front to see General Kirponos and discover the exact state of affairs. At the same time, Marshals Shaposhnikov and Kulik were sent to find out what was happening to the Soviet 3rd Army under General Pavlov's West front command facing Field Marshal von Bock.

General Pavlov, apparently unaware of the situation on his front, had delayed too long in an attempt to withdraw not only the Soviet 3rd but also the 10th Army from the dire positions developing rapidly in the Bialystok pocket. Fearing the worst, he had committed Soviet 13th Army to hold Minsk in an attempt to open the way of escape, but he was already too late. The German 47th Panzer Group had already cut the escape route, while German infantry were completing the encirclement of the Soviet troops, estimated at 290,000, in the Bialystok pocket.

No news of this impending disaster on the Central front had reached the Kremlin, and there was no news from Stalin's emissaries, one of whom was reported lost and the other sick. Even General Pavlov was unaware of the situation. In Moscow Stalin fretted and fumed and on June 30 he and Timoshenko heard the news over the German radio. Field Marshal Zhukov was at once instructed to make radio contact with Pavlov and ask him whether enemy reports that two of his armies had been surrounded was true. General Pavlov replied (according to Col. Seaton) that he thought there was a good deal of truth in it. He was at once ordered to Moscow with his Chief of Staff, summarily tried and executed. He had held his command for six days and could not have been responsible for the dispositions of his armies, which, as many thought after the event, were much too far forward and vulnerable to encirclement by the lightning armored spearheads round their flanks. The disposition of the Soviet forces was the responsibility of the Soviet High Command.

Hitler Vacillates

Hitler was elated at the opening success of his armor, and excited by General von Manstein's early crossing of the River Dvina and his establishment of a bridgehead at Daugavpils. Nevertheless Hitler soon began to vacillate, his mind ranging over the whole vast front, obsessed with early victory. In July von Leeb's rapid progress in the North and the great importance of the Baltic ports to safeguard supplies of Swedish iron ore to the Reich, led the Führer to order von Bock to switch his Northern Armored Group to strengthen von Leeb's assault on Leningrad. This was disconcerting to von Bock but he kept Moscow in his sights, as also did Guderian commanding his right flanking Armored Group. Without delay Guderian made rapid progress on Minsk, determined to open the road to Smolensk and surround the Soviet armies in the whole area.

In spite of the temporary loss of much of the left flanking armor, both von Bock and Guderian believed that Moscow should be the main target, and having taken Minsk with two encircling movements which cut off large bodies of Soviet troops at Gorodische, Bock pressed on towards Smolensk. Moving on his left through Lepel and Vitebsk to outflank the Beresina, his advance guards reached the outskirts of Smolensk on July 16, although the greatest tank battle of the campaign on von Bock's front held up his advance and the capture of the city until August 7. Losses on both sides had been heavy, and von Bock was compelled to rest his troops, refit as well as he could and prepare for his final attack on Moscow.

While von Bock was halted at Smolensk von

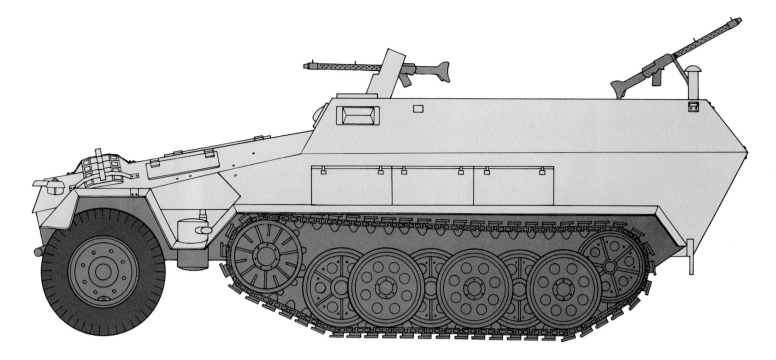

Leeb used his armored reinforcements to good effect. Rapidly he advanced through Esthonia and reached Narva in mid-August. But in the South, what was perhaps the vital battle of 'Barbarossa' was developing rapidly. Soviet readiness was not able to halt the enemy armored breakthrough in the wake of the artillery and air bombardment, but stubborn resistance was given. On the Northern flank South of the Pripet Marshes, von Kleist's Panzer Group drove a wedge between the Soviet 5th and 6th Armies, reached Rovno and pressed on to Zhitomar, and prepared to advance on Kiev. Nevertheless von Kleist's armor had been under constant harassment, mainly from Potopov's 5th Army. Withdrawing into the Pripet Marshes, Potopov held his army in being, its morale high; he was able to mount attacks on the flanks of the German armor, and held up the progress of Field Marshal von Reichenau's army following up in support.

The Appearance of the T34 Tank

Nevertheless the German advance, even in the first week had gone far enough and fast enough to threaten the encirclement of four Soviet armies, and on June 30 the Soviet High Command ordered Col. General Kirponos to withdraw 150 miles to a line Korosten – Novograd – Volymsk to Prokurov.

On July 9 von Kleist broke through the Soviet defense line, and took Zhitomar. But heavy fighting held up the Germans to the end of July, Kirponos' armies holding their positions in the area Novograd – Volymsk, while on July 10 Potopov's 5th Army struck suddenly out of the Pripet Marshes to cut the supply lines of the German 1st Panzer Group. This impeded the German 6th Army in its attempts to con-

German infantry and a
PzKpw III tank advance
through Russian
wheatfields.

solidate its gains, and Soviet 5th Army artillery concentrations, brilliantly directed, inflicted heavy casualties.

But nothing could seriously hold up the German armor. On July 5 von Rundstedt's right wing advanced across the Pruth. The resistance everywhere on the Southern front was far greater than the Germans had expected, and moreover the appearance of Soviet T-34 tanks, even when badly handled by inexperienced crews as most of them were, inflicted heavy casualties and were immune to the German anti-tank guns. It was not until the Germans had the brilliant idea of using their 88mm anti-aircraft gun in an anti-tank role that the menace was countered.

General Tyulenev, commanding two Soviet armies, had had time to know what to expect, and was ready for the Rumanians east of the River Pruth. Progress was slow but steady, the German 11th Army under Col. General Ritter von Schobert took two months to reach the Dnieper. But that was fast enough. Odessa was captured without great difficulty, but the Soviet defenses of the Perekop Isthmus, the gateway to the Crimea, were proving stubborn. Meanwhile von Schobert had been killed in an air crash, and von Manstein inherited his command to press his attack on the Perekop Isthmus.

Between August 10 and 12 the Germans had their first great success at Uman, and von Kleist's armor seized Nikolayov on the way to help force the Perekop, and open the way to

These Soviet infantrymen display a mixed bag of weapons. On the left the PPSh sub-machine gun, on the right the Simonov automatic rifle and above, the Degtyarev light machine gun.

the Crimea. On August 24 the Soviet High Command ordered the blowing up of the great Dnieper Dam, and ordered its armies in the whole region of Kiev to hold on at all costs. Already the dismantling of all plant and machinery to be moved East was proceeding rapidly, and all that could not be moved was being destroyed. Indeed, all the great wealth of the Donetz Basin was to be denied to the Germans, and they would inherit a waste land.

The Soviet Marshal Budyenny, commanding the Soviet South West front, had been alarmed from the beginning. He had withdrawn the bulk of his central armies to the Kiev area and was becoming increasingly anxious throughout August.

In mid-August Guderian's armor moving south had advanced on Gomel, and on August 20 drove on South to Chernigov. This threatened Potopov's 5th Army and all the Soviet armies covering Kiev. The German advance

continued steadily all along the line; on August 20 von Reichenau's 6th Army reached the Dnieper at Cherkassy. A Soviet catastrophe of the gravest nature was developing as von Kleist's armor advanced North from Dnepropetovsk.

Kirponos, commanding the Soviet right flanking armies quickly realised the dangers and sought permission to disengage with the utmost urgency, but Shaposhnikov, Chief of Staff in Moscow, reflecting Stalin's views, denied permission. Cautiously Kirponos began to withdraw, but the German armor, under Guderian from the North and von Kleist from the South was advancing very fast, aiming to join forces far to the West of Kiev, to cut off all Soviet armies in what came to be known as the Kiev Cauldron. Marshal Budyenny, attempting to withdraw too late, was escaping eastward with the remnants of his armies but at least a million men, fully equipped, continued to fight hard

West of Kiev. These included the armies of Kirponos and Tyulenev, whose left flank was on the Black Sea.

Marshal Timoshenko was at once sent to replace Budyenny on the South West front while Marshal Zhukov took over the defenses covering the approaches to Moscow.

Hitler had been vacillating since early July and resisting the constant attempts of von Brauchitsch and Halder, his Chief of Staff, to persuade him to keep his mind on Moscow. Together with von Bock and Guderian they believed that by pressing the assault on Moscow in all possible . strength they could overwhelm the city before winter set in. They had all, including Guderian, resisted Hitler's decision to deprive von Bock of his armored strength at a vital time. But Hitler was adamant, and no one knew his thought processes.

The final attempt to keep Hitler's mind on Moscow was made in the middle of August.

Hitler's response, embodied in a directive, was definite:

'. . . of primary importance before the outbreak of winter is not the capture of Moscow, but rather the occupation of the Crimea, of the industrial and coal mining area off the Donetz Basin, the cutting off of the Russian supply routes from the Caucasian oilfields.'

Hitler's Costly Strategy

In this new policy Hitler was entirely alone. Field Marshal von Rundstedt, the most experienced commander in the German Army, a brilliant strategist and able tactician, disagreed profoundly. Hitler at once treated him to a lecture on economics. It seemed to all the German military commanders on and off the field that the object of 'Barbarossa' had changed, and that *Blitzkrieg* was to become positional warfare seeking to defeat and bring about the surrender of the Soviet Union, not by the swift defeat of its armies, which it was already apparent had been under-estimated. It was beginning to be noted at the time that the Russians were bringing reserve armies forward with great speed and preparing for counterattacks which might develop into a counter-offensive when the Germans were at full stretch. Thus the only chance of swift victory must rest in the capture of Moscow, the seat of Government and center of a great industrial area.

Halder noted with some alarm that instead of the expected Soviet 200 divisions which the *Blitzerieg* had been planned to destroy, he had identified more than 350 divisions. At the same time German losses, while very small in comparison with Soviet losses, were severe. Moreover, not only the enemy but the whole nature of the Soviet Union, its weather, the very difficult going and the immense difficulties of adequate maintenance were taking a severe toll of manpower.

Field Marshals von Rundstedt and von Bock were both demanding replacements, and it soon became apparent that the reinforcements were not only insufficient to replace the losses but were of a lower standard of training.

It was also noted that in spite of the very

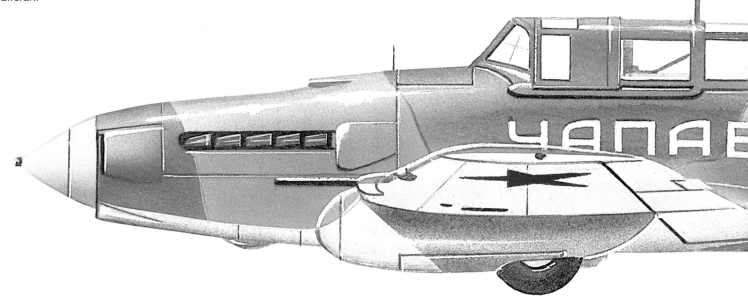

The Ilyushin Il-2 tactical bomber was known as the 'Sturmovik' or assault aircraft. Its robust construction and armor for the pilot made it a formidable tank-busting aircraft.

A formation of Sturmoviks flying over Stalingrad. Right: in the early days of Barbarossa much of the Soviet air strength was destroyed on the ground.

great German successes all along the ever-lengthening line, the experiences of Poland and France were not being repeated. In Poland and France the Poles and the French, on finding themselves surrounded, had been seized all too often with panic, and the armored spearheads were virtually able to disregard the enemy troops they had overrun, leaving them to be rounded up by the supporting infantry. In Russia, while many Soviet troops had been captured, thousands had formed into groups and continued to fight with dogged courage, drawing on arms and ammunition carefully sited and hidden against such emergencies.

In the weeks immediately preceding Hitler's directive the German armies under von Rundstedt had great success, based on von Rundstedt's tactical ideas and largely disregarding Hitler's known wishes. In early August, despite sustained Soviet resistance von

Kleist pressed his attacks and succeeded in isolating 20 divisions, a large part of the Soviet 6th and 12th Armies. Vinnitsa had been taken by von Stulpnagel's 17th Army despite powerful attacks by the Russians. The 17th thereupon continued to advance on the Dnieper, and the first considerable German victory occurred at Uman. After bitter fighting more than 100,000 Soviet troops with 300 tanks and 800 guns were taken by the Germans by August 8. At the same time the Soviet Southern armies under Tyulenev were under grave threat.

By the middle of August the Russians had lost the Ukraine but the Germans had paid heavily in casualties. When Guderian moved South with the aim of linking with von Kleist's main armor already moving North to encircle the entire Kiev area, far to the East of the city, the Russians had already suffered badly and the armies stubbornly defending Kiev and the Dnieper were in a desperate situation. Their predicament, clear to the Soviet commanders on the spot, was not accepted by Moscow. Four new Soviet armies were rapidly forming and moving westward, and the Soviet High Command ordered that Kiev and the Dnieper must be held. It was no longer possible.

Meanwhile, General Eremenko on the South of the central front had formed a new Bryansk front from remnants of the defeated armies together with 50th and 13th Soviet Armies. These moved towards Gomel to attack Guderian's flank. Eremenko expressed his confidence to Stalin but his optimism was not justified. His 13th Army was forced to retreat eastward, losing contact with the main body of his troops.

Guderian made rapid progress to complete

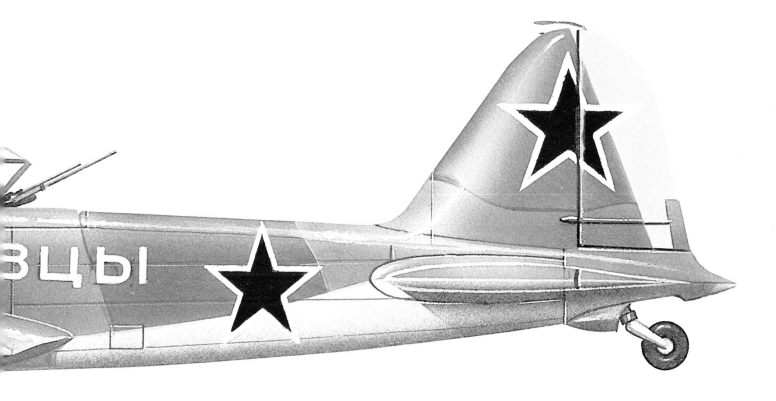

the success of von Rundstedt's drive on the Dnieper and the reduction of Kiev. In early September the German 17th Army crossed the Dnieper and the main strength of von Kleist's Panzer Group was moving North.

Neither Budyenny nor Kirponos was able to convey the urgency they felt to the Soviet High Command, and on September 13 Marshal Budyenny was replaced by Marshal Timoshenko, and Kirponos's desire to disengage and withdraw was denied. On September 16 Guderian's spearheads joined with von Kleist's armor at Lokhvitsa 150 miles east of Kiev. The area enclosed was very large, probably holding within it more than 1,000,000 Soviet troops with all their artillery, transport and services. Very large numbers of the German enemy resolved on their destruction were also in that great enclosure, which could not in fact be completely enclosed or sealed.

On September 17, at least a day too late the Soviet High Command gave the order to Kirponos to withdraw.

The huge area cut off by the Germans known as the Kiev Cauldron, was greater even than the encirclement of the Soviet armies in the 'Minsk pocket'. These names are misleading. The areas involved compared with the entire Western front, as Fuller points out. Within them were many battlefields, and although the yield in prisoners was very large – perhaps more than half a million in the Kiev Cauldron –

German losses were also heavy, and the troops involved in rounding up the prisoners were more than the Germans could properly afford. But in an area so large perhaps an almost equal number of Russian troops in large and small groups continued to fight not simply for days and weeks, but for months.

Roads were so few and poor that German infantry found it difficult to round up the enemy, nor were they able to move as fast and freely as the Russians in their own territory. Perhaps several hundred thousand Russian troops survived, determined to fight, organized into groups of all sizes, harrying the enemy for weeks and months, and many escaping eastward. Such German victories were very costly.

In the Kiev Cauldron General Kirponos, whose armies had fought well and tenaciously, was reported killed.

The way through to Kursk and Kharkov now seemed wide open, but Timoshenko, scratching together all the troops that had escaped encirclement and with Malinovsky's 6th Army, formed a new defense line. At Poltava and Krasnograd the German 17th Army was halted.

Far to the South von Manstein was deeply involved in a bitter struggle to force the Perekop Isthmus and enter the Crimea. Sustained attacks by the German 54th Corps failed on September 24, and von Manstein was unable to find sufficient strength. His 11th Army and 3rd Rumanian Army advancing

The KV1 heavy tank had been secretly developed and was to become the scourge of the panzers. The 76mm gun could deal with any German tank, while the heavy armor was resistant to all German anti-tank artillery.

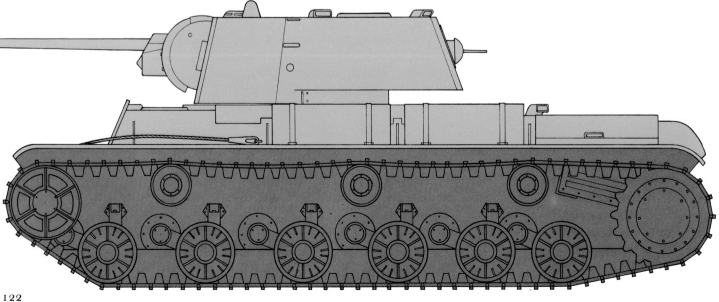

A German assault group
forces an entry into a
Russian border fort.

Eastward had met severe Soviet attacks and
the Rumanians were broken. For the time
being the assault on the Perekop came to a
standstill.

On October 7 von Rundstedt ordered von
Kleist to move South with part of his Panzer
Army and attack the Soviet South front. The
Soviet forces consisted of three armies newly
placed under the command of General Cherevichenko. Rapidly von Kleist moved on
Osipenko to join with 11th Army, moving
behind Cherevichenko and encircling two
Russian armies. Von Kleist at once turned east
to advance on Rostov while von Manstein
returned with his 11th Army to mount a final
assault on the Perekop and occupy the Crimea.
It would be a bitter and sustained struggle,
finally bogging down in the Crimea before
Sevastopol. The Black Sea was dominated by
the Soviet Fleet and the Red Air Force.

In September Hitler again changed his mind,
to the consternation of his own commanders as
well as the Soviet High Command. None could
follow his reasoning, but it seems simple. Confronted with the imminent failure of 'Barbarossa' and refusing to accept it, Hitler again
decided to concentrate on Moscow, the one
place where victory might be won before the
onset of winter.

Standstill on the Northern Front

Yet the remarkable achievement of the
Germans was undeniable, and in early September Hitler ordered Guderian to rejoin von
Bock's armies on the Central front and go all out
for Moscow. He had contrived to bring von
Bock's armies up to more than 1,500,000 men,
and there was, he believed, still time. Von Bock
also clung to this hope.

At the same time Hitler had given up all idea
of taking Leningrad. Von Leeb had done well
but not well enough, and Leningrad was more
than half surrounded. Yet Soviet counter-
attacks were constantly strengthening both
North and South of the city, and against
Hitler's will von Leeb was compelled to withdraw from Tikhvin, an area rich in bauxite,
under heavy Soviet pressure. Thus the Northern
front came to a standstill, and was committed

to a long siege of Leningrad. In the extreme South Hitler still pinned his hope on the capture of Rostov opening the way to the Caucasus and Baku oil. Von Kleist was making steady progress, advancing rapidly, but so was winter.

For Operation 'Typhoon' von Bock's Center Army Group had been built up to 70 divisions by robbing the North and South fronts. The aim was to destroy the Soviet armies before Moscow, advancing out of Smolensk, already consolidated by German infantry in the period when von Bock had been deprived of the bulk of his armor. His intention was to advance on a direct line to Moscow while his armor in a wide encircling movement bit off a very large area and encircled Vyazma.

The First Snows

On September 30 von Bock launched the attack on Moscow, with von Kluge commanding 4th Army. Progress was rapid, and the Soviet High Command had been taken by surprise. But all was not as good as it at first seemed; Guderian's armor had suffered from its long march South, and was unable to reach the Smolensk area. Instead he was ordered to attack through Gomel and advance to Tula, while his left wing with von Weich's 2nd Army, swept round to encircle Eremenko's armies caught in the Bryansk area. By October 6 Eremenko was completely out of communication with Moscow. Two days later he attempted to withdraw, but was already too late. Nevertheless the bulk of his forces continued to fight with determination. The country was heavily wooded and virtually impenetrable. On October 9 heavy rain began and in many places the ground was impassable.

Nevertheless Bryansk had been taken by one of Guderian's Panzer divisions, enabling the German engineers to open the railway through to Orel. But the first winter snow had begun, and German infantry found it difficult and often impossible to move. The German commanders right down to company commanders began to fear for their troops. Morale was lowering, and keeping alive was not easy. Sickness, vomiting and diarrhoea became common. Boots were

German armor advances through the snow to take a burning village on the steppe. Inset: the lack of surfaced roads was to prove a major obstacle to the German supply columns.

almost useless in the deep mud and slush, clothing was totally inadequate and food supplies scarce.

Yet the assault, driven forward by von Kluge and von Bock, somehow continued to advance on the Moscow defenses against stiffening Soviet resistance. Realising the gravity of the situation, Stalin at once recalled Zhukov to take command of the western defenses of the central front before Moscow, while General Artemev took over the defense of the city. Zhukov rapidly rounded up all available forces, and made no attempt to relieve the Soviet troops trapped in the Vyazma pocket. They were, in any case, part of the Moscow defenses, and still fighting.

On Guderian's right a Panzer Corps under von Schweppenburg fought a terrific and costly tank battle as it attempted to force its way to Tula, but the road was breaking up. Fuel was now very short and General Eberbach's attempt to seize the town was driven back with heavy losses by General Ermakov's Soviet Army. The weather now over the whole Central front was almost beyond German endurance. Tens of thousands of trucks were breaking up and unusable. It was the beginning of the end but urged by von Bock von Kluge pressed on.

Moscow In Danger

In mid-October a stream of people able to move began to leave the city. Government officials were ordered east to establish themselves in Kyubyshev. But Stalin and the High Command remained, together with senior officials of Government. There was no panic and the Western defenses of the city were rapidly strengthened.

In November when the rains ceased and the ground quickly became frozen von Kluge made some headway, but new troubles beset his troops. Guns and transport, previously immovable in the seas of mud, now had to be dug out of the frozen earth. Engines froze and had to be kept running. Up against the defenses of Moscow the German infantry came under constant heavy fire from artillery, small arms and mortars. The Soviet losses had abundant ammunition, while German stocks were short

General Belov's cavalry charging in December 1941, a maneuver which became more rare as the war progressed.

and rapidly diminishing. They were at the end of a line of communications 1,000 miles long whereas the Russians were within easy reach of their bases.

Meanwhile Soviet counter-attacks North and South of the city were developing into a counter-offensive, and von Kluge's exhausted troops, striving to pin down the enemy, found themselves pinned down and compelled to withdraw.

Yet Hitler, von Bock and von Kluge refused to give up. Indeed, they were hopelessly committed to such a course even when failure was obvious.

In the extreme South the German situation was also serious. The Germans had taken Rostov, although the leading commanders knew that they would be unable to hold it against growing Soviet strength and with a counter-offensive developing. The ground was frozen solid and the cold reached $-20°$ Centigrade. Soviet T-34 tanks smashed the German anti-tank guns, but with the courage of something like despair, suffering heavy casualties, the leading divisions of von Kleist's Panzer Army took Rostov, only to be

counter-attacked immediately by the Soviet 56th Independent Army. But the danger was far more grave. Marshal Timoshenko had organised a counter-offensive designed to cut off the German supply lines between Rostov and the Sea of Azov. At the same time von Kleist's 1st Panzer Army was threatened with isolation. The Germans were in fact fighting for their survival and the troops involved knew it. Only von Reichenau's 6th Army might save them, but 6th Army could do nothing and the 17th Army further South was unable to relieve the pressure.

On November 28 the Russians re-occupied Rostov to bring about the first serious set-back suffered by the Germans. Nothing like it had happened in Poland, France or the Low Countries, and the German reverse therefore seemed even worse than it was.

Von Rundstedt had long foreseen that this would almost certainly happen. Since the first days of November he had urged withdrawal and pressed on Halder and Hitler that the only wise course was to withdraw, refit and be ready to launch a new offensive in the Spring. The

Russians had established new defense lines from South to North. Nevertheless, on November 30, Hitler ordered the weary and defeated troops to stand and fight. Von Rundstedt at once asked to be relieved of his command, and it became obvious even to Hitler that he would be forced to accept a withdrawal that was already taking place. Field Marshal von Reichenau at once succeeded to the command of the German South front, and as a fanatical follower of Hitler attempted to drive the retreating troops forward. It was in vain, and all he achieved was chaos as the Germans attempted vainly to turn about. At last, less than 24 hours after von Rundstedt had been relieved, his suggested withdrawal to the Mius River was accepted. Halder commented that all that had been achieved by Hitler's emotional demands was that time, energy and von Rundstedt had been lost.

In the far North the situation was equally serious. At the end of November von Leeb abandoned his hopes that the attacks on Moscow on the central front would relieve the pressure on his troops, especially in the region of Tikhvin, where they were dangerously

The Soviet Army did not rely solely on anti-tank guns to kill tanks. In the Soviet book, all artillery was anti-tank artillery, and a 152mm howitzer could do considerable damage to any tank. Below: as the rigors of the winter enveloped the German armies, local transport was requisitioned.

A German infantryman snatches a hot drink during a lull in the fighting.

The winter snows drift over two victims of the battle.

extended. On December 8 he asked permission to withdraw, but Hitler refused. Again there was no longer an option.

On the Central front von Bock realised that the struggle for Moscow had failed. Von Kluge had reached within 25 miles of Moscow to the North of the city. His position was untenable and his troops almost incapable of fighting. A few days later Field Marshal von Bock wished to be relieved of his command, soon to be followed by Field Marshal von Leeb.

On December 19 Hitler retired Field Marshal von Brauchitsch, nominally Commander-in-Chief of the Army, and as Führer at once assumed Supreme Command in name as well as fact. He alone would be the architect of victory or defeat. It was estimated that the Soviet Union had lost six million men, but their new reserve armies more than replaced the losses. Moreover at last they were beginning to seize the initiative. Against them German losses were between 800,000 and one million, and troops of their quality were difficult, if not impossible, to replace. Condemned to a dangerous and terrible winter, they had no alternative but to wait for the spring, beat off Soviet counter-offensives, and steadily rebuild their own strength for the war in the East to which they were now committed.

'Barbarossa' had failed. It is almost certainly true that Moscow would have been taken had von Bock been permitted to press his attacks in late August without being deprived of his powerful armor groups. But it seems unlikely that Stalin and the Soviet High Command would have agreed to Hitler's demands, even if Moscow had fallen. Certainly they would have withdrawn to Kyubyshev if the position of Moscow became hopeless.

Had Rostov been forced earlier and the Caucasus opened, Nazi Germany would have been compelled to employ enormous forces and work forces, and there could not have been a withdrawal. It was clear at the end of 1941 to some senior British Staff Officers, especially in the Middle East, that the Germans were already over-stretched.

Nazi Germany failed to achieve her aims because of faulty appreciation of Soviet strength, especially reserve strength, by the vacillations of Hitler from early July to the end, by immense difficulties of adequate supply and maintenance, and by the Russian winter. The Führer blamed everyone but himself, and even blamed the Russian winter.

Nevertheless the Germans had achieved the greatest feat of arms in all military history. It was a bitter irony.

129

Soviet infantry defend Stalingrad with a variety of weapons. The crouching man in the foreground carries a PPSh sub-machine gun while his companion, holding a Mosin-Nagant rifle, prepares to throw a stick grenade.

STALINGRAD:
THE FROZEN HELL

Under the stress of combat Hitler's military instinct
was less reliable, and his obstinacy resulted in the 6th Army's
encirclement and destruction.

NEARLY 300 MILES beyond the German front-line that existed in the spring of 1942 lay the city of Stalingrad. Even farther away, over 350 miles distant, was the Caucasus with its rich oil fields. Adolf Hitler decided that these two objectives would be captured during his summer offensive against the Red Army.

At first glance, Hitler's intentions seemed to be sound, designed to destroy the Russians before another cruel winter came to their aid. If the German Army could cross the Volga in the Stalingrad area, then Russia's main north-south line of communications would be cut. And, if simultaneously the production of the rich oil fields in and near the Caucasus could be harnessed to the German war effort, then the whole situation in the East would be changed and the prospects of an outright victory considerably enhanced.

It was a gamble, however, because Hitler's objectives, being some 350 miles apart, meant that two separate, divergent operations had to be mounted. To capture two such remote and distant objectives meant bringing fresh divisions to the Eastern front and these had to come from Germany's allies – Rumania, Hungary and Italy. Prior to 1942 only élite units from these satellite nations had fought alongside their German masters. Now complete corps or even armies of one nationality were to fight at ever-increasing distances from their homelands. Such a vast increase in battalions gave some substance to Hitler's dreams. He was intoxicated by their numbers but the seeds of disaster had already been sown when he launched his offensive at the end of June. The soldiers of Germany's allies followed the spearhead of the attack with a reluctance that increased as they moved deeper into Russia.

The campaign, under the operation Code word 'Blau', began with a series of victories. In July Krasnodar on the Kuban River and Voroshilovsk close by the foothills of the Caucasus mountains were captured. Thousands of prisoners were taken. By the end of August the German flag had been hoisted on the peak of the Elbrus, the highest point in the Caucasus. At this stage, 4th Army's panzers suddenly stopped on Hitler's orders and turned north east to help 6th Army in its drive to the Volga. No further progress was to be made in the Caucasus. The attention of both sides was drawn inexorably to the Stalingrad front.

In the early days of August the Germans struck across the steppes from the south west, advancing along the Salsk-Stalingrad railway. The rail centre of Kotelnikovo, 73 miles from Stalingrad, was captured on August 2. Thereafter the forces used in these efforts swelled in mid-August from a total of 17 divisions to 23 but there was to be no dramatic breakthrough by General Friedrich von Paulus and his experienced 6th Army. By now Stalin had issued his stirring cry: 'Ni shagun nazad' (Not a step backwards). Stalingrad, in 1941 a sprawling industrial giant of half a million people, was going to be defended street by street, block by block, house by house. The German 6th and 4th Panzer Armies were being sucked into all out attacks on the city – with their long open flank on the River Don guarded by apprehensive satellite divisions.

The Luftwaffe Lashes the City

At midnight on August 23 the 16th Panzer Division had outrun the support of the other divisions and reached the outskirts of Stalingrad. Earlier on the same day the Luftwaffe began a series of terrible air raids, levelling the city until it looked as if a giant hurricane had lifted it into the air and smashed it down into a million pieces. Thousands of frightened civilians, whose presence in the smoking ruins was no longer necessary, were evacuated, crossing the Volga in a fleet of battered tugs, ferries and steamers. The Stukas tried to stampede the civilian population by bombing the jammed embankment beside the main ferry landing. Clusters of bombs found them and the footpaths near the Volga were slippery with blood, while many of the boats of the rescue fleet sank with few survivors reaching safety. For those who remained in the city, the troops of the 62nd Red Army, the civil militia armed with rifles, and the workers in certain important factories, the regular visits of the German Air Force became a part of a terrifying nightmare. Nearly 40,000 people were killed during those brutal air raids.

German infantry prepare a
mortar position in front of
one of Stalingrad's
factories.

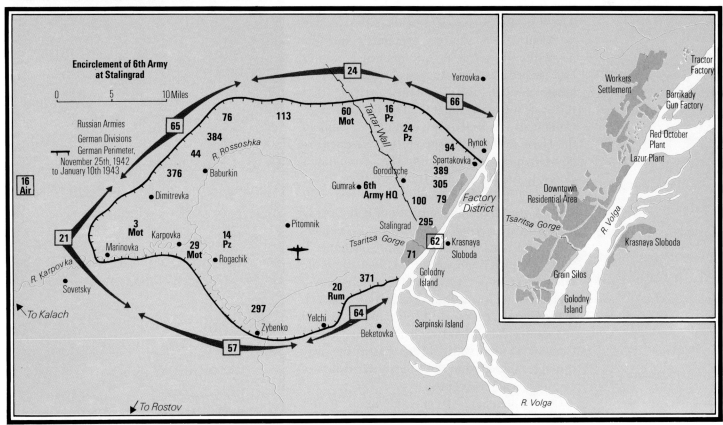

**Encirclement of 6th Army
at Stalingrad**

0   5   10 Miles

Russian Armies
German Divisions
German Perimeter,
November 25th, 1942
to January 10th 1943

24

66

Yerzovka

65

76   113   60   16
                          Mot   Pz
                                   Tartar Wall
384   24
                                   Pz
44   R. Rossoshka   94   Rynok

16   376   Baburkin   Gorodische   389   Spartakovka
Air
        Dimitrevka   Gumrak 6th   305
                                        Army HQ
                                                  100   79   Factory
21   District
        3   295
        Mot   Karpovka   Pitomnik   Stalingrad
29   Tsaritsa Gorge
Marinovka   Mot   14   62   Krasnaya
R. Karpovka   Pz   Rogachik   71   Sloboda

Sovetsky   Golodny
                                        Island
To Kalach   371
                        20   Sarpinski Island
                 297   Rum
57   Yelchi   64
              Zybenko   Beketovka

To Rostov   R. Volga

Tractor
Factory
Workers
Settlement   Barrikady
                                        Gun Factory

                                        Red October
                                        Plant
                                        Lazur Plant
Downtown
Residential Area
Tsaritsa Gorge   R. Volga
                                        Krasnaya Sloboda

Grain Silos

Golodny
Island

133

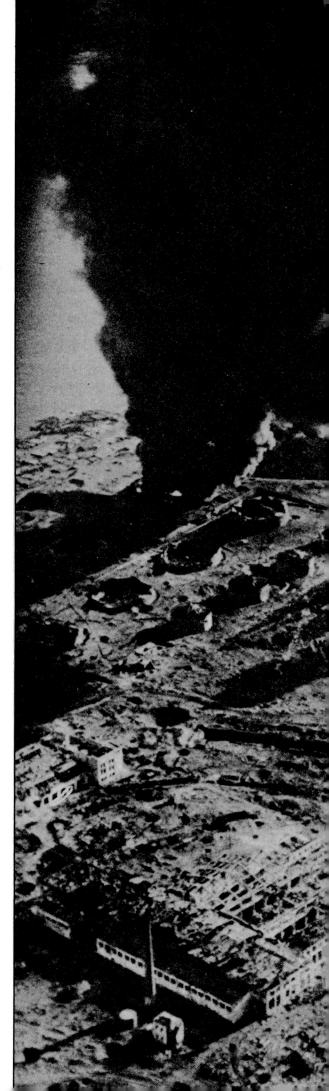

Stalin's determination to save the city that
bore his name was not always reflected in the
morale of all his troops that fought in the
Stalingrad sector during the late summer of
1942. Defection was rife, few Russian soldiers
believed that the Germans could be stopped
short of the Volga, and the numbers of prisoners
pouring into German hands became a torrent.

The Commander of the 62nd Army, General
Lopatin, admitted that he had lost confidence in
his ability to save Stalingrad. He was sacked
and replaced by the strong-willed, pugnacious
General Chuikov. From mid-September onwards
the partnership of Generals Yeremenko and
Chuikov changed the situation. Anyone who
showed any signs of defeatism or pessimism was
thrown out; they demonstrated complete faith
in the 62nd Army by bringing reinforcements
across to the west bank of the Volga when the
situation was at its blackest.

No longer could the Germans expect to take
the city by storm on the march. Gone were the
lightning advances across the steppes; now the
panzers were bogged down in narrow streets,
shot at by snipers, doused by Molotov cocktails.
The cost of victory was to increase day by day
as August gave way to September but the
possibility of such a victory lessened as winter
approached, as the Russians made plans to
break through the German 'corridor' that
thrust its way to Stalingrad. The Russian High
Command was well aware that the left flank of
the German Army Group 'B' was manned by
non-German troops, with the Rumanians
closest to Stalingrad, the Italians farther to the
west, and the Hungarians farther west still.
Indeed, the German General Staff had already
begun warning Adolf Hitler about this vulnerable flank but his answer was unchanged.
'Where the German soldier sets foot, there he
remains. You may rest assured that nobody will
ever drive us away from Stalingrad' (Speech
to the German people in October 1942). Instead
of a strategical withdrawal before winter came,
General Paulus was told to battle his way
through Stalingrad to the Volga – regardless of
cost to men and machines.

On September 13 two German assault
groups, infantry and tanks, smashed into the

A part of the industrial zone of Stalingrad photographed by the observer of a Stuka dive-bomber. Inset: large numbers of pathetic and bemused civilians fled from Stalingrad during the initial German advance.

positions held by Chuikov's 62nd Army. After a day of bitter fighting the German troops made some gains. Next day the Soviets tried to counter-attack but with the whole weight of many hundreds of guns supported by Stukas, tanks and truck-loads of infantry fought their way towards the Volga and threatened the central landing stage, the very lifeline of the besieged army. By now, the Germans were only 800 yards from Chuikov's HQ. Never faltering, he made the important and fateful decision to summon the 13th Guards Division to his aid even though more than a thousand of its members had no weapons to fire. After a hazardous crossing of the Volga in small boats and barges, strafed by Stukas during daylight hours and targets for observed artillery and small arms fire, the Guards riflemen joined the other defenders who were fighting for survival: men who had nowhere to retreat, who were lacking food and water, who were constantly under attack from air as well as being embroiled in a deadly struggle that went on by day and night. At a very high cost, the German onslaught against the center of the city was blocked and the 62nd Army won a few more precious hours.

A Battle of Attrition

Contrary to German expectations, the city did not fall into their hands rapidly nor did the Red Army pull back entirely onto the eastern bank of the Volga. Each building in Stalingrad became its own battleground. Factories, railway stations, streets, squares, even single ruined walls, were all defended with a stubborn tenacity by soldiers, militia and the workers themselves. The Central Railway Station changed hands many times. The struggle for the hillock, Mamaev Kurgan, was equally intense. On the southern boundary of 62nd Army stood a giant grain-elevator in which German and Soviet soldiers fought for several days and nights for parts of the building. Elsewhere there were dozens of strongpoints which took a heavy toll of lives, German and Russian.

The commanders on both sides were shaken by the terrible casualties, wondering whether they would run out of men before their opponents did, but by September 22 the Germans

Volunteers of the German-backed 'Russian Army of Liberation' take the oath to their colours. The Thousand-Year Reich was not able to guarantee such renegades against Soviet retribution.

appeared to be on the verge of victory. General Friedrich von Paulus was telling journalists from his own country that the city would fall 'anytime now, anytime'. In his heart, however, he had lost most of his hopes for a quick victory. Moreover, Paulus envisaged no solution other than butting his way through the factory districts, using his tired army as a human battering ram.

The 52-year old Army Commander was a typical German General Staff officer; tall and handsome, impeccably groomed at all times, the ambitious Paulus had solid grounds for thinking that the capture of Stalingrad would lead to further promotion. Nevertheless, he was worried by the long open left flank in his rear, guarded by the puppet forces of Germany's Allies. Stubbornly sticking to his earlier tactics Paulus continued to hurl his army against Russian defenses. Weakened by nagging dysentry, he sent a series of complaints back to his superiors, asking for more of everything; instead he received a sapper battalion specially flown out from Germany to help in the house-to-house fighting which was decimating his infantry units. The build-up meant that by the first week in October General Chuikov considered that he was facing nine German

divisions, with the Volga less than 4000 yards behind the front line.

There could be no retreat. There was none. By the middle of October nearly 100,000 Russian reinforcements had been ferried across the river into Stalingrad. They were killed so quickly that in less than a month the 62nd Army had lost more than 80,000 men, killed, wounded or missing. The German 6th Army was in no better plight. In a period of six weeks they had lost over 40,000 casualties. The struggle for the key to the city, the factory area, continued throughout October with the northern sector under constant siege. The Germans narrowed their attacks down to sectors, two to four hundred yards wide, concentrating on taking the shortest way to the Volga. Such tactics were to bring some success. In four places they broke through the narrow-waisted city to the river. General von Paulus set up his HQ in a basement store on Heroes of the Revolution Square, in the center of Stalingrad. Like his army he was committed to stay in Stalingrad. For a few days both sides stood limp and exhausted from their murderous struggle in the smoking ruins, the graveyard of a city.

The Germans take Stalingrad

The 6th Army had all but taken Stalingrad; they had a death-grip on the ruins along the Volga. An order of the day from Paulus to his exhausted army claimed an outright victory adding, 'the actions of the leadership and the troops during the offensive will enter into history as an especially glorious page. Winter is upon us . . . the Russians will take advantage of it. It is unlikely the Russians will fight with the same strength as last winter'.

Brave but ill-considered words. The Germans held most of Stalingrad but all around them was gathering a storm, a storm that was due to break on November 19. For while the 6th Army had been hurling itself against Stalingrad, only limited German operations had been continuing in the Caucasus, and elsewhere along the front the German High Command had left the other Red Armies alone, free to re-organise, able to regroup. Under Stalin's supervision, Marshals Zhukov and Vasilevsky were

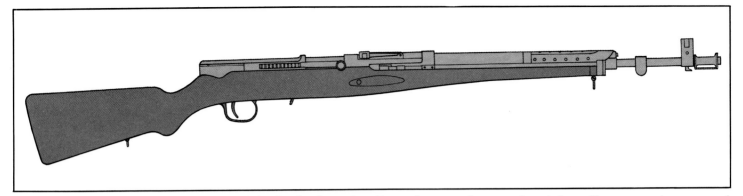

drawing up their final plans for Operation 'Uranus', designed to encircle and trap their enemy within the gates of Stalingrad. Such a counter-offensive, which involved three fronts, Stalingrad, Don and South-Western, meant that thousands of Russian troops were on the move days before the date Stalin had selected far the attack to begin – and the Germans were fully aware that an onslaught was about to be launched to coincide with the Russian winter.

On many occasions, Hitler had been told that the left flank of Army Group 'B' was exposed, the Achilles heel of Paulus and his army. General Zeitzler, Chief of the Army General Staff advocated a withdrawal westward from Stalingrad, which would shorten the front and would do away with the long corridor with its vulnerable flanks.

Such a solution proved totally unacceptable to Hitler. To even suggest the abandonment of Stalingrad, the hard-won prize of his summer and fall offensives, was enough to cause the Führer to rant and rave. For him the retention of Stalingrad had become a question of personal prestige. Nobody, and nothing, could make him change his mind.

In desperation his General Staff devised other expedients. A small reserve was created behind the threatened flank. It consisted of a single weak Panzer corps, comprising two armored divisions, one German and the other Rumanian. In addition, small German units,

such as anti-tank battalions, were interspersed amongst the satellite divisions. These units were intended to bolster the threatened front. In the event of the non-German units being overrun, the 'bolster units' were to stand fast, to limit the enemy's gains, and in holding out in such a manner, to create more favorable conditions for a German counter-attack. In theory there was some merit in the plan but should the allied troops collapse too quickly, or too completely, then it was obvious that the German units would find themselves hopelessly swamped by sheer weight of numbers. Other measures included posting liaison groups, containing German General Staff officers and signal units, to the senior headquarters of the non-German formations.

The Counter-Attack

Radio deception was practised on a large scale, with the purpose of concealing from the Russians the fact that there were no German troops along the threatened flank and also of giving them a false picture of the German strength in that sector.

These were but some of the precautions taken but, efficiently though they were put into operation, the Russian High Command was not deceived. During the first half of November the picture of the future Russian offensive became increasingly clear. That they were going to attack north-west of Stalingrad became obvious. German Intelligence felt that the sector held by the Rumanians would be the one selected but what they could not gauge was the date on which such an attack would be launched. Even the puppet allies had begun sounding the alarm. The Commander of the Rumanian 3rd Army, in position on 6th Army's left flank at the Don, sent a cry for help that was forwarded to East Prussia for Adolf Hitler's consideration. What was the German Army going to do about the build-up opposite his Army? Hitler gave his reply in a political speech during which he said: 'I wished to reach the Volga at a certain point, near a certain city. That city happens to bear the name of Stalin himself . . . I wished to take that city; we do not make exaggerated claims and I can now tell you that we have captured it

A deadly game of hide-
and-seek amid the ruins
of Stalingrad.

This Ju87D-1 of III Gruppe /Stukageschwader 3 operated on the Eastern Front in the spring of 1942. Against proper opposition the Stuka soon lost its awesome reputation and proved to be very vulnerable. Below: a Stuka flies over the vast emptiness of the Russian landscape.

. . . Now people may ask: Why does not the Army advance faster? But I do not wish to see a second Verdun. I prefer it to reach my objectives by means of limited assaults. Time is of no importance . . .'

In Moscow, the Russian General Staff was overjoyed when the Germans continued to rivet their attentions to the ruined city near the banks of the Volga. The German Luftwaffe did what it could to harass the Soviet build-up. Planes were sent to the Kletskaya and Serafimovich bridgehead areas to strike against rail lines and troop concentrations. Long-range artillery bombardment was used to maximum effect but the most that this could hope to achieve was a postponement of the date fixed for the attack. The Germans did not possess total, overwhelming air supremacy nor did they have an air force of the requisite size on the Eastern Front.

General Richthofen, the aggressive, flamboyant Air Fleet IV commander, wrote in his diary on November 12, 'The Russians are resolutely carrying on with their preparations for an offensive against the Rumanians . . . When, I wonder, will the attack come? The guns are beginning to make their appearance in artillery emplacements. I can only hope that the Russians won't tear too many big holes in the line!'.

The Horrors of a Russian Winter

Such was the situation when the Russian winter broke upon the Germans with all its fury. Now they knew that the counter-offensive would not long be delayed. Three days later the outspoken Richthofen, in a telephone conversation with General Zeitzler, gave vent to his anger and frustration: 'Both the command and the troops are listless . . . we shall get nowhere. Let us either fight or abandon the attack altogether. If we can't clear up the situation now, when the Volga is blocked and the Russians in real difficulty, we shall never be able to'.

Zeitzler agreed – but there was nothing that he could do. The final authority lay with Adolf Hitler.

Early on the morning of November 19, 1942, the Russian offensive opened. The liaison staff

with the Rumanians reported, 'Very heavy artillery bombardment of the whole Rumanian front north-west of Stalingrad'. The single reserve corps under command Army Group 'B', Panzer Corps 'H', the 48th Corps, was made ready for action immediately – but application had to be made to Hitler for its release from reserve. It required, as usual, a tremendous effort to convince the Führer that the reserve had to be used at once. Meanwhile the Russian shelling of the Rumanian positions had redoubled in intensity; then, under cover of a heavy snowstorm and with the thermometer showing 20 degrees below zero, the Red Army attacked. For Chuikov and his Army, it meant that the 68 days of fighting in Stalingrad were about to be rewarded. Their stubborn defense had bought time and enabled the gigantic counter-offensive to be prepared and launched. Now he and his men would wreak their vengeance on the German 6th Army.

Three Red Army Groups launched the carefully planned offensive from north-west and south-west of Stalingrad. The Russian 5th and 21st Tank Armies burst through the Rumanian Army in the wake of the heavy artillery bombardment. The bewildered, frightened Rumanians offered little resistance, with only a few staying to fight the Russian tanks. The German 48th Panzer Corps was sent to challenge the Russian 21st Army rampaging south of the Don. Its efforts were hampered by the fleeing Rumanians who were scattering in terror across the snowfields. The foul weather grounded both air forces so that General Richthofen was unable to help the stricken Rumanians, whose officers had defected, leaving thousands of soldiers to wander aimlessly around the steppes, nor was he able to assist 48th Panzer Corps in seeking out the Russians. The prospects of a successful counter-attack soon diminished. The Panzer Corps was incapable of stabilizing the situation and became hopelessly embroiled in the general confusion, fighting desperately for its own survival.

South of Stalingrad more Russian forces massed along a 125-mile front. The 64th, 57th and 51st Armies were facing the vastly over-extended 4th Rumanian Army. Its task was to protect the German 6th Army's right flank. At 1000 hours, on November 20, General Yeremenko began his attack. The soldiers of the Rumanian 4th Army fled and within a matter of hours, 10,000 prisoners had been taken by the Russians. The Russians swept forward, trapping units as they retreated into defensive pockets where they were isolated without communication with each other or Higher Command. In the fading afternoon light of November 21 the Germans gained victory. The 29th Motorized Division thrust at the right flank of the Russian mechanized column. A sudden counter-attack caught the Russians off guard and many of their tanks were lost in the ambush. Before the Divisional Commander could annihilate the burning enemy force he was ordered to pull back to guard 6th Army's rear at the Don. Such a victory brought a brief respite only; its significance was soon forgotten as disaster followed disaster elsewhere. The Stalingrad Army was thus threatened with encirclement from both flanks and it was only a question of hours before the two Russian pincers closed behind 6th Army's rear. When General Paulus suggested that his Army should withdraw to the south-west, a sharp command was received to hold fast, to stand firm.

'To HQ 6 Army, Führer Order.

'6 Army will hold position despite threat of

Soviet gunners man a 57mm anti-tank gun amid the dust of a Stalingrad factory.

temporary encirclement.... Keep railroad line open as long as possible. Special orders regarding air supplies will follow.'

The order implied that the 6th Army would be supplied from the air after forming their defence. General Richthofen is reported to have phoned Göring's deputy and said: 'In the filthy weather we have here, there's not a hope of supplying an army of 250,000 men from the air. It is stark staring madness.' Such considerations were brushed aside by Hitler and

A grim American cartoon captures the essence of Stalingrad.

GATEWAY TO STALINGRAD
NOVEMBER 25, 1942

A tenuous air-supply link was maintained to the German 6th Army. This HeIII has just delivered rations and ammunition and will be used to evacuate wounded.

The air-supply lifeline
was rapidly curtailed as
Soviet troops overran
the airfields.

After their tank had been stopped by an anti-tank gun this German crew were cut down by machine-gun fire as they attempted to escape.

on November 23 the Russian pincers met at Kalach. The encirclement movement was complete. The Rumanian divisions had been defeated, most of them caught and slaughtered by the surprise Red Army crossing of the unfrozen river Don. Inside the Red Army ring were 22 divisions, 20 German and two Rumanian. There were also troops from the engineers, artillery, assault gun battalions, pioneers, in addition to the headquarter staffs of five corps and General Paulus's own Army Headquarters. The Luftwaffe was represented by parts of an anti-aircraft artillery corps and by the ground staff personnel. It is impossible to establish the exact number of troops encircled, the figure given ranging from 215,000 to something approaching 300,000. Small elements of 6th Army were not caught

in the encirclement when it was first formed while units belonging to other armies were. The only means of communication between the entrapped Army and the outer world was by airplane and radio. Initially, there were three or four airfields within the pocket and an efficient radio-telephone link was established between General Paulus and the Commander, Army Group 'B'.

One of the first orders that Hitler issued after the Russian pincers had met ran as follows: 'The forces of the 6th Army encircled at Stalingrad will be known as the troops of Fortress Stalingrad'. However, Stalingrad was a fortress in name only, even if the German civilian population were hoodwinked into thinking that the army could withstand a long siege. There were no

Straw overboots abandoned by the German garrison later served as fodder for Russian Army horses.

fortifications, the bombastic and meaningless title bestowed upon the 6th Army did nothing for the morale of the soldiers. Sixth Army was to hold a pocket of some 25 miles from east to west and about 12 miles, north to south. Outside the ruined city, the country was steppe, with scarcely a tree or bush to be seen. Sections of Stalingrad were still in Russian hands with its eastern boundary on the right bank of the Volga. And now the stricken army, in conditions of extreme cold, in blizzards, with the thermometer far below freezing point, had to build fortifications where none had existed before. Although General Paulus was convinced his Army should begin its retreat towards the west, he continued to wait for Hitler's approval, putting all units on the alert to move quickly in case permission was granted. The authorization was never to be forthcoming – although Zeitzler and his colleagues tried to persuade Hitler that Paulus must be given freedom to act on his own and be allowed to break out.

Occasionally, Hitler lost all self-control, crashing his fist down on the table, shouting: 'I won't leave the Volga! I won't go back from the Volga!'. He put his faith in the efforts of Army Group 'D' and the arrival, on the Russian front for the first time, of the new heavy tank, the Tiger. Efficient though the prototype Tigers were, it was stretching fantasy to extremes by expecting a single battalion of tanks not only to succeed in breaking through the Russian lines but to keep the 'Corridor' open thereafter.

If relief was to come, then it had to be in the shape of a force commanded by Field Marshal Erich von Manstein, the newly appointed Commander-in-Chief of Army Group Don. Before Manstein's attack was to begin, however, an even more crucial problem had to be resolved. Could Reich-Marshal Göring and his Luftwaffe keep 6th Army supplied by air?

The Reich-Marshal had assured Hitler that this was possible but the beleaguered army in Stalingrad required some five hundred tons of resupply each and every day. Early figures were not encouraging; 110 tons, 120, sometimes 140 tons. On many days no supplies arrived at all. This was not the fault of the German air crews nor of their immediate commanders who did their utmost, but Göring had undertaken a task which was far beyond the capacity of the Luftwaffe. The winter weather meant that there were many days when planes could not fly. The pilots had to run the gauntlet across a belt of enemy-held territory which became wider and wider as the Russians pushed the German forces further to the west. As more and more German planes were shot down so the capacity to lift in the required tonnage decrease. In the 'Fortress' the situation deteriorated as shortages became more and more acute. The soldiers of the 6th Army called the Fortress 'Der Kessel' (the Cauldron). It was a tragedy for 6th Army that General Paulus was not able to act against the wishes of the Führer, especially when he knew in his heart that to stay in Stalingrad meant disaster. The only hope for Paulus and his men lay in Field Marshal Erich von Manstein, conqueror of Sevastopol, hero of the French campaign whose plan to out-

The Soviet M1895 Nagant revolver, a 7.62mm weapon of unusual design. The cylinder was automatically moved forward to mate with the barrel and form a gas-tight seal.

flank the Maginot Line had led to the downfall of France within six weeks. If anyone was to save Paulus and his army, it was Manstein – but he needed more troops and armor than circumstances allowed him in the middle of December 1942. In addition, 6th Army would have to abandon Stalingrad and fight their way west to meet him.

The Bear's Embrace

Meanwhile, the Russians had been surprised by the success of their Operation 'Uranus'. In their wildest dreams they never expected to trap nearly 300,000 men within their giant encirclement. But now seven Soviet Armies were hugging 6th Army in a hostile embrace. There remained the problem of exterminating such a big force. There is a Russian tale about a hunter who bet a friend that he could catch a bear single-handed. He went out, grappled with the bear, and called back to his friend: 'See, I've got him. The only thing is, now, he won't let me go'. The question was whether the 6th Army would let its encirclers go or would they try to break out without help from a relief force? Zhukov predicted that they would stand fast, that a relief force would attempt to evacuate the trapped army and, in his opinion, the 6th Army pocket should be cut in half. But before this could be put into effect, Operation 'Winter Storm', the attempt to break through to 6th Army had begun.

From the suburbs of Kotelnikovo, tanks and trucks of the 6th Panzer Division fanned out and raced for Stalingrad. To begin with, General Hoth and his Fourth Panzer Army advanced steadily and six days later they were little more than 40 miles from the southern perimeter of Stalingrad. Three days later the city was only 30 miles away. For the first twelve days, as Manstein and Hoth pushed forward, the Russian resistance was negligible, then the opposition hardened with Soviet T-34 tanks and anti-tank guns being thrown against the Germans. The attack slowed to a snail's pace.

On December 17 the Russians struck another blow, this time against two Italian divisions, fifty miles west of Serafimovich. The attack was aimed at seizing the city of Rostov, thereby entrapping the entire German Army in Southern Russia. The Italian army failed to hold and it was clear that Manstein would have to go to their rescue. He urged Hitler to issue an order for Operation 'Thunderclap', an order that would mean that 6th Army, weakened though it was, would begin to move back westwards across the steppe, fighting the Russians on all sides in a bid for salvation and safety. But the Führer forbade Paulus to withdraw from Stalingrad. His reasoning was arrogant and typically blind, adding that 'too much blood has been spilled there by Germans'. Manstein sent his intelligence officer into Stalingrad by air so that he could discuss the situation with Paulus. By now it was clear that 4th Panzer Army could only continue to drive forward for a very limited period; that some divisions might have to move away and go to the assistance of the Italians. It was doubtful whether General Hoth's tanks could advance many more miles towards Stalingrad. Could Paulus extend his own drive a further 25 kilometers to the south? In Paulus's opinion this was not feasible as 6th Army was desperately short of fuel for its tanks and all arms needed urgent supplies of food and ammunition. General Paulus was not prepared to accept the risk of making the link-up until more supplies had been received or unless his Führer so ordered a complete evacuation of Stalingrad.

Hitler Remains Adamant

Before his attack ground to a halt some 30 miles from Stalingrad, Field Marshal von Manstein made one more attempt to persuade Hitler to change his mind. Zeitzler spent many hours with the Führer, arguing and pleading. Eventually Hitler said that a message could be drafted addressed to Paulus, asking him how far he could get if he was ordered to break out. Zeitzler immediately drafted the signal in Hitler's presence and gave it to him to sign. The Führer read it, picked up a pencil and inserted the words: 'the condition being that you continue to hold the line of the Volga'. Such a condition missed the whole purpose and nature of the proposed operation. Instead of a full-scale evacuation, Hitler intended a link-

70.000

up which was intended to bring further supplies into the Stalingrad garrison. Paulus's reply came, 'about 25 miles', a shorter distance than that which separated him from the vanguard of Field Marshal von Manstein's force. Once again, salvation had been denied Paulus and his besieged army by Adolf Hitler. That was the very last moment at which the 6th Army might still have been saved. All it could do was to defend Stalingrad against increasing pressure from all sides – without any hopes beyond death or captivity.

Demoralization Sets In

On December 24 the Red Army under General Malinovsky struck against Manstein. In three days he pushed the relieving forces back to their starting point and on December 29 captured Kotelnikovo. The distance between 4th Panzer Army's foremost troops and the outposts of the 6th Army was increased, once again, to over sixty miles. Another successful attack of the Russian winter offensive, west and south of Stalingrad, was beginning to threaten the German Army Group 'A' in the Caucasus. If the Russians captured Rostov the whole of that Army Group would be in imminent danger of encirclement. At first it appeared as if the Führer would not withdraw from the Caucasus but eventually he relented, thus saving his armies from the fate that had befallen their fellow countrymen in Stalingrad.

At the end of December the situation within the fortress had badly deteriorated, although, as yet, the Russians had not undertaken any major direct assaults. The airlift was totally inadequate and shortages became more and more acute. The troops' rations were cut and cut again; these were now insufficient to keep the men alive for any length of time. It was obvious that a further reduction would soon be inevitable. The failure of the attack by 4th Panzer Army had demoralized both the commanders and the troops – all the more so since they had been encouraged to hope and believe that salvation was on its way. The defenders dug deep in the basements of the city and hacked holes in the frozen earth. They received 25 to 30 cartridges daily, with orders to use them only in self-defense. Four ounces of bread and a ration of horse meat, with the temperature well below zero, with a burning cold wind from the east which whipped across the barren earth: such was their lot. To describe such conditions is virtually impossible, and those who have survived invariably maintain that the last days in Stalingrad were akin to Hell – but that the weeks and months spent as prisoners of the Russians were far worse – quite beyond description and outside the comprehension of those who were not there to share their sufferings.

January 8, 1943 was the date which marked the beginning of the end for General Paulus's Army. This was the day on which the Russians

Their hopeless task: German light machine gunners in the frozen hell of Stalingrad.

Automatic Weapons at Stalingrad

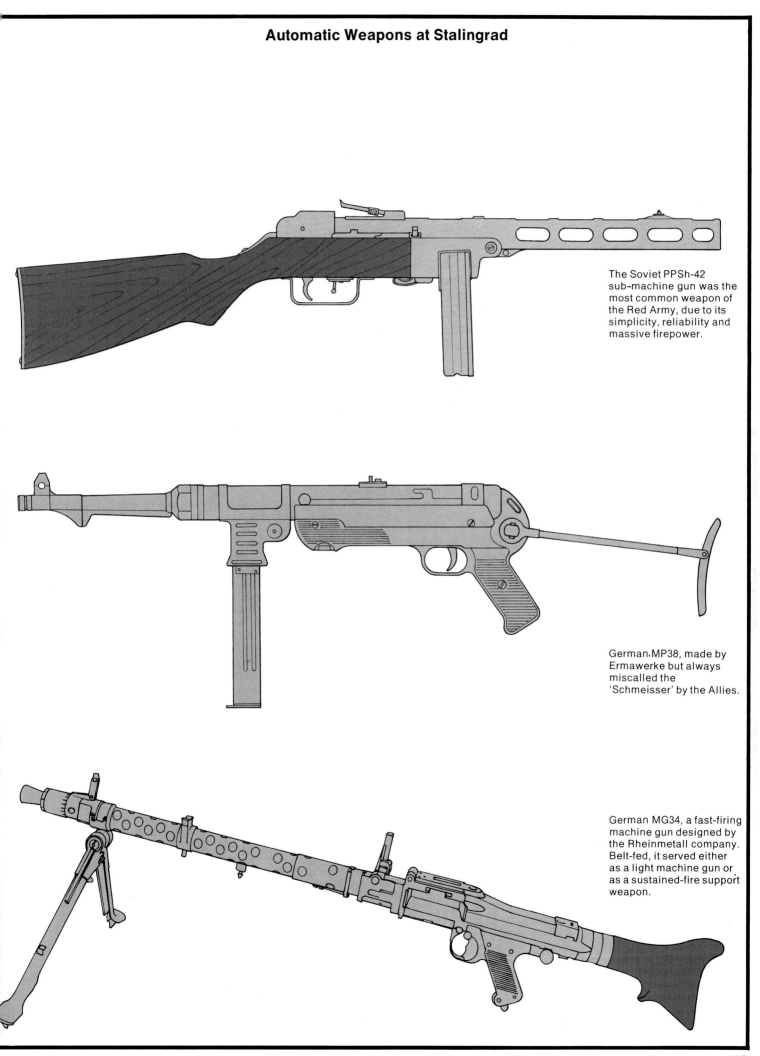

The Soviet PPSh-42 sub–machine gun was the most common weapon of the Red Army, due to its simplicity, reliability and massive firepower.

German MP38, made by Ermawerke but always miscalled the 'Schmeisser' by the Allies.

German MG34, a fast-firing machine gun designed by the Rheinmetall company. Belt-fed, it served either as a light machine gun or as a sustained-fire support weapon.

sent two officers, accompanied by a bugler and carrying a white flag, towards the German lines. As their bugler sounded a call, the Germans answered them with a hail of fire, which sent the Red Army men scampering for cover; but they came back, waved their flag, sounded their bugle again, and on this occasion the German lines were silent. The Germans blindfolded them and took them to Paulus in his headquarters.

The emissaries carried an ultimatum, a demand for surrender, addressed to General Paulus and signed by the Russian General commanding the Don Front, Lieutenant-General Rokossovsky. In it the Russian Commander-in-Chief described the hopeless position of the encircled 6th Army and promised that if the soldiers surrendered they would be guaranteed life, security and their return to Germany, or whatever other country they came from, as soon as the war was over. The document ended with the threat that if the Army did not now capitulate, then it would be annihilated. The time limit fixed for the reply was 1000 hours, January 9, 1943.

There was no need to send a delegation to seek a reply from the Germans next day, and the Russians never came. The ultimatum had been turned down. Paulus had contacted Hitler at once and asked for freedom of action. The General's request was immediately and curtly refused. Hitler ordered his army to fight to the death and that they would do. Again, Soviet loudspeakers called on the Germans to surrender, but to no avail. Firing was resumed and two days later, on January 10 the Red Army launched an offensive against the starving, desperate Germans.

Why?

Why did Hitler condemn a whole army to death and destruction? He was a man of such varying moods. It is impossible to say whether he really understood the significance of his 'last round, last man,' edict. In his New Year message to the Stalingrad army he promised them they would be relieved and delivered from the hands of the Russians. To the German people he repeated over and over again that the sacrifice and fortitude of Paulus and his men had been vital and had enabled other fronts to be preserved intact. Their defense would yet be crowned with victory – said the Führer. There is no direct evidence as to Hitler's true feelings except that General Jodl, his most intimate military crony, said at his trial at Nuremberg:

'I feel great compassion for General Paulus. He could not know that Hitler considered his army lost from the moment when the first winter storms began to blow about Stalingrad'.

We can only assume that Hitler was a prisoner of his own obstinate conviction that where the German soldier once set his foot, there he remained.

The Russian Strike

Early on the morning of January 10, the Russian artillery laid down a heavy barrage which heralded a major attack against the 'Fortress'. Their infantry began an assault against its northern, western and southern flanks. The defenders, weak with hunger and short of ammunition, fought with desperation and heroism. Casualties on both sides were severe. But the 6th Army could not stop the Russians breaking through on all flanks and large sections of the defensive front had to be abandoned: the pocket was being steadily constricted and this continued throughout the next few days.

By January 16 the pocket was barely 15 miles long and about nine miles deep at its widest. The most serious loss was that of the Pitommik airfield through which the defenders had been supplied. Now even Hitler's blind optimism could not continue. For the first time the German people were told about the serious situation which was developing in Stalingrad. Nevertheless, the Führer still refused to give Paulus the freedom of action which the Army commander had repeatedly requested. In Stalingrad, Paulus found that several of his subordinate generals were plotting mutiny, convinced that further resistance was futile. He seemed dazed by the calamity that had overtaken him. An observer wrote, 'Sorrow and grief lined his face. His complexion was the color of ashes. His posture, so upright otherwise,

The snows of Stalingrad overwhelmed man and beast.

By a twist of fate the German victims of Stalingrad resembled their own victims of the concentration camps.

was now slightly stooped'. Indeed, his Chief of Staff, Lieutenant General Artur Schmidt, had begun to assume control of the defeated army. Schmidt was a bulwark of strength, shining in adversity, bullying defeatist officers and threatening would-be deserters with the firing squad.

Like a Greek play, the tragedy was drawing to its close. By January 26, the Russians had broken the German force into two small, isolated groups, one west and the other north of Stalingrad. For the ordinary soldier fighting there, each day simply brought a renewed dose of hunger, privation, bitter cold, hardship of every sort, fear of freezing or starving to death, fear of being wounded when little could be done to tend the wounds. For supplies had ceased almost completely. If something was lost, then

it was gone for ever and could never be replaced. There was no shelter for the wounded, no bedding, no medicine. Surgeons and doctors alike were powerless because they had nothing to work with to alleviate pain or suffering.

The once proud 6th Army began to disintegrate. Senior commanders who could no longer endure the strain either committed suicide or went out in the open, firing at the Russians until at last a bullet put an end to their agony. Some junior officers and men set off to try and reach the main German front. In March one solitary sergeant managed to reach the German lines after weeks of incredible hardship. He died a few days later, worn out by the privations he had suffered.

The Surrender

The Führer's reply to General Paulus, when he asked, once again, for freedom of action, was to promote him to Field Marshal as well as issuing dozens of decorations and promotions to the starving, dying survivors in Stalingrad. Within Germany, Dr. Goebbels' propaganda machine began to extol the exploits of Paulus and his men. Reich-Marshal Göring spoke of the greatest and most heroic fight in all the annals of the German race and compared the 6th Army to the Greek heroes that fought to the last man at Thermopylae.

On January 31 the western group was smashed and Paulus, the general who had subordinated himself completely to Hitler's whims, and in so doing had lost control of his destiny, was captured. Unshaven, but immaculate in his full dress uniform, Friedrich von Paulus went into captivity after being reassured that his men would be given proper rations and medical care.

Unfortunately neither of these conditions was to come to pass. Hundreds of defenseless and wounded German troops were killed where they lay. When the final attack was made early in the morning of February 2, Germans who had fired their last ammunition at the attackers were beaten to death by the enraged Russians.

The battle for Stalingrad was over. In five months, 99 per cent of the city had been reduced to ruins and rubble. Of the half million

The haggard figure of the newly promoted Field Marshal von Paulus stumbles towards his interrogation.

inhabitants of the previous summer, only some 1500 civilians remained. Of the 500,000 Germans, Italians, Hungarians, Rumanians, who were captured in the Stalingrad sector or in the city itself, it is estimated that in three months, between February and April of 1943, more than 400,000 of them were to perish somewhere in Russia. The Russian High Command had never expected to take such numbers into captivity. They left most of them to their own devices and to the cruel mercy of a harsh Russian winter. Those that survived did so, in many cases, by accepting Communist indoctrination because co-operation meant at least some food – and life.

The Effect on Germany

For Paulus, too, there was to be no happy ending. Hitler raged against his newly appointed Field Marshal, one who preferred captivity to death. Hitler said that he had not expected this; had he done so, he would never have promoted Paulus. In captivity, Paulus eventually let it be known that he believed that Communism was the only hope for post-war Europe and lent his name to the Anti-Fascist Officers group which flourished in Soviet prisons. Paulus was to spend the rest of his life behind the Iron Curtain, living in Russia until 1952, when he moved to East Germany. His final years were bitter ones. Stung by memoirs that accused him of subservience to Hitler and of apathy in adversity, he wrote copiously to rebuff these charges.

The disaster at Stalingrad profoundly shocked the German people and armed forces alike; indeed, it truly horrified them. Never before in Germany's history had so large a body of troops come to so dreadful an end. It is true that the Eastern Front was stabilized during 1943 and there were to be some notable German successes. But the gap torn in the ranks of the German Eastern Army, when the 20 divisions of the 6th Army, almost all formations of the highest class, were annihilated, could never be made good. The Battle of Stalingrad was the turning point of the entire war. Adolf Hitler not only condemned an army to death; he ensured that the German Nation could not win the struggle against the Allies.

Good as the PzKpw V
Panther was, it was no
match for heavy Soviet
guns at short range.

KURSK:
THE GREATEST TANK BATTLE IN HISTORY

In trying to draw the Russians into a tank battle
the Germans themselves were trapped, and lost large numbers
of tanks without any result.

General, Feldmarschall, Eastern Front 1943. The General Officer's standard greatcoat had a blue-grey felt collar and scarlet piping. The lapel turnbacks showed the scarlet lining. Riding boots, gold cap cords, distinctions and oak-leaf collar patches kept the Prussian military traditions alive for Generals at least.

THE BATTLE OF Kursk in 1943 has been described as the 'Waterloo of Hitler' and the turning point in the Eastern Campaign. Even at this late date it is a little difficult to assess its importance, because it was very little known or written about in the West until well after the war. It is the Soviets who have insisted on its significance; the Germans seem less concerned, though they admit that it was, in many respects, the watershed of their endeavors. And it was certainly the biggest tank battle which took place in any theater of war.

The events leading up to the battle form a good example of tactical reasoning by astute commanders, basing their assumptions upon their knowledge of enemy dispositions, a feeling for the enemy's possible moves, and a sound military training.

The situation at the beginning of 1943, from the German point of view, was that first there was little hope of mounting a major offensive during the coming summer. The grave losses of troops and equipment at Stalingrad and the gradual attrition throughout the winter had so depleted the German fighting strength that major operations on the scale of those in 1941 and 1942 were out of the question. But the German Army was by no means beaten, and there seemed good reason for thinking that provided there was sound planning and adequate leadership, the war could be turned into one of attrition; the object being to form a solid barrier against which the Soviets could beat in vain without making any material gains. The line of reasoning here was much the same as that which had precipitated the battle of Verdun in the First World War, to present the enemy with the opportunity of wasting his manpower in a meat-grinder. Eventually, the German High Command hoped, the Soviets would become disenchanted with this expensive pastime and settle for a stalemate, from which the Germans could hope to force a draw and persuade them to accept some form of peace agreement.

But to achieve this end, it was no use thinking about a static line of defense; the 'solid barrier' was a concept, and not a blueprint. The plain fact was that with a front some two thousand

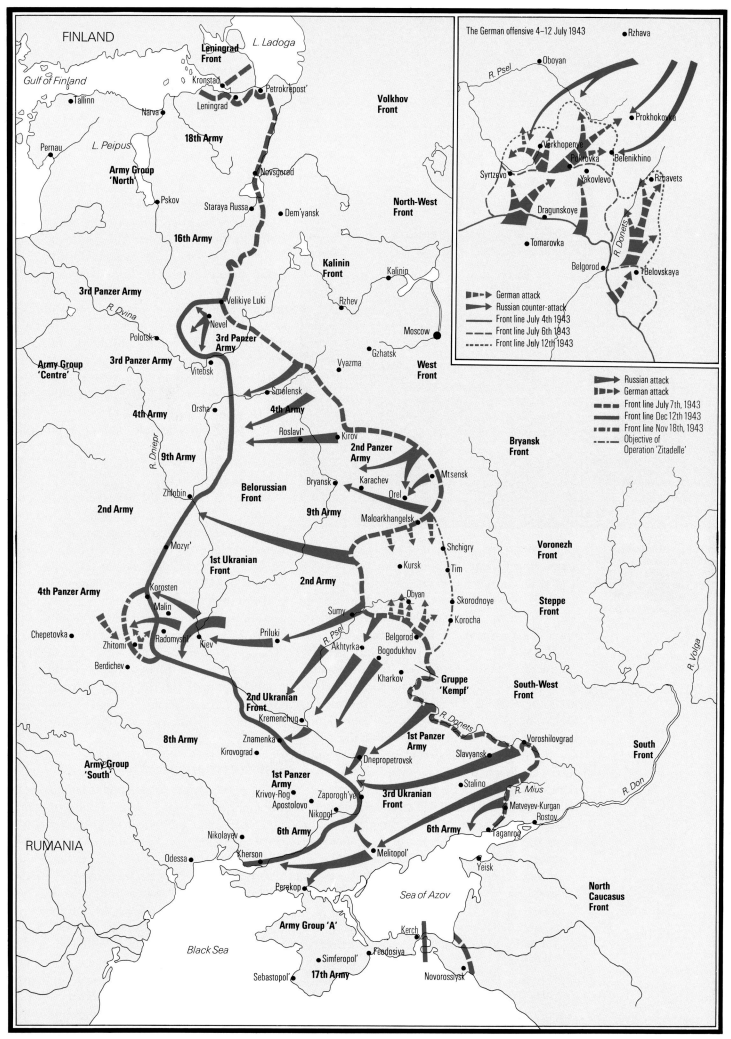

FINLAND

Gulf of Finland

L. Ladoga

Leningrad Front

Kronstad

Petrokrepost'

Leningrad

Tallinn

Narva

L. Peipus

18th Army

Volkhov Front

Pskov

Army Group 'North'

Novsgorad

16th Army

Staraya Russa

Dem'yansk

North-West Front

3rd Panzer Army

R. Dvina

Velikiye Luki

Nevel

3rd Panzer Army

Kalinin Front

Kalinin

Rzhev

Polotsk

Army Group 'Centre'

3rd Panzer Army

Vitebsk

Smolensk

Vyazma

Gzhatsk

Moscow

West Front

4th Army

Orsha

4th Army

R. Dniepr

9th Army

Roslavl'

Kirov

2nd Panzer Army

Bryansk Front

Zhlobin

Belorussian Front

Bryansk

Karachev

Orel

Mtsensk

2nd Army

9th Army

Maloarkhangelsk

Mozyr'

1st Ukranian Front

2nd Army

Shchigry

Chepetovka

4th Panzer Army

Korosten

Malin

Kursk

Tim

Voronezh Front

Obyan

Skorodnoye

Steppe Front

Zhitomir

Radomysl'

Kiev

Priluki

Sumy

R. Psel

Korocha

Berdichev

R. Psel

Belgorod

Akhtyrka

Bogodukhov

2nd Ukranian Front

Kremenchug

Kharkov

Gruppe 'Kempf'

South-West Front

8th Army

Znamenka

R. Donets

1st Panzer Army

Voroshilovgrad

South Front

Kirovograd

Dnepropetrovsk

Slavyansk

R. Don

Army Group 'South'

1st Panzer Army

Krivoy-Rog

Zaporogh'ye

3rd Ukranian Front

Stalino

R. Mius

Matveyev-Kurgan

Apostolovo

Nikopol

6th Army

Rostov

RUMANIA

Nikolayev

6th Army

Taganrog

Odessa

Kherson

Melitopol'

Yeisk

North Caucasus Front

Perekop

Sea of Azov

Army Group 'A'

Kerch

Black Sea

Feodosiya

Simferopol'

17th Army

Novorossiysk

Sebastopol'

R. Volga

The German offensive 4–12 July 1943

Rzhava

R. Psel

Oboyan

Prokhokovka

Verkhopenye

Pokrovka

Belenikhino

Syrtzevo

Yakovlevo

Rzbavets

Dragunskoye

R. Donets

Tomarovka

Belgorod

Belovskaya

German attack

Russian counter-attack

Front line July 4th 1943

Front line July 6th 1943

Front line July 12th 1943

Russian attack

German attack

Front line July 7th, 1943

Front line Dec 12th 1943

Front line Nov 18th, 1943

Objective of Operation 'Zitadelle'

161

A simulated tank turret reproducing the movements of a tank in difficult terrain, used to train tank gunners at the German armor school.

miles long the Germans had no hope of amassing sufficient troops and material to form a solid line of defense. Furthermore, there was every likelihood that in the near future British and American troops might land somewhere upon the continent of Europe now that the North African campaign was within sight of completion, and as soon as this happened German troops would have to be withdrawn from the Russian Front in order to reinforce other areas. Too, there could be little doubt that the Soviets had also appreciated this point and would probably be content to wait until such a landing had taken place before beginning their own attacks, in the hope of thus gaining an advantage over the depleted German defenses.

From consideration of all these points the German General Staff came to the conclusion that the only worthwhile tactic was to take up what they called a 'Strategic Defensive' posture. Taking advantage of the better quality of German staff work and troops, there would be a succession of heavy but localized attacks which would be sustained with the minimum effort by the Germans but which would suck the maximum Soviet strength into the meat-grinder. To plan these, the next German step was to make some assumptions about what Ivan was likely to do when the spring thaw arrived.

Broadly speaking the Soviet options resolved themselves into two choices; either to sit tight and wait for the Western Allies to invade and begin the long-promised 'Second Front', or to begin an offensive. The latter seemed to the Germans to be the more likely course. In the first place the Allies in the West were unlikely to make many concessions in their planning in order to simplify Stalin's problems, and in the second place the Soviet troops had gained a good deal of confidence during the course of the winter, having disposed of von Paulus' 6th Army at Stalingrad and made several smaller but equally worthwhile gains. With their avowed intention of sweeping the invaders from Russian soil, it was a fair bet that their choice would be an offensive.

With that decided the next question was the location of their attack, and this also seemed fairly obvious to the German Staff. South of Kharkov the front swung eastward in a sudden curve to form a vast salient enclosing the Donetz Basin, an area which covered valuable coal-mining, engineering and manufacturing centers. It was an obvious place for an attack; as von Manstein, the German commander, said 'The whole salient was just begging to be sliced off'. A successful breakthrough in this area would give the Soviet troops a clear route to the Ukraine and put them into a good position to begin clearing the German forces out of the Crimea.

The Germans in Wait

Once this appreciation had been made by the Germans they set about making preparations to counter the move. Their planning also revolved round two basic options; either they made a pre-emptive strike and hit the Soviets before they made their attack, or they waited for the Soviets to move and then made a counter-attack. They chose the latter course, the basic idea being to wait for the Soviet attack, give ground before it, falling back to a prepared line on the Lower Dniepr River, and then unleashing a powerful armored force from the Kharkov region to take the Soviet advance in its flank when its supply lines were well stretched out. This would cut off the spear-

The 76.2mm divisional gun was the basic support gun of the Soviet artillery. As well as being a field gun it had an excellent anti-tank performance.

head and encircle it while also smothering the rear echelons. Such a move would produce the maximum destruction of Soviet forces for the minimum exertion of the German, and it was a sound and sensible plan.

The Choice of Kursk

It had, however, to be approved by Hitler, and as we now know and the High Command ought to have known by then, Hitler was always violently opposed to any plan which as much as suggested giving up ground which had already been won. The plan also contained an element of risk in allowing the Soviets to make some gains and gather momentum before the counter-stroke went into action. But, like most amateurs playing at being soldiers, Hitler had little stomach for taking calculated risks in battle. The plan was turned down.

So the General Staff went back to their maps and set to work to produce a blueprint for a limited offensive. Here the prime factor was to mount an attack fairly quickly while the enemy was still weak from his losses during the winter and before the Russian factories could increase the number of tanks and guns arriving at the front. It was known by the Germans that the Soviet formations in the front lines were still using tanks which had seen a good deal of combat during the winter; if these could be brought to action there was a fair chance that mechanical trouble would cause as many casualties as would the Panzers, but any delay would allow these tanks to be reinforced and eventually replaced by new machines, with a correspondingly smaller hope of German success.

Examination of the map again pointed the Germans to the obvious choice for the location of their offensive – the Kursk Salient. This bulge in the front line, north of Kharkov, thrust about 60 miles into the German area and was about a hundred miles from side to side. It was a perpetual curse to the Germans since it permitted the Soviets within it to make raids into the flanks of the German line. There were sizeable Soviet forces in the salient and it seemed probable that as and when the Soviets opened their offensive in the South, these units

would jump out of the salient and begin making diversionary attacks, drawing German troops away from the main Soviet thrust. And so 'Operation Citadel' was born; a two-pronged attack from North and South to pinch out the Kursk salient, straighten the line, catch the Russians off balance, and put large numbers of them out of action. The German Southern Army Group, composed of two armies, the 4th Panzer Army and the 'Battle Group Kempfe', would strike northwards from Belgorod towards Kursk, while the Central Army Group provided 9th Army to attack from the North near Orel. The only drawbacks to these decisions were that the Southern Army Group would have to thin out some of its defenses in order to provide the troops for the attack, while the 9th Army would have to assemble inside the Orel Salient, a curve which thrust into the Soviet lines and which the Soviets were doubtless itching to eliminate. If they decided to do so while 9th Army had their backs to them and their eyes on the South, the results could well be fatal.

So 'Citadel' was planned and the dates set; the Panzers would roll in the first half of May 1943, as soon as the ground had dried out from the spring thaw sufficiently to allow armor to move across the steppes and before the Soviet troops would be refitted with new equipment.

Russian Plans

But while all this planning and preparation was going on, the Russians weren't sitting in idleness. They too had a planning section which was working for its living, and they too had been looking to the coming spring and summer and calculating what the possibilities might be. It took very little calculation to see that the Kursk Salient was the most likely place for a German attack; there were seven Soviet armies inside this bulge, and a successful move by the Germans could well cut this force off and destroy it. The Soviet assumptions were rather more grandiose than the actual German plan, in as much as they expected that the Germans would, if their move in the Kursk area succeeded, swing southwards and try to roll up the South-Eastern salient. While the Soviet view was that the Germans had insufficient troops

A 57mm anti-tank gun M1943 in use at Kursk.

A 45mm anti-tank gun is run forward by its crew to take up a firing position. Inset: the 8in howitzer on a tracked chassis was the heaviest field artillery weapon used by the Red Army. This camouflaged gun is being used in the Kursk Salient.

for a major offensive, they nevertheless prepared their appreciations by taking the most serious case and assuming that the Germans might, after all, just manage it. So the decision was taken to do exactly what Hitler had refused; to allow the Germans to make the first move, check them, and then throw them back and destroy them. After which the Soviets would go over to their own offensive and eliminate all the salients thrusting into their front.

Early in April the Soviet plans were laid, and the collection of a massive reserve force was begun. A series of defensive line was prepared within the Kursk salient, lines composed principally of anti-tank obstacles, mines and anti-tank guns, for the Soviets were well aware that their primary task was to stop the Panzer thrust. Additional anti-tank guns were brought in from other parts of the front, as well as being delivered directly from the factories as they were turned out, until there was a density of some 48 to 50 anti-tank guns to each mile of defensive line in those areas where the threat was deemed to be greatest.

The Soviets had learned several lessons from their successful defense of Stalingrad, and utilised the same system of 'zone' defense in the Kursk area. This method of defense rested on the knowledge that German attacks always came in three distinct stages. First there was a reconnaissance by light armor in the form of feint attacks intended to explore the Soviet defenses and locate the weapons. Second came the 'Preparation by Fire', a mixture of air support dive-bombing and strafing the discovered positions and artillery bombardment of the forward defenses. Finally came the main attack, either while the preparation by fire was still in progress or immediately after it finished. This attack was led by armor, with accompanying infantry, their task being to occupy the gains made by the tanks and to deal with anti-tank weapons.

The Soviet defense took all this into account and thus became primarily an anti-tank defense, with the infantry and their machine guns protecting the anti-tank weapons. And these anti-tank guns were not, as in every other army, specifically designed as high-velocity

A pensive General
Malinin, Chief-of-Staff of
the front, outside his dug-
out at the Kursk Bulge.

guns; in the Russian view, any gun capable of shooting at a tank was, *ipso facto*, an anti-tank gun, irrespective of what the designer might have had in mind when he designed it. One way or another, practically all Soviet artillery was capable of use against tanks.

The Artillery Zones

The method of achieving this was to arrange the artillery in 'zones' behind the front. The first zone, in the front line, contained the artillery sited so as to fire directly at approaching tanks. These guns were grouped in strongpoints, mutually supporting and protected by infantry. In sectors which appeared to be well suited to armored attack, battalions of field artillery designated as 'tank-destroyers' were sited so as to cover the lines of approach thoroughly and swamp them with fire. These tank-destroyer units were so firmly committed to this role that they were deliberately excluded from the general artillery command system and thus were incapable of receiving any orders or fire missions for indirect fire; their target was tanks, and nothing but tanks.

Behind this forward zone was the 'zone of field artillery' in which the normal field guns for indirect fire support were located; behind this the 'zone of medium artillery', and behind that the 'zone of heavy artillery'. Finally, at the rear, was a massive reserve of all types of guns and howitzers which could be moved in to reinforce any threatened area or used as replacements for weapons damaged in battle. Again there was no sectarian division; when a replacement gun was wanted, the first available weapon was sent, irrespective of type or caliber. An anti-tank gun casualty might well be replaced by a field howitzer, or a field gun with an anti-tank gun. If it could shoot, it went.

Having zoned their defensive area, the Russians now carried the same system forward and divided up the enemy area into corresponding zones. From the front line to the nearest skyline was the zone of direct fire and this was reserved to the direct fire weapons in the line. The next zone, corresponding to the 'zone of field artillery' on the Soviet side, was reserved for the fire of the field artillery, and similar zones of fire were delineated for the medium and heavy artillery.

When an attack developed, the heavy artillery was the first to go into action, firing into its own zone on the enemy side, hoping to break up the attack in its early stages. As the attack persisted and moved forward, so the medium artillery would come into action as the enemy came into the medium fire zone and, in turn, the field artillery would engage targets as they appeared in their zone. Finally, as the oncoming assault came over the skyline the tank-destroyer battalions and direct-fire artillery in the front line would go into action. In this way the strength of the defensive fire increased as the attack came closer. Moreover in the initial stages of the attack, when the Germans were probing for information, only the heavy and medium guns would engage from positions well back, and the forward weapons would remain silent and thus not give away their positions prematurely.

New German Armor

On problem which faces the historian looking at the Battle of Kursk is the question of the relative strengths involved. The official German figure merely quotes 27 divisions without going into detail about how many men or tanks were involved, and since, by that time of the war, a German division was unlikely to be in accordance with the Tables of Organization, it is impossible to calculate a figure. Soviet sources give the German strength as 33 divisions, however, and a German strength of 900,000 men, 10,000 guns, 2700 tanks and assault guns and 2000 aircraft; the Soviet strength is quoted as being 1,300,000 men, 20,000 guns, 3600 tanks and assault guns and 2400 aircraft. The Soviet strength may well be correct, but it seems likely that their estimate of German strength is somewhat exaggerated in order to present the Soviet success in an even better light.

At the beginning of May Hitler issued orders postponing 'Operation Citadel' until June, so that more of the new weapons, just beginning to come from the production lines in quantity, could be provided. The High Command pointed out to him that this sort of argument could

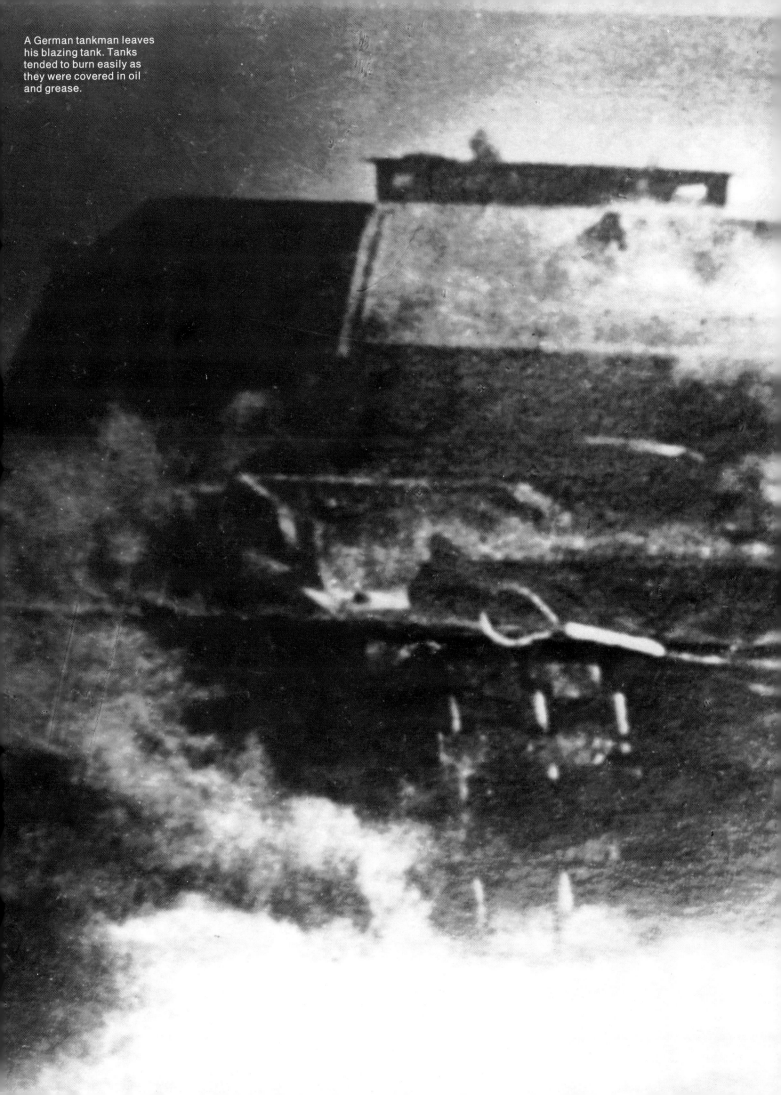

A German tankman leaves his blazing tank. Tanks tended to burn easily as they were covered in oil and grease.

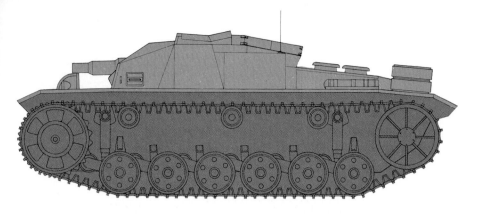

The Sturmgeschutz III armed with a short 75mm gun was the principal assault artillery which accompanied the infantry in their final assaults.

be applied both ways, and that the Soviets would have the same amount of breathing space in which to produce new tanks and guns, and that since the Russian industrial potential was greater, they could undoubtedly produce more in the time than the German factories could. Moreover every day's delay brought the possible invasion of Europe nearer. But their arguments were in vain, and since tank production was slower than even the Führer had anticipated, it was not until early July that 'Citadel' was ready to roll.

These new weapons that Hitler had considered sufficiently valuable to warrant delaying the operation were the Tiger, Panther and Ferdinand armored vehicles and the Focke-Wulf 190 fighter aircraft. Both the Tiger and the Panther had been produced in response to the shock appearance of the Soviet T-34 in the previous year. The speed, toughness and powerful armament of the T-34 led to a panic-stricken cry for a tank which would be at least its equal, and the Army High Command quickly put together a specification

for a 30-ton tank and called upon various makers for designs. Almost immediately the specification was superseded by Hitler, who demanded in its place a 45-ton tank mounting a heavier gun. This conflict of demands could well have led to disaster, but, by good fortune, it actually led to the two finest German tank designs ever to appear.

Two companies, Daimler-Benz and the Maschinenfabrik Augsburg-Nürnberg, kept to the original 30-ton specification, and after comparative tests of the prototypes the MAN design was selected for production. It used sloped armor, copied to some extent from the T-34, and was originally fitted with a 48-caliber 75mm gun. Hitler intervened once again, and insisted on having a much more potent 70-caliber 75mm gun, and by the time this had been done and one or two changes made, the 30-ton tank tipped the scales at 45 tons. Nevertheless, it went into production as the Panther and soon established a reputation as a first-class fighting tank.

The 45-ton specification went to the com-

Russian soldiers inspect a captured Ferdinand. Though solidly armoured and powerfully gunned, this was a sluggish tank, which was later appropriately termed 'Elephant'. Its main armament was an 88mm gun.

The PzKpw V Panther armed with a long 75mm gun was one of the most successful German tank designs. It combined mobility, protection and firepower with mechanical reliability.

panies of Henschel and Porsche, and of their designs that of Henschel was judged to be superior and was selected for production. This mounted an 88mm gun derived from the famous anti-aircraft weapon and, like the smaller design, exceeded its weight limit by a considerable amount, finishing up as the 56-ton 'Tiger'. The Porsche prototype was more complex mechanically, but the Army asked for it to be converted into a tank destroyer, mounting the same 88mm gun as the Tiger but with limited traverse. In order to save time and machining the turret was done away with, the sides and front of the hull made higher, and the 88mm gun mounted in a ball mounting in the front plate of the fighting compartment. The result was called 'Ferdinand', after Dr. Porsche, and carried 185mm of armor and weighed 68 tons. It promised to be an all-conquering Behemoth, and the entire output, some 90 in all, went forward to take part in the Kursk battle.

June came, and with it a further postponement of 'Citadel', and finally, after repeated urgings by the High Command, a date was set.

A column of T-34 tanks accompanied by the Red Air Force and carrying 'tank-riding' infantry, moves into action in the Battle of Kursk.

July 5 would see the battle open; the Soviets, however, soon got wind of this and resolved to upset the German schedules by a spoiling bombardment. Having discovered from interrogating a prisoner that the German attack was due to begin at 0300 on July 5, at 0220 every available Russian gun and rocket-launcher opened fire on the German assembly areas. Precise shooting was not possible since the Soviets did not know the location of all the likely targets, but the guns were directed on to the obvious areas likely to be used for forming-up troops and concentrating armor, with instructions to spread their fire around these areas.

So far as German losses were concerned this bombardment was less successful than the Soviets hoped, since chancy shooting into large areas of Russia left plenty of room for missing, and most of the German troops were, in fact, under cover. But it certainly disrupted the plans for the attack since, under such a bombardment, it was hopeless to try and assemble units or move them about. The 0300 deadline came and went, and it was not

The Soviet T-34/76 tank was the major factor in Russian tactics once it became obvious that the Germans had nothing comparable. Of outstanding mobility, it was well armored and carried a powerful gun.

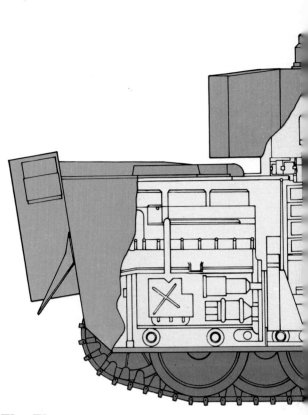

until 0430 that the German artillery began its opening bombardment of the Northern flank of the Salient. With the aid of air support the tanks and infantry moved into action on a wide front at 0530, the blow falling on the Soviet 13th, 48th and 70th Armies. An estimated 500 tanks, led by the new Tigers and Ferdinands, were flung into the attack and in spite of heavy losses to the direct-fire guns, the momentum was preserved and the German attack penetrated to a depth of nine miles before being brought to a halt against a powerful defensive line on high ground.

Panzer Thrust

The German 9th Army then paused to draw breath and re-organize, intending to take up the attack after a day or two's break, but this idea was forestalled as the Soviets moved into the second phase of their planned tactic, a powerful counter-thrust. On July 11 the West and Bryansk Fronts under Rokossovsky and Popov launched attacks into the Orel Salient, threatening the flanks of the German positions there, and in order to deal with this move the German 9th Army had to abandon any idea of resuming its attack and concentrate its efforts on trying to contain the Soviet advances. To do this it was forced to break off, turn about, and move north once more to go to the aid of the other German troops in the Orel Salient. And with them went any hope of cutting the neck of the Kursk Salient from the northern side.

On the Southern edge of the Salient the German attack, though moving slowly, was much more successful. 4th Panzer Army under Colonel-General Hoth formed the spearhead of this attack, with some 700 tanks, and the Soviet defenses were outnumbered by three-to-one, which is always considered to be the optimum figure for a successful break-in. The German attack pierced the Soviet defenses and moved forward in the direction of Korchka for some ten or twelve miles before being brought to a halt by the third defensive line, in which hundreds of Soviet tanks had been dug into the ground as immobile pillboxes. With only their turrets showing they were extremely difficult targets, and prolonged hammering against this

The Tiger

This sectional drawing of the PzKpw VI Tiger tank illustrates the mechanical arrangements and the mounting of the 88mm gun. A second version, known to the Allies as the King Tiger or Royal Tiger, was even more massive, but both types were plagued by mechanical problems.

Weight: 56 tons.
Speed: 25 mph.
Armor: 100-mm.
Engine: 590 hp Maybach HL230 P45.

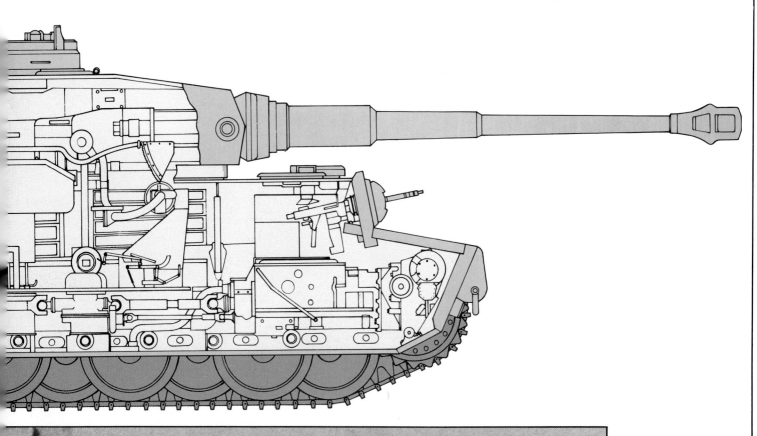

The remains of two Panther tanks caught by Soviet artillery in the Prokhorovka area of Kursk. Inset: two Russian tankmen wearing their protective helmets inspecting the damage to a Tiger turret done by their 76mm gun.

line only served to increase the German loss rate. So, while retaining a holding force against this line, the German commanders now shifted the direction of their thrust further north to head for the towns of Prokhorovka and Oboyan. This sudden change of axis took the Sovie by surprise and allowed the German troops to make some spectacular advances, capturing 24,000 Soviet prisoners, 1800 tanks and about 1200 guns in the process. Faced with this sudden surprise, the Soviets decided to throw in their reserves in an attempt to stop the German advance once and for all, and for this they called out the 5th Guards Army and 5th Guards Tank Army, both of which had been awaiting the call in the area behind Prokhorovka.

The Tanks Clash

On July 12 this Soviet armored reserve swept into the Prokhorovka area to confront the Panzers of General Hoth. It has since been estimated that 1500 tanks met that day on the battlefield, the greatest tank battle the world has ever seen or is ever likely to see. For once all the visions of years before, of great tank fleets sweeping across open country and maneuvering like fleets of warships, came true. Across the open steppe, in clouds of dust and smoke, the two armored forces thundered into action. The T-34s and KVs struck across the flank of the Panzers, but within minutes of the engagement beginning all semblance of order was lost as tanks charged hither and thither, firing furiously at anything which crossed their path, separated from their companions and commanders, even crashing head-on into each other in the dust clouds. Like Inkerman, it soon became a 'soldier's battle', since the commanders had little hope of being able to control affairs. The clouds of dust and the smoke from burning tanks soon obscured the battlefield, so that nobody could have the slightest idea of how the battle was developing, and it all came down to the individual tanks and their crews, fighting it out in single combat, tank by tank. In such conditions as these the superior training of the German Panzer troops was sufficient to balance the superior numbers of the Soviets for some considerable time, and the battle thus became a prolonged and bloody business. From dawn until nightfall it raged, and when the affair finally came to an end the Germans had lost some 350 tanks and an estimated 10,000 men. The Soviet losses have never been published, but common-sense suggests that they could not have been less and were probably a good deal more. In the end the superior Soviet numbers had told, and Hoth's force was prevented from making any further advance.

German Hopes Collapse

This tank battle, by which Kursk is always remembered, marked the high point of the German advance. On that same day the Soviet attack on the Orel Salient began, and three days earlier on July 10, the long-awaited move against the Continent had come with the Anglo-American invasion of Sicily. On July 13, while the Germans were still counting the cost of the Prokhorovka tank battle, the two Army Commanders, von Manstein and von Kluge, were summoned urgently to Hitler's Headquarters where they were apprised of the Allied landings in Sicily and of the fact that the Italians looked like suing for peace. With this threat on the Southern flank, and the imminent possibility of landings in Italy or even the Balkans, German reinforcement of these areas was imperative, and 'Operation Citadel' had to be called off forthwith in order to provide the necessary troops. Things had fallen out precisely as the German High Command had predicted; the Soviets had immensely strengthened their tank forces and the Allies had moved against the German flank, and between the two, the prospects of further German offensive operations in Russia were ground into dust. Although the Germans estimated (probably correctly) that the Soviet forces had suffered something like four times the casualties in men and equipment as the Germans the offensive was called off; the Germans disengaged and fell back, and the Soviet counter-offensive rolled irrevocably forward. The gamble had failed, and the Soviets, confirmed in their conviction that they could now take on the best the Germans could produce and defeat it, were able to set out on the road to Berlin.

An armored command post being dug into the sand for protection in the desert.

THE DESERT PENDULUM:
THE CUNNING FOX

**After his Italian allies had suffered a series of
defeats in North Africa, Hitler despatched General Rommel and
the Afrika Korps to restore the situation.**

BEFORE DESCRIBING THE activities of General Erwin Rommel and his celebrated Afrika Korps it might be as well to set the stage by examining what had gone before and, most basic of all, why the far-off deserts of Cyrenaica and Libya became one of the major battlefields of the Second World War.

The importance of the Western Desert began with the Italian declaration of war on Britain and France in June 1940. With the Italian Navy in the Mediterranean, and with the major portion of its shores now enemy or enemy-held territory, the British supply-route to and from the Far East was immediately placed at hazard.

Field Marshal Wavell (right) talking to General O'Connor, commander of the desert forces, outside Bardia.

Malta took on a new importance as an unsinkable aircraft carrier and as a naval base, and it became the key to British control of the sea, while at the same time the problem of supplying it by convoys in the face of a hostile fleet and between hostile shorelines became a considerable logistic problem. By using the air and naval forces based on Malta it was possible to threaten and disrupt the Italian supply lines to their forces in Cyrenaica, but this advantage was offset by the ease with which Malta could be bombed and by the sizeable naval forces which Italy could deploy.

Britain's operational requirements were thus easily defined. The Royal Navy had the twin tasks of dealing with the Italian Fleet and disrupting the Italian supply line, the Royal Air Force had to protect Malta, combat the Italian Air Force and, in its spare time, also upset the Italian supply-routes, while the Army had to clear the Italians out of the African continent. The naval and air sides fall outside our sphere of interest, but they must be constantly borne in mind since their operations had important repercussions on the land battles. But at first it seemed as if the British Army was more than capable of taking care of its side of affairs, even though hopelessly outnumbered.

By great good fortune the British commander in the Middle East was General Wavell, a brilliant and clear-sighted soldier. He had been appointed to this command in August 1939, before the war had even begun, and had marked his appointment by producing an 'appreciation' which sized up the situation and forecast the future in an astonishingly prescient manner. He saw the importance of the Mediterranean, presuming an Italian declaration of war, and came to the conclusion that the task of the British Army in the Middle East was not to act simply as a defensive garrison but 'to take such measures of offense as will enable us and our Allies to dominate the Mediterranean at the earliest possible moment.'

From this appreciation Wavell laid his plans, which included offensive operations against the Italians as soon as war was declared. His other major step was to begin building up a massive base of operations in the Nile Delta and Canal

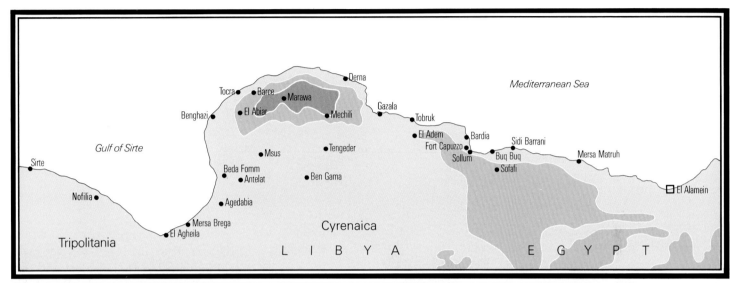

Derna
Tocra • Barce • Marawa
Benghazi • El Abiar • Mechili
Gazala
Tobruk
Mediterranean Sea
El Adem • Bardia
Fort Capuzzo • Sidi Barrani
Msus • Tengeder
Sollum • Buq Buq
Gulf of Sirte
Sofafi • Mersa Matruh
Sirte • Beda Fomm • Ben Gama
Antelat
□ El Alamein
Nofilia • Agedabia
Mersa Brega • Cyrenaica
Tripolitania El Agheila L I B Y A E G Y P T

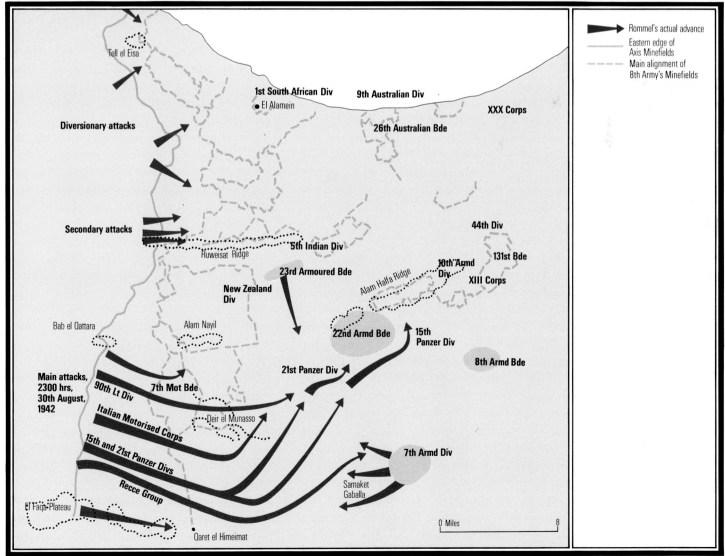

Rommel's actual advance
Eastern edge of
Axis Minefields
Main alignment of
8th Army's Minefields

Tell el Eisa

1st South African Div   **9th Australian Div**
• El Alamein

Diversionary attacks

26th Australian Bde   **XXX Corps**

Secondary attacks

44th Div

Ruweisat Ridge   **5th Indian Div**

23rd Armoured Bde   **10th Armd Div**   **131st Bde**

Alam Halfa Ridge   **XIII Corps**

New Zealand Div

Bab el Qattara   Alam Nayil

22nd Armd Bde   **15th Panzer Div**

21st Panzer Div   **8th Armd Bde**

Main attacks, 2300 hrs, 30th August, 1942
90th Lt Div   **7th Mot Bde**

Italian Motorised Corps

Deir el Munasso

15th and 21st Panzer Divs

Recce Group   **7th Armd Div**

Samaket Gaballa

El Faqa Plateau

0 Miles   8

Qaret el Himeimat

Italian 47mm anti-tank gun and its crew ready for the advancing British armor. This was an effective gun but was not available in sufficient numbers to make an appreciable difference.

Zone capable of supporting fifteen divisions in action. As a result, when Italy finally did declare war, there was a logistic back-up available and functioning, a logistic back-up which enabled the spearhead of the army to carry the war to the enemy in the knowledge that fuel, rations, ammunition and replacements were ready and that a line of supply and communication existed to produce all these items for the fighting troops as and when they were needed.

General Richard O'Connor took command of the forces in the Western Desert two days before Italy declared war, armed with orders from Wavell that as soon as a formal declaration was made, he should proceed to take offensive action. The 7th Armoured Division was concentrated in the area of Mersa Matruh and on June 11, the day after Italy's move, the 11th Hussars mounted an offensive patrol across the border of Libya which ambushed an Italian column near Fort Capuzzo. Some 50 prisoners were taken, whose interrogation soon made it plain that the Italian Army was in no way prepared to make any offensive moves against Egypt. Indeed, some of the soldiers were not even sure that a war had begun. As a result of this information O'Connor decided to take the initiative, and within a few days the Hussars set

forth and captured Forts Capuzzo and Maddalena by way of announcing their presence.

This stung Marshal Graziani, the Italian commander, into action; he had, under his command, the better part of a quarter of a million men, while the British strength stood at no more than 36,000 troops in Egypt with about 30,000 scattered across the Middle East, few of whom were up to strength in equipment. In the middle of September Graziani began a ponderous and half-hearted advance, the British outposts falling back before him, and took four days to move the 65 miles to Sidi Barrani. Having arrived there he despatched a boastful telegram to *Il Duce*, 'All is quiet. The trams are running again in Sidi Barrani', and his force proceeded to dig themselves into defensive positions.

Wavell by this time, had begun planning a major offensive against the Italians, and had arranged for such scarce items as tanks and guns to be shipped from England to bring his force up to its paper strength. But while waiting for these supplies and planning his campaign Wavell was forced to strip away some of his forces in order to begin operations against the Italians in Eritrea and to reinforce the Greek defense against the Italian invasion of that country. Nevertheless, by December Operation

'Compass' was ready; it had been prepared in the strictest secrecy and was presented in the guise of a five-day limited-objective raid. Only Wavell and his closest advisers knew that the whole plan was so constructed that at the end of the five days, if the Italians were showing signs of collapse, the operation could be extended to a full-scale invasion of Cyrenaica. On the other hand if the Italians proved tougher than Wavell believed, then at the end of the fifth day the battle could be broken off without much difficulty.

'Wavell's Thirty Thousand'

In the event Wavell's assessment of the Italian Army's capabilities turned out to be correct. They crumbled before the British attack and the five-day jaunt turned into a major military coup. General O'Connor's force of 30,000 troops, which went down into history as 'Wavell's Thirty Thousand', made a swing through the desert, outflanking the Italian positions on their southern side, to take the Sidi Barrani garrison in its flank and rear. At the same time the 7th Armoured Division headed further west and then swung north to come up well behind Sidi Barrani, on the coast road,

and thus cut off the escape route. Within three days the Sidi Barrani area was in British hands and the Italian Army had lost 38,000 troops, 237 guns and 73 tanks, over a thousand 'soft' vehicles and four general officers. The British losses totalled 624 killed, wounded or missing.

At this juncture Wavell had to reduce his forces once more, removing the 4th Indian Division who had taken Sidi Barrani, in order to send them to the Sudan to prepare for the forthcoming Eritrean campaign, leaving only the 7th Armoured Division to mop up and follow the retreating Italians into Cyrenaica. But by keeping up the pressure of their original attack, and giving the Italians no time to reform and reorganise, this small force forged ahead, knocking over one Italian garrison after another, until it came up against the perimeter of Bardia, where the Italians had managed to pull together something like a formidable defense. Here there were some 45,000 troops together with about 400 pieces of artillery, all of which came as something of a surprise to O'Connor, who had been given to believe that half that number of men and a quarter the gun strength would be the most he might find.

At this point 7th Armoured Division were re-

The British 2-pounder anti-tank gun. Capable of all-round traverse, it was probably the best gun of its type ever designed but it was hopelessly outclassed by German armor in the desert.

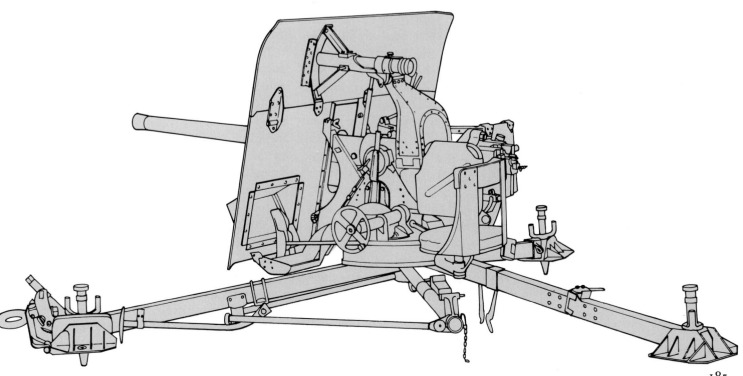

A desert fort with a mixture of German and Italian artillery in the foreground. On the left is a German 88mm gun, while the trucks carry Italian 75mm anti-aircraft guns.

inforced by the arrival of the 6th Australian Division from Palestine, fresh, well-trained, and immensely confident of their own abilities. At dawn on January 3, 1941 they stormed the wire defenses of Bardia while battleships of the Royal Navy stood off to sea and bombarded the place. By noon the Italians were surrendering in droves, and within two days the entire area was firmly in Australian hands. Another 38,000 Italians headed for the POW cages, while 465 guns, 120 tanks and over 700 soft vehicles were taken.

With Bardia cleared the advance now swept on to Tobruk, the next major town on the coast and the next major defensive post for the Italians. This fell on January 21, providing another 30,000 prisoners, 87 tanks, 200 guns, and so much assorted transport that nobody ever got around to counting it for the record. Losses such as these showed that the Italians were not particularly keen about disputing ownership of their African colony, and also that

there couldn't be a great deal of Graziani's army left. The Commonwealth troops now strained every muscle in an attempt to put a quick end to the whole campaign. O'Connor was convinced that the Italians were about to evacuate Cyrenaica completely, and he despatched what was left of 7th Armoured Division across the desert in a left hook, while the Australians followed the coast road and rolled up the defenses of Derna and Barce *en route* to Benghazi. And as the Italians took their leave of Benghazi in the face of this advance, so a tiny outpost of 7th Armoured Division managed to get astride the coast road west of Benghazi at a village called Beda Fomm. Here the 11th Hussars, the 2nd Battalion of the Rifle Brigade, 'C' Battery, Royal Horse Artillery with eight 25-pounder guns and the Lancashire Yeomanry with nine 37mm Bofors anti-tank guns set up a road block and awaited the arrival of the fleeing Italians. Soon a column estimated at $11\frac{1}{2}$ miles long and containing some 30 tanks ran up

distance away near Sirte, Hitler sent for General Erwin Rommel and appointed him to the command of two divisions, one Light and one Panzer, which were to be sent to North Africa. From then on, things moved very quickly indeed. Rommel arrived in Tripoli on February 12, and two days later the first German troops followed him. These units, the 3rd Reconnaissance Battalion and an anti-tank gun battalion, were disembarked overnight and moved off to the front, to be in action by February 16.

British Forces Cut to the Bone

On the British side, the forces had been cut down to a dangerous level. 7th Armoured Division had been sent back to Egypt to rest and re-fit, and they had been replaced by half of the 2nd Armoured Division, fresh from England and with no battle experience (the other half of this division had been sent to Greece). The 6th Australian Division had also gone to Greece, its place being taken by the 9th Australian Division, though again, this formation was not up to its full strength; part of it was kept at Tobruk, because there was insufficient transport available, to maintain it further forward. Besides being at reduced strengths, both these divisions were short of transport since a large quantity of their equipment had been taken from them to reinforce the Greek Front. Finally General O'Connor himself had been sent back to Egypt to become General Officer Commanding-in-Chief, and his replacement in the field, General Neame, knew little of either desert warfare or the handling of armor.

Wavell, for his part, appreciated this weakness in the west, but he was the victim of conflicting priorities and political demands. Greece had to be given assistance on political grounds, even though it was obvious to a trained military mind that it was a forlorn hope. The campaign in Eritrea was entering its final and decisive phase and nothing could be diverted from that theater. Finally, there was the over-riding responsibility for protection of the whole Middle Eastern theater, from Palestine across to El Agheila and down to the Sudan, to be taken into the reckoning. Faced with all this,

against this tiny force. For a day and a half the Italians battered, but they lost 27 of their tanks to the cunningly-sited guns and failed to get through. Meanwhile the Australians had taken Benghazi and the 7th Armoured Division had come up on the Italian flank. The Italian Army in Cyrenaica was surrounded, and surrendered forthwith. As General O'Connor wrote later, 'I think this may be termed a complete victory, as none of the enemy escaped'. The Italians had lost ten divisions, and the Commonwealth troops had taken 130,000 prisoners, 850 guns, 400 tanks and untold quantities of other equipment and stores, against a loss of 500 killed, 1,373 wounded and 55 missing.

Such was the opening phase of the Desert War, and it was such a setback for the Italian Army and for *Il Duce's* pride that Hitler had to come to the rescue. In the early days of February, while the British and Australian troops were establishing their outposts at El Agheila and the Italians theirs at a discreet

Wavell's appreciation of the threat in the desert was that the Italians would be unable to mount much of an offensive, and that although he knew of the impending arrival of German forces, they would not be in a position to make an impression for some time. Similarly, the appointment of a new German general might eventually mean problems, but it was unlikely that a new broom would start sweeping very quickly, until he had taken a few weeks to find out the situation and familiarize himself with his new responsibilities. On balance, then, it seemed to Wavell that no move against his desert forces was likely until at least the beginning of May, by which time the situation would be improved by the replace-ment of worn-out armor and the arrival of reinforcements in Egypt. This was a perfectly valid assumption, given that

the thinking was performed on conventional lines. Indeed, had Wavell known it, much the same line of reasoning had been followed and the same conclusions reached by von Brauchitsch, the German commander, when he had originally briefed Rommel for his new post. But neither Wavell or von Brauchitsch had reckond on Rommel's fighting spirit.

The difference of approach between Rommel and Wavell – and many other British and German generals of the time – can be seen in the matter of defensive lines held at the time. Wavell had been told that the escarpment south of Benghazi was a natural obstacle which could be used as a defen-sive line; he assumed it to be a precipitous cliff with only a few points passable for vehicles. When he actually saw the escarpment a long time afterwards, he found that it was, in fact, a

After his victory at Fort Mechili, only seven weeks after reaching North Africa, Rommel (second from left) talks with his prisoner, Major-General Gambier-Perry (right).

Rommel's personal aircraft, a Fieseler Storch in which he carried out frequent reconnaissance. Right: armor and artillery for Rommel's Afrika Korps being unloaded from a freighter in Tripoli harbor.

gentle slope which could be driven up with impunity almost anywhere along its length, and was a poor obstacle at the best of times.

On the other side of the fence, Rommel had the same problem of determining the lie of the land, but he elected to get into an airplane and fly over the country to see for himself – He actually flew up to the front on a reconnaissance on the same afternoon that he had landed in Tripoli; no second-hand information for Rommel.

The German Thrust

Within hours of their arrival Rommel's troops began thrusting forward from Sirte and mining sections of desert so as to channel any British advance into the coastal strip. Having thus ensured their front, the anti-tank battalion became part of the Italian defenses of Sirte, while the reconnaissance battalion began making forays into the desert so as to familiarize themselves with their new environment. Meanwhile the rest of the *Deutsche Afrika Korps* was arriving in Tripoli with its equipment and supplies. During February and March almost a quarter of a million tons of supplies came into Tripoli harbor, the Royal Navy's ability to interfere with this stream having been impaired by heavy German bombing attacks on Malta and the Fleet. On March 11 the 5th Panzer

Rommel's headquarters in the desert. His caravan can be seen among the scrub. Inset: two German staff members take breakfast in the sun, suitably camouflaged against air observation.

Regiment, disembarked with 120 tanks in Tripoli, and on the following day Rommel's headquarters moved out to the front at Sirte. This too was indicative of a new spirit; the *Afrika Korps* headquarters was to become a light and fast-moving unit which was always close up to the front line and from which Rommel always had first-class knowledge of what was happening. By comparison, General Neame's headquarters was an over-grown and static unit, 80 miles or more behind the front, ill-informed, slow to react, and usually out of touch with what was going on at the sharp end of the battle.

Rommel's orders were, in essence, to devote himself and his force to reconnaissance and to act in accordance with the wishes of the Italian commander, General Garibaldi. But neither of these instructions were to Rommel's liking. He could see, better than could the far-off *Oberkommando* in Berlin, that the British forces in the desert were overstretched and off balance, and he had little patience with the Italian views on warfare. On March 24 Rommel moved off; the Italian Brescia Division pushed up the road to El Agheila while the 5th Light Division, assisted by the Italian Ariete Armored Division, swept across the desert in an out-flanking move. As his forward elements made contact with the British outposts at El Agheila, so these fell back in accordance with their orders. Wavell had ordered Neame not to try and hold ground, but Neame's reading of this order seems to have been carried too far, and the British troops simply retreated. With El Agheila secured, Rommel now moved to deal with the small concentration of British armor which his air reconnaissance had found at Mersa Brega, a few miles further along the coast. This position was defended by the Support Group of 2nd Armoured Division, a scratch collection composed of an infantry battalion, a regiment of field guns and a regiment of anti-tank guns, nominally supported by the 3rd Armoured Brigade some five miles behind it. In fact the 3rd Armoured Brigade was no more than a grouping of two medium tank regiments and a light tank regiment; one of the medium regiments was equipped with captured Italian tanks, while the other two

A German officer examines a two-pounder shot, part of the ammunition from the wrecked Matilda tank in the background.

were outfitted with a collection of decrepit and obsolescent machinery more fitted for the scrapyard than for armored combat. The Support Group managed to hold the German attack for several hours before having to call for the services of the armored reserve, who could then have effected a counter-attack and pushed the Germans back. But the commander of 3rd Armoured Brigade considered that it was too late in the day to start thinking about armored battles; it would soon be dark and the tanks could easily get lost. So the armored reserve never came in, and, with a final burst of effort, the Germans pierced the defenses of the Support Group and chased them into the open desert. Little was it realised at the time, but Mersa Brega was the touchstone of Rommel's whole operation; had he been held there, and had his forces been beaten off with bloody noses, it is very unlikely that he would have escaped Hitler's extreme displeasure for exceeding his orders (which were only to reconnoiter). He would probably have been pulled back to Sirte and told to stay there until the *Oberkommando* authorised an attack in May or June, by which time the British forces would have been in much better shape to receive him. But as it was, he found that the British could be induced to retreat, and this encouraged him to continue his advance. Nothing succeeds like success, and a general who is on a winning streak is rarely required to make excuses.

By April 2 Rommel's forces had reached Adgedabia, and there split into three columns. The first, headed by 3rd Reconnaissance Battalion, took the coast road for Benghazi, which it entered on April 4 without opposition. The second column, principally made up from 5th Panzer Regiment under Colonel Olbrich, headed across the desert to Msus in the hope of catching up with the British 3rd Armoured Brigade and bringing it to battle, while the third prong of the advance swept even deeper into the desert via Tengeder. These two desert columns aimed to link up once more at Mechili before swinging around to fall upon Derna from the east, as the 3rd Reconnaissance Battalion came up from the west. Taking a leaf from O'Connor's book, this bold stroke swept around the British Army and placed a roadblock on the Derna-Tobruk road, so that much of the British strength was surrounded and captured, including Generals Neame, O'Connor and Gambier-Parry.

By April 7 Derna had fallen and the Germans, waiting only long enough to bring up fuel and supplies, turned about and set their sights on Tobruk, Bardia and Egypt. But by this time

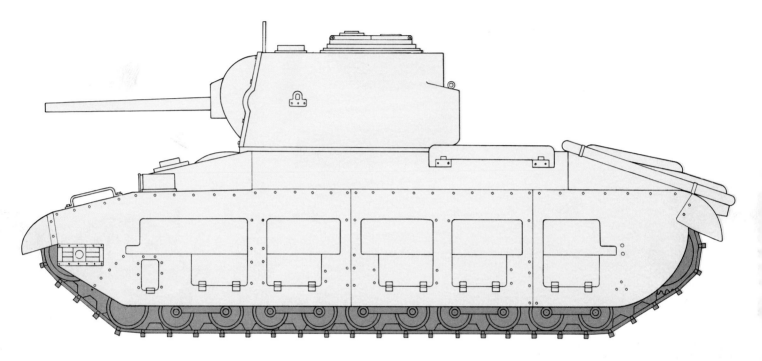

The Matilda Mark 2 tank, formidably armoured but undergunned, having no more than a two-pounder to match the opponent's 75mm gun.

there had been some frantic scurrying around in Cairo; Wavell had held a meeting with his advisers, together with Anthony Eden and Field-Marshal Dill, both of whom were visting Egypt at that time, and had given orders for the reinforcement and holding of Tobruk and the preparation of a defensive position at Mersa Matruh which would keep the Panzers out of Egypt. Churchill followed this up by cabling Wavell that 'Tobruk must be held to the death', but it seems probable that their reasons for wanting to hold on to Tobruk differed. To Churchill Tobruk was, or certainly became, a symbol of defiance, a thorn in Rommel's side and a possible 'sally-port' from which to attack the German flank. Wavell's view was much more immediate and prosaic: if Rommel took Tobruk he would have a working port that much closer to his front line. As things stood, all Rommel's supplies had to come through Tripoli and then be trucked or flown forward, a logistic handicap which was to the British advantage. If Tobruk fell into Rommel's hands this tenuous supply line was immediately replaced by a port which allowed him to land his supplies directly behind his front line. It followed that Tobruk had to be held and that the Royal Navy and RAF had to make some impression on the Tripoli supply-line.

Much has been written and said about the 'Fortress of Tobruk' but in truth, Tobruk was no more a fortress than was Anzio; it was simply a piece of desert surrounding the land side of a small seaport, and not particularly suited to defense in the first place. The defensive line was a 28-mile perimeter, with little defense in depth and with no permanent fortifications whatsoever. What saved Tobruk was not the geography of the place but the people inside it, notably the 9th Australian Division commanded by General Morshead and their supporting artillery. The perimeter could not be brought closer in so as to thicken the defense, because it was vital to keep the Germans out of artillery range of the docks, so the line of defense consisted simply of a shallow ditch line, barbed wire, and insufficient mines, dotted with dispersed defensive posts up to half a mile apart.

Two Able Opponents

Tobruk was now to demonstrate a very interesting tactical problem, a defensive position held by a general who was resourceful and a master of the defensive battle, confronted by a German force who were specialists at mobile warfare and who were commanded by the uncrowned king of *Blitzkrieg*. The irresistible force had come up against the immovable object.

Had Morshead simply sat tight and let Rommel call the tune it is doubtful whether he would have lasted for very long, but Morshead and his Australians were not disposed to let anyone tell them how their battle was to be run, and they proceeded to go out and take the battle to Rommel, much to his surprise and much to the discomfiture of his troops.

Rommel Repulsed

Rommel arrived at the Tobruk perimeter on April 14 and forthwith decided to attack, in the hope that his normal speedy attack would catch the defenses off-balance. His plan was to blow in the perimeter ditch and lift the mines, then inject tanks through the gap and make for the air-strip and harbor. Behind this initial thrust would come more tanks and supporting infantry to widen the gap and gradually roll up the defenses. But Morshead had instructed his infantry to sit tight and let the tanks go past them, concentrating their effort on destroying the infantry follow-up and leaving the armored thrust to be dealt with by artillery. The Australians chose to place their own interpretation on these orders and opened the ball by dashing forward and dealing harshly with the infantry and pioneer force who were supposed to be dealing with the ditch and mines, which rather upset the German timetable. Next the assembling German infantry were mauled by artillery fire and by long-range fire from the Australian heavy machine-guns, so that they were badly disorganized by the time the advance began. As a result the Panzers went forward without their accompanying infantry, and also without very much accompanying artillery fire, since most of the gun detachments had been shot by the Australians before they could bring their guns into action.

Deadly Anti-tank Guns

Those German tanks which got through the breached perimeter came under intense artillery fire from field guns, which had been sited for just this task, and by anti-tank guns mounted 'portee' on the back of trucks so that they could be rapidly maneuvered. Whichever way the Panzers turned they were greeted with more

artillery fire, and tank after tank was left burning. Eventually, they turned back and fought their way out through the gap in the wire, and Rommel had sustained his first setback. The defenders lost 26 killed and 64 wounded, 2 tanks and 6 guns, while the attacking force lost 17 tanks, 150 dead and 250 prisoners. Two days later the Italian Ariete Division made a half-hearted attack, but gave up as soon as they met serious opposition, most of the assaulting force electing to continue forward but with their hands above their heads. Rommel later claimed to have lost 1200 men in these attacks, but a large proportion of this figure must have been Italian defectors.

There being no future, for the time being, in further attempts on Tobruk, Rommel now turned his flagging troops and set them on the road once again, though aggressive patrolling by the Australians from the Tobruk perimeter meant that a sizeable besieging force had to be kept in place there, another tactical advantage to the British. And so by April 25 the remainder of the British forces were back at Mersa Matruh, and all the gains made by O'Connor's spectacular dash had been wiped out.

New Tanks for the 8th Army

This sudden reversal demonstrated that the arrival of Rommel and his forces had placed a very different complexion on the Desert War, and it was apparent that British strength was barely sufficient to hold the position at Matruh, and certainly insufficient to begin any worthwhile offensive action. Operation 'Brevity', an attempt to roll back the forward Axis positions and take the Halfaya Pass, key to the coast road, was thrown back somewhat summarily, and a worried Churchill despatched a special convoy, codenamed 'Tiger', to deliver 238 new tanks to Egypt on May 12. These tanks were principally the new 'Crusader' model, a fast and maneuverable vehicle but one which had been insufficiently developed and tested, due to pressure of events, and which was completely strange to the troops who had to use them. As a result they had to go into action with insufficient training and familiarization with the new weapon, a grave handicap in battle at any time

195

and particularly so when their opponents were highly-trained Panzer troops using first-rate equipment with which they were thoroughly at home.

The next major operation to be mounted was 'Battleaxe', a British thrust to harry Rommel from his forward positions and, if possible, relieve Tobruk; it was, indeed, 'Brevity' all over again, but with more muscle behind it, thanks to the 'Tiger' convoy's tanks. But it was to reveal some amazing defects in British tactical thinking. General Beresford-Pierce intended the battle to be spear-headed by the heavy 'Matilda' infantry tanks, using the lighter and faster Crusader models as a sort of flank cavalry. The Matildas were secure in the knowledge that their armor was more than a match for the guns of the German tanks and for the divisional anti-tank guns too, and thus a tank-versus-tank battle had the odds well in the British favor. But Rommel had learned a lesson at Tobruk from the manner in which his Panzers had been punished, and he had no intention of allowing his tanks to go up against the odds when there was a more effective way of conducting affairs. The British, on the other hand, had entirely failed to appreciate the lessons of the Tobruk action, and as a result the Battleaxe was soon to lose its edge.

The Debut of the '88'

The key to the affair lay in the Halfaya Pass, through which the coast road ran. Rommel seeded this area with anti-tank guns, and, in addition, removed a number of 88mm anti-aircraft guns from the Divisional Anti-Aircraft Regiment and had them dug into the ground so that only their muzzles were visible. The potentialities of the 88mm Flak gun as an anti-tank weapon had been briefly explored by the Condor Legion in Spain, and because of their reports an armor-piercing shell had been developed and was on general issue, in addition to the conventional high-explosive shell. The first use of the 88mm as an anti-tank gun in the Second World War appears to have been at Arras in 1940 when troops (also under Rommel) had finally stopped a breakthrough of British armor (also Matilda tanks) by throwing in

some of these guns as a last-ditch measure. Now, with the Matildas threatening again, Rommel turned back to these guns, and with good reason; the Matilda tanks had 80mm of armor plate, and the standard German anti-tank gun, the 50mm PAK 38, could only defeat this at ranges of 400 yards or less. The 88mm, on the other hand, could pierce 105mm at 1000 yards and could take on the Matilda at 1500 yards with a very good chance of success.

Battleaxe Fails

So as Battleaxe got under way, Rommel held his Panzers clear of the action and allowed the Matildas to rumble forward into the killing-ground of the 88s. Once they had stopped the advance, the Panzers were released for the inevitable German counter-stroke. By that time most of the British armor was out of action, either shot to pieces by the 88s or victims of their own mechanical unreliability, and with pitifully few anti-tank guns the British infantry had little hope of checking the Panzer advance. Within 48 hours of its start, Battleaxe was finished and the survivors were back at their start line, distinctly the worse for wear, and with two-thirds of their armor lying wrecked on the desert.

The failure of Battleaxe led Churchill to take action which he had been contemplating for some time; to change the leadership in the desert. While Wavell was one of the best generals produced by any army during the war, Churchill's penchant for directing his every move by a stream of minutes and telegrams sat hard upon him, and one cannot help feeling that it was with some relief that he handed over the reins to General Auchinleck. Beresford-Pierce was also fired, and Auchinleck brought in a fresh set of commanders, in the selection of which he was less than usually astute. General Cunningham, selected to head the 8th Army, had conducted the campaign in East Africa with some distinction but was a complete stranger to massed armor, while Ritchie, who later replaced him, had not commanded in battle since 1918.

Auchinleck's strong suit was his refusal to be prodded into hasty and premature action by

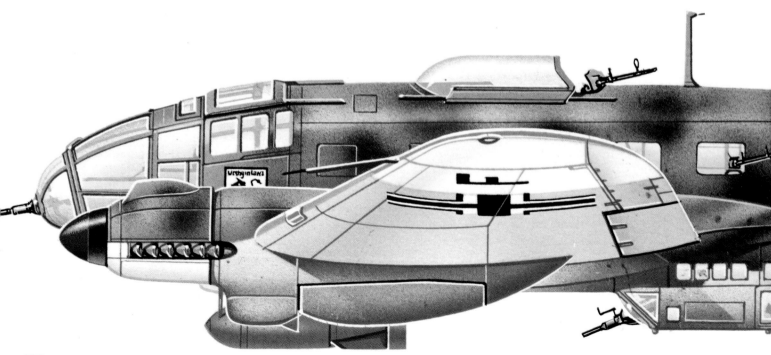

Churchill. After considering the situation as he found it, he decided that there would be no offensive move by the Desert Army until its strength had been built up and some vital training performed, which meant early November at the earliest before battle was resumed. During this period Rommel was also retraining and consolidating, accumulating more troops and tanks, building up his supply dumps, and generally preparing to advance into Egypt. But his first priority was to remove Tobruk from the reckoning, and, basing his calculations on much the same sort of factors as had Auchinleck, Rommel decided that he would attack Tobruk some time in November.

Auchinleck's instruction to Cunningham was simple: go and capture Cyrenaica. And the sure and certain way of doing this was to bring Rommel to battle and destroy his armor. Two plans were advanced for the forthcoming operation, either a deep-into-the-desert out-flanking move through the Jalo Oasis to arrive at El Agheila and thus cut off the entire Cyrenaican bulge in one swoop, or to slog along the coast road with a desert swing as a second-dary thrust. While the first plan stood a good chance of succeeding, there was no guarantee that Rommel would come out to do battle, and

it might simply leave the 8th Army sitting at the end of a long and vulnerable supply-line. The second plan was better since it also brought in the possibility of relieving Tobruk, a target for which Rommel would undoubtedly be pre-pared to fight. So the final plan, now named 'Crusader', envisaged one prong of attack through the area between Fort Maddalena and Sidi Omar, bypassing the ill-fated Halfaya Pass. Meanwhile 13 Corps would contain the Halfaya Pass area and keep the Axis forces there occupied. An 'Oasis Force' would sweep through the desert via Jarabub and Jalo Oases to secure these two places and generally give the impression of an attack developing along this axis. Finally the Tobruk garrison, acting in concert with the main attack, would break out of their perimeter and join up with 8th Army as it arrived. It was an ambitious plan, depending on fine timing and concerted action, and General Cunningham was convinced it would put Rommel back to his start line in his turn.

A Luftwaffe bomber crew rests in the shadow of their aircraft. Below: this Heinkel HeIII H-6 of II Staffel of Kampfgeschwader 26 operated from Sardinia against British shipping.

The crew of a PzKpw III surrender at bayonet point during the Battle of El Alamein.

ALAMEIN:
THE END OF THE BEGINNING

The German failure to control the Mediterranean
sea-routes robbed Rommel of vitally needed supplies, while his
enemies grew strong enough to drive him out of Africa.

ROMMEL HAD DECIDED to reduce Tobruk in the latter part of November; on November 14 he flew to Rome to attend a conference, and then to Greece. On the morning of the 18th, while he was still in Athens the British attack opened, the tanks of 7th Armoured Division rolling forward all day with no opposition other than the occasional German armored car, which soon sheered off at the approach of the tanks. On the following day action was finally joined when 22nd Armoured Brigade met the Ariete Division. 22nd Armoured were a fresh unit, with little desert experience, and they were also, as was commonplace with British units, going into battle with a new and untried tank, the latest 'Crusader' design. As a result the Italians managed to beat off the attack, destroying 40 British tanks in the process. In the center 7th Armoured Brigade met little opposition and pushed ahead until they were brought up short at Sidi Rezegh, only ten miles from the Tobruk perimeter. But on the right of the thrust the 4th Armoured Brigade were severely handled by air attacks and by the sudden and un-expected appearance of 21st Panzer Division;

A German tank crew refresh themselves with a sea bathe after the Battle at Sollum.

by the time night fell the Brigade had lost 66 tanks out of its original strength of 164.

From this point onwards, 'Crusader' lost its pattern and became what one participant later described as an 'American Sandwich' with layers of opposing troops fighting in all directions. The Tobruk garrison was making a sortie against the German 21st Corps; below this came the 7th Armoured Brigade and the 5th South African Brigade attempting to capture Sidi Rezegh; beneath them came 21st Panzer Division versus 4th Armoured Brigade, and beneath them the Ariete Division against 22nd Armoured Brigade. In response to these alarums and excursions units of both sides would turn about and dash to the other end of the battlefield before turning and charging back again. A complete analysis of this stage of the operation would take far more space than can be spared and at the end of it one would be little wiser. The one fact which stands out through it all is that the British forces never moved concertedly, but were thrown into battle piecemeal; at one stage of the affair, it is said, General Freyberg, commanding the New Zealand Division, sent a signal to 4th Armoured Brigade to ask whether they were engaged in a private fight or could anybody join in? Units stood idle while waiting their turn to be thrown to the Panzers, and mutual support by all arms seems to have been forgotten.

However, more by good luck than good management, one feels, the British attack finally succeeded in pushing the Germans back, though not before Rommel had made a valiant attempt to turn the tide by making a sudden advance which caught many of the British units off balance. Unfortunately it also dis-organized his own side; not everybody had such a quick mind as Rommel, and his sudden change of direction brought administrative chaos in its wake. Faced with the prospect of being cut off, he fell back along the coast road, fighting his usual masterly rearguard action, until finally coming to rest on his defensive line at El Agheila. Tobruk had been relieved (though there are some cynics who claim that it was the Tobruk Garrison which relieved the 8th Army and not the other way round) and

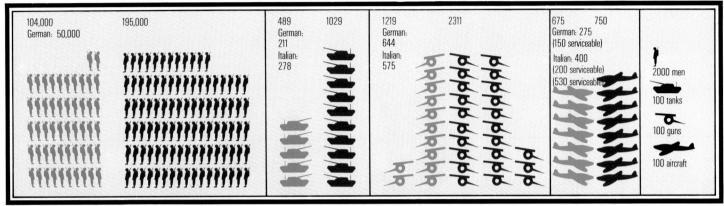
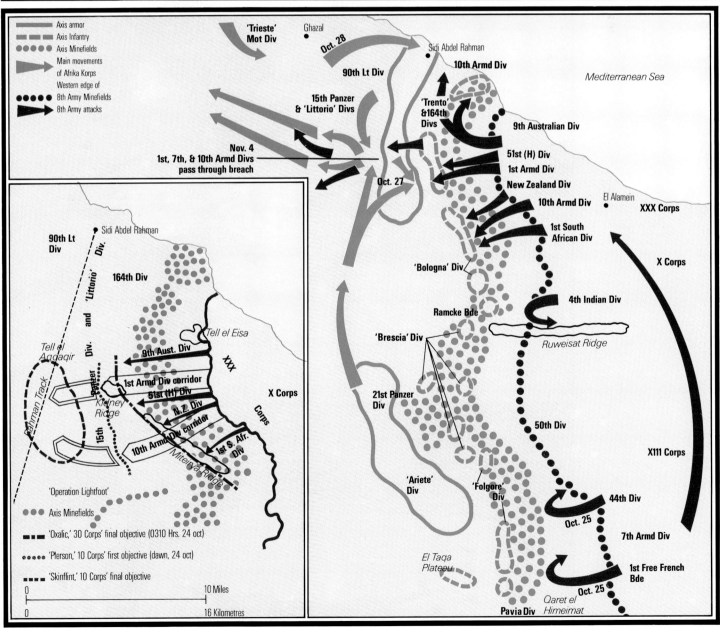

General Erwin Rommel examining a captured British 'Crusader' tank.

Cyrenaica had been cleared. Cunningham had, it seemed, achieved his object, but in fact he had been within an ace of throwing in his hand in the course of the battle, and it was only Auchinleck's firm grasp and direction which carried the affair through. Cunningham was replaced by Ritchie in the middle of the operation, but it was Auchinleck's direction which controlled the battle – insofar as it was ever under control.

Rommel Attacks Again

Because of Rommel's quick reaction to the attack and his tenacity in retreat, 'Crusader' turned out to be a long and wearying affair instead of the short and sharp sortie which Cunningham had visualized. It was not until January 6 1942 that Rommel was back in his defense line, and the process of getting him there had been a succession of small battles and bitter actions every few miles along the coast. Axis losses were estimated at 38,000 men and 300 tanks, while Commonwealth losses were some 18,000 men and 278 tanks; so on figures and gains the British were the victors, but the one prime demand of the plan had not been met. Rommel's armor had not been brought out *en masse* and destroyed. It was still a force in being, despite its losses, and as soon as Rommel had made up those losses he would once again set forth from El Agheila with blood in his eye. The only question was, when?

The riposte, when it came, was totally unexpected. During December, while the battle was still raging, fresh tanks had arrived for Rommel at Tripoli, and with these at his disposal he was ready to try his strength against the British outposts within a fortnight of his arrival at El Agheila. The British, for their part, were quite sure that Rommel had been given a blow which would keep him quiet for three months or more, and apart from a thin screen of outposts were spending most of their effort in tidying up Cyrenaica and organising their forces there. Rommel assumed that the next, indeed the obvious, British move would be another attack in the hope of driving him still further to the west, and in order to upset any preparations which might be in progress he mounted a spoiling raid, intending merely to disorganize the opposition and give himself more time in which to prepare for his own next offensive. On January 21, 1942 the Afrika Korps, outfitted with new armor and accompanied by the 90th Light Division and elements of the Italian 20th Motorized Corps, thrust forward against Mersa Brega. Taken by surprise the British outposts fell back to Adgedabia and were followed hot-foot by the Panzers. On arriving at Adgedabia they found it only lightly held and managed to take it without much trouble. The Italian Commando Supremo, nominally Rommel's masters, were happy to satisfy themselves with this. They were resigned to the loss of Cyrenaica, and they instructed Rommel to consolidate his gains and take up a defensive posture. But Rommel, having seen the alacrity with which the British had fallen back, was convinced that by keeping up the pressure he could re-take Cyrenaica. Unconvinced, the Italian commander, Cavallero, withdrew from Rommel the command of the Italian 10th and 21st Corps, ordering them to remain at Mersa Brega. Undaunted by this Rommel elected to continue his advance, using only the Afrika Korps and the two accompanying formations.

Faulty Tactics

The British weakness was due to two things; first, there had been considerable troop withdrawals to reinforce Iraq, and second the 8th Army had succumbed to its near-fatal delusion that 'small is beautiful'. After 'Crusader' the cry was for smaller units since, for some unfathomable reason, it was decreed that the division, that autonomous battle unit, was too unwieldly to handle in the desert – and this in spite of Rommel's demonstrations of what he could do with two at once. And so began the ephemeral fancies for 'Brigade Groups', 'Jock Columns', 'Battle Groups' and similar splintered forces, which had the overall effect of weakening mutual support and, most important of all, of dismantling the artillery command structure, so that the field artillery were no longer linked in an all-embracing network of control which could switch massed fires from

General Rommel, accompanied by his staff, walks over the ground after the Battle of Sollum.

concentrates his force, has a definite aim in view and seizes opportunity as it occurs will inevitably succeed over he who dissipates his force, knows no aim and commands at such a distance from the battle as to be unable to see an opportunity, let alone take advantage of one.

This fragmentation of forces found its final reward when Rommel attacked once more, after a short lull, on May 26, intending to take Tobruk and push the British back to the Nile. While the Italian divisions held the front, Rommel took a wide southward swing with his armor to cut behind the British positions at Gazala and take them in the rear while also placing Tobruk at risk. The British forces were dispsersed all over the desert in individual 'boxes' and, in spite of great gallantry and fierce fighting, they were inevitably defeated one by one by the concentrated application of all Rommel's force at each place. British armor, newly reinforced by the arrival of American 'Grant' tanks which were a considerable improvement on some of the earlier models, was cut to pieces by concentrations of anti-tank guns, artillery and armor; in three days the 8th Army tank strength went down from 300 to 70 tanks. Tobruk fell, and 33,000 men went into captivity, and the British were pushed further and further East. An attempt to form a line in the familiar area of Mersa Matruh was rapidly bypassed by Rommel. A panic started in Egypt, for it seemed that nothing could possibly halt the headlong charge of the Panzers.

Return to First Principles

Basically, what did stop them was a return to the fundamental principles of war. Auchinleck had taken charge of the 8th Army during the retreat, and he had decided to try and hold the enemy advance at Fuka or, if that failed, at the El Alamein-Ruweisat Ridge-Qattara line, which had been put into some sort of shape as a possible last-ditch defensive line some time before. In order to make this defence credible all the artillery coming east was seized and placed in positions commanding the line.

For the first time for many months, it was properly tied together and organized, so that

one area to another when called for. Now the individual gun regiments were parcelled out to these new sub-formations and by their own unaided effort the unit would sink or swim. To pit this sort of fragmented army against a concentrated thrust of German armor was foolishness of the worst order, and the 8th Army duly paid the price of its folly. In a series of swoops and thrusts the Afrika Korps chased the British out of Cyrenaica, hammering the splintered formations in turn and defeating them in detail and causing the army to abandon much of its equipment as it fled. By February 5 Rommel had reached Tmimi, a few miles west of Gazala, and came to a halt there solely because his supply line was stretched to the point of collapse. The British forces had left behind 1,600 tanks and armored vehicles, 2,500 trucks, 10,000 dead and 12,000 prisoners to record their activities in Cyrenaica during the winter. The resurgence of Rommel was a re-statement of the basic principle of war: he who

General Rommel, in his 'Kubelwagen' was a frequent sight in the front line; his command system involved constant communication with the fighting units.

on July 1, when the 90th Light Division came up against this line and tried to 'bounce' it, as it had 'bounced' so many British positions in the past, it was brought up short by a concentration of artillery fire of an intensity never before seen in Africa. The 90th took fright, dug in, and nothing would move them further. Rommel himself, who went forward to see what was holding them up, was also pinned down, unable to go forward or back. It was the beginning of the 8th Army's return to first principles, and an augury of things to come.

The Alamein position had one great advantage denied to most other defensive positions in the desert; it could not be outflanked. It was bounded on the North by the sea and on the South, 38 miles away, by the Qattara Depression, a vast inland sea of soft and shifting sand which was quite impossible to cross. Thus Rommel was forced to abandon the tactic at which he was best, the wide outflanking sweep, while the British were put into a position to do

the thing at which they were best, a solid defense to be followed by a set-piece battle and a frontal attack. From the moment that 90th Light Division was brought to a stop, Rommel had lost the initiative and his mobility availed him little.

The team having suffered a defeat, the natural recourse was for the board of directors to change the manager and coach in the hope of better results at the next game, and that is exactly what happened. Auchinleck made way for Alexander, and Gott was designated as commander of the 8th Army. Lieut-General Gott had been commanding 7th Armoured Division, and later 13th Corps, and his selection for this post has always been considered one of the minor mysteries of the desert war, since he had never been a particularly successful commander. Unfortunately, he was the victim of a fatal flying accident when flying to take up his new post, so his potential worth as an army commander was never revealed. Instead, the

207

The British 25-pounder

This versatile gun-howitzer had no equivalent in other armies. It was capable of use as a field-gun, howitzer and anti-tank gun, and was the mainstay of the divisional artillery. Firing a 20lb armor-piercing shot, it became the foremost tank-killer on the British side.

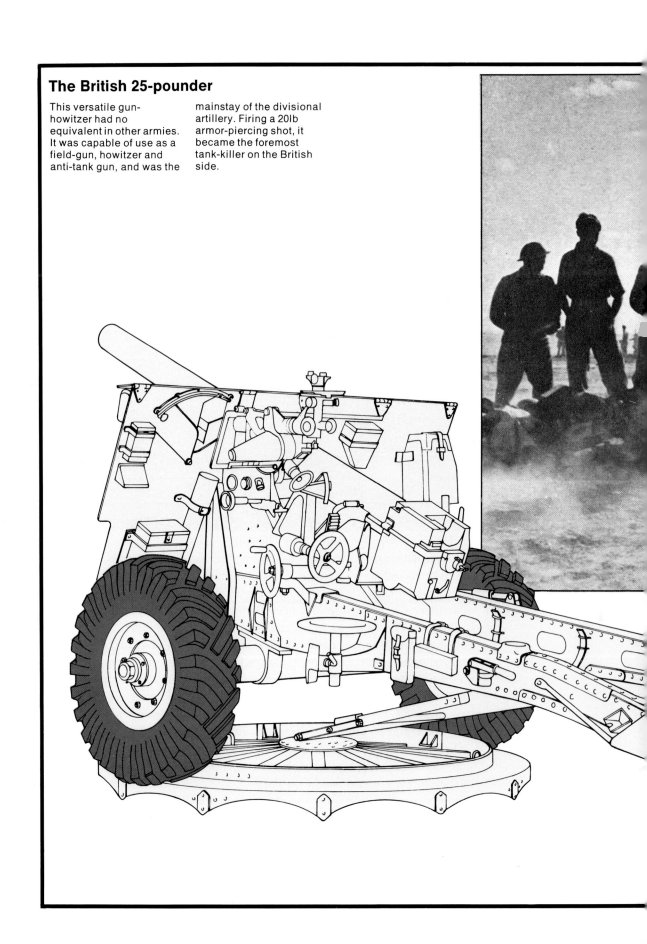

The breech of this 25-pounder recoils to its full extent, while the muzzle blast throws up the desert dust.

relatively unknown General Montgomery was appointed in his place, and he proceeded to pick the 8th Army up by its heels and give it a good shaking.

Montgomery had some military attributes which appeared strange, almost archaic, to the 8th Army. In the first place he was an autocrat; he left room for reasonable discussion before laying down his orders, but once his plan was set forth, that was the end of the matter. The days of battlefield soviets, divided commands, and interminable arguments about orders were over. His second quality was his avowed excellence as a trainer of men, and only by hard training and firm orders could the 8th Army be shorn of its bad habits and turned into the sort of striking force Montgomery wanted. Third, he was a strictly orthodox soldier. This is not to say that he would ignore opportunities to surprise or confound an enemy, simply that he adhered to the tried and tested principles of war and was not to be seduced from his path by the get-rich-quick school of tactics, the school which had brought the 8th Army within a hand's breadth of ruin. One of Rommel's strengths lay in this same orthodoxy, this same adherence to the basic laws, plus a keenly-developed readiness to see opportunity and grasp it. But Rommel never tried to be too clever, never attempted any unorthodox tactics. Both he and Montgomery knew very well that in spite of pronouncements to the contrary from fashionable military pundits, unorthodox generals always get beaten in the long run.

Rommel Faces Auchinleck

During this period of change, though, the two sides continued to spar and feint like boxers, each probing the other's weaknesses in the hope of finding a loophole capable of being exploited. After the advance of 90th Light Division had been stopped by the defences of the 'El Alamein Box', Rommel made his usual move to outflank the obstacle. But since the Alamein position was only 38 miles long he had little hope of a wide swinging move, and he sent the Afrika Korps slightly south of 90th Light to take the Miteiriya Ridge, a minor eminence in itself but of considerable tactical value in the relative flatness of the desert. Meanwhile Auchinleck had his own ideas about how things ought to develop, and he had dispersed his available forces about the desert, not in the usual static 'boxes' but loosely grouped so as to provide an interlocking defense in depth and also poised so as to be able to move quickly should an opportunity occur to make a counterstroke. He also grouped his artillery into formations capable of delivering massive fire at almost any point on the battlefield, another innovation for the 8th Army.

A Hornet's Nest

The Afrika Korps, finding no position on the Miteiriya Ridge, swung further south to go for the next major feature, the Ruweisat Ridge, and here, at Deir El Shein at the western end of the ridge they ran into trouble. The 18th Indian Brigade held this area, supported by two field artillery regiments and a quantity of six-pounder anti-tank guns, and the Afrika Korps struck this hornet's nest at noon on July 1. At the other end of the ridge was the armored reserve, the 22nd Armored Brigade, a unit with an unfortunate record of arriving late. On this occasion it was the recipient of a misleading report from the divisional armored car regiment, to the effect that all was quiet on the western front, so the Brigade stayed where it was for most of the afternoon, finally coming up at 5 p.m. to push 15th Panzer Division back, During this time the 21st Panzer Division. despite losing 18 tanks to the Indian Brigade, had managed to take the Deir El Shein position.

During the night Rommel, realising that 90th Light were making no impression on the South African defenses at El Alamein, ordered the Afrika Korps to move northeast to cut the coast road east of Alamein, sweeping along both sides of the Ruweisat Ridge. Auchinleck, however, beat him to the punch; 1st Armoured Division was to move off the ridge to attack the Panzers, while a column from 10th Indian Division would occupy the ridge with anti-tank guns. This effectively checked Rommel's move; twice the Panzers advanced and twice

German reinforcements arrive at Tunis airport in the ubiquitous Junkers Ju52 transport aircraft.

they were beaten back by Grant and Valentine tanks, 6-pounder (57 mm) guns and field artillery fire.

Rommel's next move was to combine the Afrika Korps and 90th Light Division in an attempt to cut up to the coast while two Italian divisions, the Ariete and Trieste, were sent south to 'contain' 13th Corps. Again Auchinleck's dispositions checked the move; the Afrika Korps was held up by 1st Armoured Division, while the Ariete Division, which Rommel considered to be the best of his Italian formations, was torn to pieces by the New Zealand Division, a motorized infantry column which captured 350 prisoners and 44 guns.

This was the furthest point of Rommel's advance. After holding his gains for a short time, he was forced to withdraw, his Panzer divisions badly in need of rest and replenishment. And now Auchinleck, instead of sitting tight as the British had usually done, followed him up with a series of concentrated attacks which eroded the Panzer strength, demolished another Italian division, and fought Rommel to a standstill. Mussolini, who had flown across to Tripoli ready to lead the victory parade into Cairo on a white horse, flew home again on July 20.

Although Montgomery is generally credited with breaking Rommel, it is plain from this brief description of the series of actions now lumped together as the 'First Battle of Alamein' that Auchinleck was the man who stopped him and threw him back on his heels. General Bayerlein, Rommel's Chief of Staff, later said 'If Auchinleck had not been the man he was – and by that I mean the best Allied general in North Africa during the war – Rommel would have finished him off.' Nevertheless, this wasn't enough for the War Cabinet, and Auchinleck departed to become, in due course, C-in-C, India, as had Wavell before him.

Rommel was not yet ready to throw in his hand, and after obtaining reinforcements, new armor and, most of all, gasoline for his tanks, he prepared another attack for August, hoping to be able to crash through the British line before the new commanders had had time to size up the situation and before British and Commonwealth reinforcements made the defenses too strong. He made his attack conditional upon receiving at least 6000 tons of gasoline and, assured that the first of this supply was on the way to him, on August 31 he began the 'Battle of Alam Halfa' or, as the German soldiers eventually came to call it, the 'Six-Day Race'.

As usual, his tactic was the flanking movement; diversionary attacks were put in to hold the defenders at the north and center of the British line while the main force was applied at the southern end, just clear of the Qattara Depression. The Afrika Korps, 90th Light Division and the Italian 20th Corps attacked with the intention of piercing the line and then making a deep advance before swinging northward, well east of the Alam Halfa Ridge. The

move up by the assaulting force began on the night of August 30/31 and almost immediately ran into trouble; the Royal Air Force now dominated the sky over the desert and, preceded by relays of flare-dropping aircraft, a constant stream of bombers came out of the night to pound the German and Italian columns.

The next setback was the discovery that the British had laid thick minefields, which held up the German advance, and this, coupled with an unexpected stubbornness in the British defenses, so delayed the planned advance of the Afrika Korps that Rommel became fearful of a flank attack from British armor, which by now had had ample time to assemble for battle. Rommel therefore altered the plan of advance to turn north sooner than previously arranged; this meant attacking the ridge of Alam Halfa head-

General Montgomery, wearing his famous two-badged beret, takes afternoon tea with a tank crew in the Desert.

The 'Desert Rat' insignia of the British 7th Armoured Division. It was adopted after a raid on Fort Capuzzo caused Mussolini to denounce them on Rome Radio as 'despicable desert rats'.

on, and in spite of the knowledge that it was well defended, he was convinced that he had the strength to do it.

On September 1 the leading elements of 15 Panzer Division approached the Alam Halfa positions to find it a good deal more heavily fortified and defended than they had expected. But, worse than that, the promised 6000 tons of gasoline had never arrived; 2600 tons had gone to the bottom of the Mediterranean, and 500 tons delivered by the Luftwaffe was virtually self-consuming and barely supplied the trucks detailed to carry it forward, leaving little for the tanks themselves. Rommel's advance came to a halt because he had no fuel to go any further, his troops were unable to repeat their old-time trick of existing on captured supplies, and the powerful British defenses failed to give way at any point. On the evening of September 2 Rommel called off his final attempt to reach the Nile and fell back, still in good order and fighting, to his starting line.

British Double Bluff

Alam Halfa, though important, was no more than a holding action preparatory to the build-up for the coming offensive. It demonstrated to Rommel that he could no longer expect to push his way through the British lines with the ease of earlier days, and he now set about preparing his own lines in some depth in order to withstand the assault. His foreboding about this attack was increased by an ingenious deception plan, called 'Sentinel', which was carried out in the desert behind the British lines. Dumps, vehicle parks, tank parks, gun batteries, and ammunition supply points began to appear in the wasteland; tracks ran from one to another, pipelines were laid, even canteens appeared, with trucks casually parked outside. All this grew until within a month aerial reconnaissance would have been satisfied that two armored divisions and all their supporting units had moved into the rear area and were concentrating ready for action. The fact of the matter was that the whole lot was bogus, a collection of painted canvas and wood which had been put together by a handful of camouflage experts and a squad of soldiers. The same technique was

used to swell up the apparent size of genuine defensive positions, thickening them with dummy guns and tanks. As new equipment appeared, such as the 300 Sherman tanks and 100 Priest self-propelled 105-mm howitzers sent from the USA, these were sent forward to replace their dummy equivalents.

From this it was a short step to building up a complete bogus army to divert the gaze of German intelligence from the chosen point of attack. Montgomery had little room for cleverness, since his entire front was so compact, and it left small scope for surprise. In order to obtain the greatest advantage, therefore, a massive deception plan went into operation. Montgomery had decided to attack at the Northern end of the line, close to the sea, and the camouflage experts were told to conceal this fact, suggest that an attack was going to take place in the South, close to the Qattara Depression, and slow down the apparent rate of build-up of forces so that when everything *was* in position, an enemy observer might reasonably conclude that it would still be some days before the British would be ready to make a move. This difficult problem was solved with some remarkable cases of deception. One outstanding case was an exercise in double-bluff; dummy artillery batteries were installed in the South but were deliberately not maintained so that, after a time, the dummies sagged and the camouflage nets slipped, revealing the fake for what it was. Then, as the attack opened in the North, the dummy guns were removed during the night and replaced by real batteries under the same ailing camouflage. Thus when a counter-attack was launched in this sector by the Germans, it was stopped by concentrated gunfire from an area which they had been schooled to ignore.

The First Plans

The greatest problem confronting Montgomery was that Rommel had locked himself in behind a series of overlapping minefields. Until this time the mine had been a relatively small problem in the desert, since the speed of the mobile operations had precluded their use in any great numbers. But now they were being

Afrika Korps Panzer-leutnant, 1942.
The German forces in North Africa soon adapted their already practical tropical clothing to the conditions of desert fighting. This tank man wears the tropical tunic and shorts with lace-up canvas boots. Peakless caps were favoured by tank crews and 'Totenkopf' badges were often pinned straight on to the tunic.

planted by the hundreds of thousands, and the prime British task was to carve lanes through these minefields to allow the armor to pass through and come out on the other side. This, in turn, meant that the attack could not be headed by armor. It had to be headed by a combination of infantry and engineers, the infantry to fight off the opposition while the engineers cleared and marked the lanes. And since the infantry could hardly be expected to walk up to the enemy's front door without protection, they were to be preceded by artillery fire on a scale never seen before in Africa, and, indeed, never seen anywhere since 1918. Some 950 field and 60 medium guns were made available for the attack, their first task being to bombard every known German and Italian gun or mortar position so as to impair their capability for interfering once the assault began. Then the guns were to fire a good old-fashioned barrage ahead of the leading infantry, to carry them to the forward positions. Then the gunfire was to switch to bombarding various defensive localities and posts detected by aerial reconnaisance and which were the objectives of the infantry attack. Finally the guns were to be in touch with forward observers advancing with the infantry so that 'targets of opportunity' could be taken on as required.

Montgomery's Change of Plans

Montgomery's basic idea was to punch a hole in the Northern end of the Axis defensive line, opening a 'gate' through which his armor could then advance, spread out, and begin the pursuit of the (it was hoped) retreating Axis forces. 30th Corps would force two corridors through the minefields and hold these open while the armor of 10th Corps roared through. But after familiarizing himself with the abilities of the troops at his disposal, Montgomery changed the plan. He felt that it was too ambitious for the state of training of the various units of 30th and 10th Corps and so, instead of demanding a penetration through the entire depth of the Axis defensive zone, to be followed by an aggressive move against Rommel's armor, the plan was changed so as to be more limited in scope. The corridors would cut the minefields

German infantry, marching along the coast road, pass by a motorized column at rest.

and the first layer of Axis defences, and 30th Corps would then establish a 'bridgehead' (codenamed 'Oxalic'). Once holding this, 30th and 10th Corps would 'crumble' the defenses, wearing away the infantry while the tanks held off any German armor seeking to interfere, thus reducing the defensive strength of the Axis line. With the infantry reduced, there would no longer be a secure base from which the Panzers could operate, a situation which would place them for once at a disadvantage. Once this 'crumbling' had gone on long enough to weaken the defense, 10th Corps' armor would move forward once again and attempt to seek out and destroy what was left of the *Panzerarmee*.

While all this was getting under way 13th Corps, at the Southern end of the line, was to stage two diversionary attacks, one against Himeimat and the other toward the Djebel Kalakh. These would involve at least three Italian divisions and, it was hoped, generate sufficient panic among them to prevent them disengaging to go North and add to the principal defense against 30th Corps. These attacks had to be carefully balanced; serious enough to be taken as a genuine threat but not so serious as to cause many casualties among the attacking troops, so that they would remain in good fighting trim against the day they would be needed to reinforce the main attack.

The 4th Indian Division was also detailed to mount a diversion in the vicinity of Ruweisat Ridge; this was to be little more than a quick raid and noisy demonstration, but it would help to occupy the Bologna Division and take their minds off things happening further North. And as a final diversionary touch a dummy amphibious landing was planned to take place on the coast, behind the Axis lines, about three hours after the start of the main attack. Tanks and men were loaded into ships in Alexandria harbor with sufficiently lax security to ensure that word of it would get back to the German headquarters. But after leaving harbor in conspicuous fashion, the bulk of the force slipped away in the darkness, secretly disembarked the men and armor to return to their rightful roles in the reserve of the main attack, while a few small, fast naval vessels went on to the landing area and put up a fine display of gunnery and pyrotechnics guaranteed to draw defensive reinforcements. To make this seaborne attack even more worrying, the 9th Australian Division made a feint attack along the coast road, close to the sea.

In spite of all the red herrings, Rommel knew very well that a frontal attack would inevitably come, and he had made his dispositions accordingly. The forward defensive line, behind the minefields, was largely held by Italian troops; the Trento and Bologna Divisions in the North, Brescia, Folgore and Pavia in the South. Behind them lay two German Infantry Divisions, the 164th and 90th Light, covering the vital area of the coast road, and disposed in two groups was the armor, 15th Panzer and the Littorio Divisions in the North and 21st Panzer and the Ariete Divisions in the South. These two 'pools' of armor were carefully positioned so that they could move rapidly to any sector of the front in order to contain an attack. All told the Axis had 104,000 men, 489 tanks, 475 field and medium guns, 744 anti-tank guns and 675 aircraft. Against this Montgomery mustered 195,000 men, 1029 tanks, 908 field and medium guns, 1403 anti-tank guns and 750 aircraft,

The remains of a 'General Grant' tank spread across the desert. In the foreground is the main turret with its 37mm gun; the 75mm gun can be seen in the wreckage. Below: a British 'Bren Carrier', its track broken by a mine. The gasmask was often worn by carrier drivers in an endeavour to survive the clouds of dust.

which tends to reflect his credo that to ensure success you need strength.

The Desert Air Force had an important part in the action. Well before the battle was scheduled to begin the fighter element had begun a war of attrition to weaken the Axis strength, while bombing attacks had taken a considerable toll of Axis stocks of gasoline, supply dumps and aircraft on the ground. As a result the day of battle found only 350 of the 675 Axis airplanes in a serviceable condition.

Alamein Barrage

On October 23, 1942, at 9.40 pm, the artillery opened fire in the now-famous 'Alamein Barrage' and the battle was on. For an hour and fifteen minutes the guns systematically bombarded every known Axis gun position, so effectively that they were able to offer very little opposition for the remainder of the night. Then after a few minutes of silence, during which the guns were re-laid onto fresh targets, the bombardment began again, a series of concentrations on to known Axis locations, headquarters, defensive areas, observation posts, likely forming-up areas and indeed every area considered remotely likely to be useful to the defenses. After this seven-minute storm the pattern shifted as each divisional artillery unit began firing on targets best suited to conform to the movements of the divisional infantry as they advanced, usually a pattern of concentrations, but in one or two cases small creeping barrages. Although to many of the 8th Army the word 'barrage' connoted '1918 thinking', it was indisputable that the regular alignment of a barrage was extremely useful in giving direction and pace to the infantry, who were mounting a night attack across featureless and dusty desert.

Breaching the minefields turned out to be a good deal more difficult than had been anticipated; it was, after all, the first time this task had been performed on such a massive scale, and there were still a lot of lessons to be learned. The general scheme was that the infantry would advance through the uncleared minefields, followed by a special Royal Engineer force to actually clear the corridors. This advance was less hazardous than it sounds, since the majority of the mines in the field were of the anti-tank type and could be safely crossed by men on foot; a small engineer party accompanied the infantry to deal with any anti-personnel mines which might be encountered. This infantry screen, together with artillery fire, gave protection to the mine-clearing parties which followed, their task being to initially clear a path 8 yards wide and later extend it to 24 yards wide. The methods used were varied since nobody could be certain which was best; electronic detectors, then in their early days, were the principal method since they had the virtue of silence, but 'flail' tanks, roller attachments in front of trucks, and even 'pilot vehicles' – trucks with reinforced floors protected by sandbags – were used. As the gaps were cleared they were marked with white tape and coloured lamps and regulated by MPs, for hard on the heels of the clearing parties came the first of 10th Corps armor, the 1st and 10th Armored Divisions, which had rolled across their start lines at 0200 hours.

When daylight came, however, only the leading armored brigade of each division was clear of the gaps and in contact with the infantry screen beyond. 9th Armored Brigade

moved forward of the Miteiriya Ridge but ran into more minefields and the usual efficient screen of German anti-tank guns, and could make no more progress. It was obvious that insufficient armor had got through the gap to make any sort of break-out, and the gaps themselves were now coming under heavy artillery- and mortar-fire, the Axis gunners having recovered from their hammering of the previous night. The 15th Panzer Division moved in to perform the usual counter-attack, but much of the drive and purpose went out of them when their commander, General Stumme, suffered a sudden heart attack and died. Moreover the Allied side now had the Sherman tank and the 6-pounder anti-tank gun, and they were able to take on the Panzers at much greater ranges than previously, and destroy them into the bargain, so the counter-attack was beaten off and the gains were consolidated during the day.

Rommel Returns Just in Time

The following night saw another attempt to breach the mines and force the armor through. This attack, supported by more massive artillery fire, began at 10 p.m., but this time the Axis troops were expecting it and the minefield gaps were the target for heavy retaliatory fire. Nevertheless, the two armored divisions passed through, although with losses, and by dawn they were in the 'Oxalic' zone between the minefield belts. 15th Panzer made more counter-attacks but these were all beaten off and the German forces suffered heavy losses in tanks which they could by now ill afford. The Allied positions were held all day, and during the night the front was widened to the North by the Australian Brigade.

On the following day (October 26) Rommel, who had been on sick leave in Germany since September 23, returned and assumed control of the forces. His first move was to move 21st Panzer Division to join 15th Panzer, and release 90th Light Division from their coast-watching role, since he was now able to assess more correctly the degree of danger from the various attacks and feints. On the morning of the 27th Rommel launched a succession of

powerful counter-attacks by both divisions, all of which were thrown back with severe losses in tanks.

But the Allied attack seemed to be running out of steam just at a crucial moment, the same phenomenon which can be seen in almost every one of the British desert battles. The infantry had slowly and methodically improved their hold on the 'bridgehead' by limited and local attacks, but the overall drive had petered out. Montgomery was prepared for this, and to restore the initiative he re-grouped his forces, abandoning the original plan to break through by a thrust from the area of the Miteiriya Ridge; he made the break to the North, taking advantage of Rommel's movement of troops away from the coast area. After three days of hard slogging the 9th Australian Division punched completely through the Axis line, swung North and reached the coast. Rommel rapidly switched his panzer force to try and contain this new threat; and on November 2, under a fierce bombardment from eleven field regiments and two medium regiments – one gun for every 12 yards of the attack frontage – the 2nd New Zealand Division with elements of the 51st Highland Division and 50th Division, together with two armored Brigades made the final attack which forced open the gate to allow 10th Armoured Division to pass through the last Axis defensive line and into the open desert beyond.

Rommel, however, was a past-master at covering a withdrawal, and the leading armor ran into a hornet's nest of anti-tank guns, some 25 88-mm guns amply supported by 76-mm, 75-mm and 50-mm weapons, all well dug in and manned by fiercely determined gunners. The subsequent fighting was bitter in the extreme; 9th Armoured Brigade lost 98 of their 133 tanks, but their sacrifice allowed more armor and artillery to come up behind them. The bridgehead was gradually extended until Rommel's anti-tank screen could be out-flanked; on November 4, 12 days after the battle had begun, the last opposition was either swept aside or out-maneuvred, the gate swung wide open, the armor began to pour through, and the race for Tunis had begun.

GIs wade ashore from a landing craft during the buildup after D-Day. On June 6 the scene had been very different.

D-DAY:
THE STORMING
OF THE FORTRESS

The Atlantic Wall, built at vast expense to defend Europe against invasion, crumbled quickly under a massive seaborne assault in June 1944.

THE INVASION OF Europe was the prime objective of Allied strategy in World War II. It would be fanciful to say that planning began as the last soldier of the British Expeditionary Force scrambled ashore after Dunkirk, but the fact remains that planning for the eventual return in triumph began very soon after the debacle of June 1940. Before the end of 1940 Operation 'Round-up', an outline plan for landing a force on the Continent of Europe, had been drawn up by the British. When the United States entered the War in December 1941 'Roundup' was accepted in principle by the US Chiefs of Staff, in the light of President Roosevelt's decision to 'finish Germany first'.

'Roundup' was naive by comparison with later ideas of what constituted a properly planned amphibious operation, and it was very quickly modified. The 'Torch' landings in North Africa, to say nothing of the disastrous Dieppe raid, added vastly to Allied knowledge of the problems associated with an opposed landing. Dieppe established beyond doubt that it would not be possible to hold a port, and also indicated that heavy bombardment would be needed to soften the defenses; 'Torch' showed that large numbers of landing craft were needed, not only to land the assault troops but also to keep the supplies moving during the vital period of the buildup, as the troops fought to establish their bridgehead.

In the spring of 1942 the British Chiefs of Staff initiated Operation 'Sledgehammer', but this differed from 'Roundup' in being only a limited diversionary landing to take pressure off Soviet Russia. In June 1942 Vice-Admiral Sir Bertram Ramsay was appointed to a new body, the Combined Commanders, with Lieutenant-General Dwight D Eisenhower and the British C-in-Cs Fighter Command and Home Command to plan 'the invasion of France and the Low Countries'. The appointment of Ramsay had a certain irony, for it was his genius for logistic planning that had made the evacuation of Dunkirk possible, and he was to play a vital role in the next two years of intensive planning, despite having to plan 'Torch' and the invasion of Sicily in 1943.

The main problem was the lack of trained troops and sufficient shipping. The US Chiefs of Staff held stubbornly to a simple and almost Clausewitzian belief in a direct assault on Europe in 1942 – the enemy's main base was North-West Europe and so that was where the blow must be directed. Fortunately for the Allies a more circumspect strategy was adopted; by testing their resources and not over-extending themselves the Allies were able to amass invaluable experience in North Africa and the Mediterranean. It had been hoped to mount the invasion of Europe in 1943, but Operation 'Husky', the invasion of Sicily, made such enormous demands on material, particularly the humble landing craft, that a postponement until 1944 was inevitable. Landing craft had been given reduced priority while the issue of the Battle of the Atlantic was in doubt, but in August 1943 the Quebec Conference put them back at the head of the list, and so the planners could at least be certain of getting the troops as far as the beaches.

'Overlord' is Born

At Quebec the Allied leaders saw the first serious results of the months of planning, when the 'COSSAC' (Chief of Staff to the Supreme Allied Commander) Plan was unveiled. It received conditional approval and on September 7, 1943 the authorities concerned were told to proceed with Operation 'Neptune', the naval side of what had been known as 'Overlord' for the previous four months. The area chosen for the landing was the Normandy coast between the Orne and Vire rivers, but in other respects the invasion plan at this stage was a much more modest conception than the final assault. The front was narrow, and only three divisions were to land, followed by a further two The choice of the landing area was based on many factors, gradient of beach, tides, distance from English harbors and airfields, the availability of ports and the strength of German defenses.

Across the Channel the German Navy faced the prospect of invasion with calm but no great optimism. Since 1942 there had been no large ships on the Atlantic coast, and with only five destroyers and six torpedo boats between Le Havre and the Gironde there was no hope of

The German Navy hoped to use its midget submarines to attack invasion convoys and landing craft off the beaches, but they inflicted very few losses. These 'Seehund' midgets were small enough to be transported by road.

the invasion fleet, while U-Boats attacked the convoys en route to the beach-head.

The German Army's contribution was massive but less positive. Field Marshal Gerd von Rundstedt, the Commander-in-Chief in the West, had little faith in the Atlantic Wall defenses, and maintained in private that they were an illusion created to fool the Germans as much as the Allies. But even if this were true, a quarter of a million Todt workers and garrison troops toiled away at building a 2000-mile chain of fortresses.

Rommel in the Fortress

Faced with the appalling task of defending the Atlantic coast Rundstedt's first reaction was to ask for more troops, but the Third Reich was rapidly running out of men, and could only spare the still-resplendent Field Marshal Erwin Rommel. Rundstedt had no hope of stopping the landing, and planned to defend the major ports like Cherbourg and Brest and the most vulnerable part of the coastline. Rommel's first appointment was merely to inspect the defenses of Festung Europa between Denmark and Spain, but in February 1944 Hitler gave him command of VII and XV Armies and the opportunity to quarrel with Rundstedt's dispositions. Rommel believed (rightly as it turned out) that Allied air power would cripple Rundstedt's plan to counter-attack by holding up troop-movements. Rundstedt hoped to delay and even prevent a breakout from the bridge-head by heavy counter-attacks, and push the

The Schnellboot, known to the Allies as the E-Boat, was fast and deadly. Torpedo-attack posed a considerable threat to the D-Day forces, but Allied bombers and destroyers kept the E-Boats at bay.

diverting Allied strength. But the large number of S-Boats (motor torpedo boats), small patrol craft and coastal radar stations could guarantee surveillance of the Channel. The Army knew that the invasion would happen sooner or later, and devoted all its energies to reinforcing the coastal defenses, Hitler's vaunted 'Atlantic Wall' of concrete gun-emplacements and beach obstacles. The Navy laid minefields off the coast, and hoped to use its new 'oyster' or pressure mine, which was virtually unsweepable, but refrained so as not to reveal its existence prematurely. Once the invasion started light forces, including new 'assault units' of midget submarines and 'human torpedoes', would harry the flanks of

Part of the massive defences of the Atlantic Wall under construction.

invaders back into the sea, and his staff clearly underestimated the Allies' ability to throw a large expeditionary force ashore. Rommel, on the other hand, predicted that if the Allies ever achieved a bridgehead they would inevitably break out, and therefore he urged that the place to defeat them was on the beaches. As so often happens, the dispute between the Commander-in-Chief and his headstrong subordinate resulted in an unsatisfactory compromise. The armor was kept back, but most of the infantry were kept forward near the coast. This disposition proved faulty when the day came, for the Panzer divisions failed to concentrate in time to deliver a co-ordinated blow.

Rommel's precautions went ahead notwithstanding the disputes over strategy. Dense rows of 'Czech Hedgehogs' or concrete tetrahedrons and mined stakes would impale landing craft, and 'Belgian Grilles' and 'Maginot Portcullises' would take care of any tanks that escaped the minefields. All open fields and spaces a distance of seven miles from the coast were sown with mined stakes to prevent a glider-borne landing, and low-lying areas were inundated. But no matter how many obstacles were put up the lack of troops was critical. There were 60 German divisions in the West, but only the SS and Panzer Divisions could be called well-trained. The infantry was diluted with the very young and the very old, as well as 'volunteers' from Eastern Europe.

German Illusions

In practise Oberkommando West (OKW) miscalculated badly. Allied control of the airspace over the Channel meant that the light forces could only put to sea on moonless nights, bombing of German factories and the railroad network held up deliveries of mines and other ordnance. Thus the intelligence which was so vital to give the defense a chance to prepare for the assault became harder and harder to gather. What did not help was the German's limited experience of amphibious warfare. This led them to make a very poor guess at the likely objectives, and they chose the Pas de Calais for the very short-sighted reason that it was the shortest route – the one which they would have

Mulberry Harbour

Right: an aerial map showing the layout of the Mulberry harbor. The photograph shows the vast area of water enclosed. Below left: the concrete caissons which formed the break-water of the Mulberry harbor. The gaps were filled by sinking old ships filled with concrete. Opposite page, right: the floating roadways carried road traffic to and from the pierheads. Opposite page, left: the old battleship HMS *Centurion* was one of many obsolete warships sunk to form the breakwater of Mulberry. Most of the bigger block-ships and the caissons carried AA guns to defend the anchorage. Bottom: tugs position one of the concrete caissons.

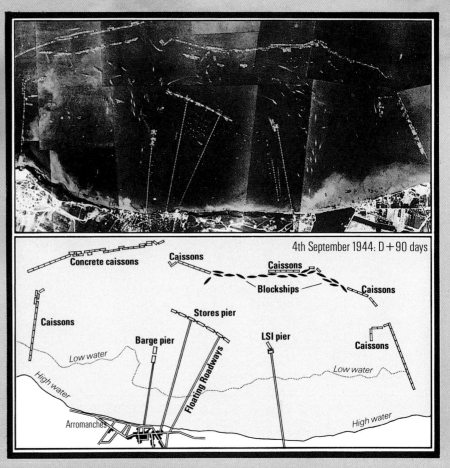

4th September 1944: D + 90 days

Concrete caissons · Caissons · Caissons · Blockships · Caissons · Caissons · Stores pier · Barge pier · LSI pier · Caissons · Low water · Floating Roadways · Low water · High water · Arromanches · High water

The most ambitious D-Day scheme was PLUTO, the Pipeline Under the Ocean which supplied fuel direct to the invasion troops. Here PLUTO piping is ranged in three-quarter mile lengths along a roadway in England, prior to being wound onto drums for laying.

chosen themselves. As the buildup in the South of England continued through the early months of 1944 the intelligence flowed in to OKW but it merely confirmed what everybody knew, that when the blow fell it would be a heavy one.

The Allies did their best to nourish German illusions about the destination of the invasion fleet. To pander to Hitler's obsession with Norway a bogus army group was created in Scotland with dummy radio-traffic, unit names etc, and dummy barges were concentrated opposite the Pas de Calais. The British Home Fleet made a number of offensive sweeps off the Norwegian coast, with the dual purpose of cutting off the iron ore traffic and of suggesting that an invasion of Norway was imminent. If intelligence was vital to the defenders it was far more so to the attackers. Small parties crossed the Channel in landing craft to gain information on tides and currents, and in January 1944 a midget submarine carried out an audacious survey of beaches and obstacles. To confuse the defenders other reconnaissances were carried out in areas far from the main invasion beaches. One of the most bizarre schemes discussed at

Quebec in August 1943 was the 'Mulberry' artificial harbor. All experience showed that the Germans would defend the big French harbors of Cherbourg and Le Havre as long as possible and would then demolish them so efficiently that they would be out of action for months. As the Allied armies would need vast quantities of supplies to maintain themselves ashore it was imperative to provide port facilities, but Dieppe had shown that a port was almost impossible to capture. Gradually the design of 'Mulberry' evolved, until the final version was settled early in 1944. Briefly, a breakwater would be created by sinking enormous concrete caissons off the beaches, backed up by sunken blockships; in the lee of this barrier against wind and weather, ingenious floating piers resting on piles would be connected to the shore by floating roadways half a mile long. Two 'Mulberries' were provided, and they were intended to be ready within three weeks of the assault, with a capacity of 7000 tons of supplies daily.

Another remarkable idea was 'Pluto', the Pipeline Under the Ocean. This was a scheme to lay an underwater pipeline from the Isle of Wight to Querqueville to supply both British

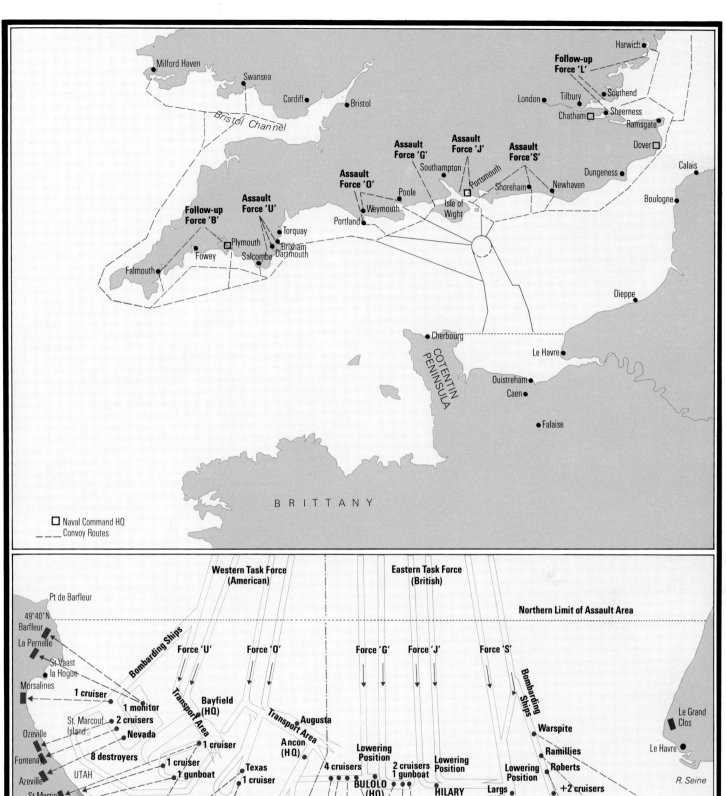

Top Map

Milford Haven
Swansea
Cardiff
Bristol

Bristol Channel

Follow-up Force 'B'

Plymouth
Fowey
Falmouth
Salcombe
Torquay
Brixham
Dartmouth

Assault Force 'U'

Assault Force 'O'

Weymouth
Portland
Poole
Southampton

Assault Force 'G'

Assault Force 'J'

Isle of Wight
Portsmouth

Assault Force 'S'

Shoreham
Newhaven

Follow-up Force 'L'

Harwich
Southend
London
Tilbury
Chatham
Sheerness
Ramsgate
Dover
Dungeness
Calais
Boulogne

Dieppe

Cherbourg

COTENTIN PENINSULA

Le Havre
Ouistreham
Caen

Falaise

BRITTANY

☐ Naval Command HQ
- - - Convoy Routes

Bottom Map

Western Task Force (American)

Eastern Task Force (British)

Pt de Barfleur

Northern Limit of Assault Area

49°40'N

Barfleur
La Pernelle
St Vaast la Hogue
Morsalines

Bombarding Ships

Force 'U'   **Force 'O'**   **Force 'G'**   **Force 'J'**   **Force 'S'**

Bombarding Ships

Le Grand Clos

1 cruiser
1 monitor

Transport Area

Bayfield (HQ)

Transport Area

Augusta

Warspite

Le Havre

St. Marcouf Island

2 cruisers

Nevada

8 destroyers

Ancon (HQ)

Lowering Position

Lowering Position

Ramillies

Roberts

R. Seine

Ozeville
Fontenay
Azeville

1 cruiser

1 cruiser

4 cruisers

2 cruisers
1 gunboat

Lowering Position

+2 cruisers

St Martin de Varreville

UTAH

1 cruiser
1 gunboat

Texas
1 cruiser

BULOLO (HQ)

HILARY (HQ)

Largs (HQ)

Frobisher

Dragon

12 destroyers

2 cruisers
Arkansas

13 destroyers

11 destroyers

2 cruisers
13 destroyers

Villerville

OMAHA

Grandcamp
Maisy

Pointe du Hoe

St. Laurent

St. Honorine

Port en Bessin

GOLD

Mont Fleury

JUNO

SWORD

Benerville

Isigny

Longues

Asnelles

Ver sur Mer

Courseulles

Houlgate

Carentan Canal

R. Vire

Carentan

Arromanches
Vaux sur Aure

Bayeux

Moulineaux

Riva Bella

Merville

Le Mont

Colleville sur Orne

Ouistreham

Caen Canal

R. Orne

R. Dives

Caen

Naval bombardment targets
5.30 am – 8.00 am on D-Day
◾ Batteries
⋯ Beaches
— Swept channels to H-hour
—·— Task Force boundary
— Area boundary

Nautical Miles (approx)
0   5   10

231

The South of England became a single vast armed camp as troops, vehicles, and aircraft were concentrated. This convoy is passing through a busy London suburb on its way to an embarkation point.

Overleaf: a small part of the massive 'umbrella' of aircraft over the invasion beaches on D-Day.

and American armies with gasoline, to save time and tankers. Neither Mulberry nor Pluto could help during the assault phase, however, and for the first few days every round of ammunition, every gallon of fuel and all the food needed by a million men would have to be landed over open beaches by landing craft. Shortages of landing craft had hampered previous landings, but this time over 4,000 landing craft were provided. They ranged from big attack transports and headquarters ships down to small assault craft and specialized craft for laying smokescreens, providing anti-aircraft fire etc. With so many landing craft there even had to be provision for landing craft to refuel other landing craft.

The most spectacular part of the battle plan was the bombardment force of seven battleships, two monitors, 23 cruisers and over 100 destroyers, which was to neutralize the shore defenses. Obviously nothing could be done until just before the assault, and all preparatory work had to be done by aerial bombardment. In the early months of 1944 heavy bombing raids disrupted communications in Northern France, disorganized the German radar-chain and destroyed the Luftwaffe. Intensive aerial mine-laying also helped to neutralize the threat from surface warships. U-Boats were to be checked before the assault by strong anti-submarine forces 'corking' either end of the English Channel.

Detailed Planning

Moving on to the forces which actually performed the assault, the US Navy provided a Western Naval Task Force under Rear-Admiral A G Kirk, while the British Eastern Naval Task Force was commanded by Rear-Admiral Sir Philip Vian. Between them the commanders had 1,200 warships in addition to 400 landing ships and craft. The British sector covered three beaches, code-named 'Sword', 'Juno' and 'Gold', while the American forces had 'Omaha' and 'Utah' (see map). By May 1944 the planning of the assault was ready down to the minutest detail, the troops were trained to concert-pitch, and all that needed to be done was to choose the moment.

Organization of Operation Neptune/Overlord Assault Forces

Omaha Beach (*St Laurent*)	1st Division (US) 116th Regimental Combat Team 16th, 115th RCTs 18th RCT
Utah Beach (*Varreville*)	4th Division (US) 8th, 12th, 22nd RCTs
Sword Beach (*Ouistreham*)	3rd Division (British) 9th Infantry Brigade Group 185th Inf. Brigade Group 8th Inf. Brigade Group
Juno Beach (*Courseulles*)	3rd Division (Canadian) 7th Inf. Brigade Group (Can.) 8th Inf. Brigade Group (Can.) 9th Inf. Brigade Group (Can.)
Gold Beach (*Asnelles*)	50th Division (British) No. 47 Royal Marine Commando 231st Inf. Brigade Group 69th Inf. Brigade Group 56th, 151st Inf. Brigade Groups

In addition there were follow-up forces:
7th Armoured Division (Br.)
22nd Armoured Brigade Group
153rd Inf. Brigade Group
29th Division (US)
26th, 175th and 359th RCTs

In addition to these assault forces the British 6th Airborne Division was to be landed in gliders near Benouville to seize the Caen Canal and the River Orne. Within half an hour 3rd and 5th Brigades would be dropped East of the Orne to silence a gun-battery at Merville, destroy bridges and clear a landing site for gliders bringing in heavy equipment such as guns and vehicles. Simultaneously the US 6th Airborne Division was to secure the Eastern flank of the beach-head by landing in the South-East corner of the Cotentin Peninsula near Ste. Mere Eglise and Vierville. These airborne landings were to take place three to four hours before H-Hour with the specific intention of capturing causeways which led across the inundated areas behind the landing zone.

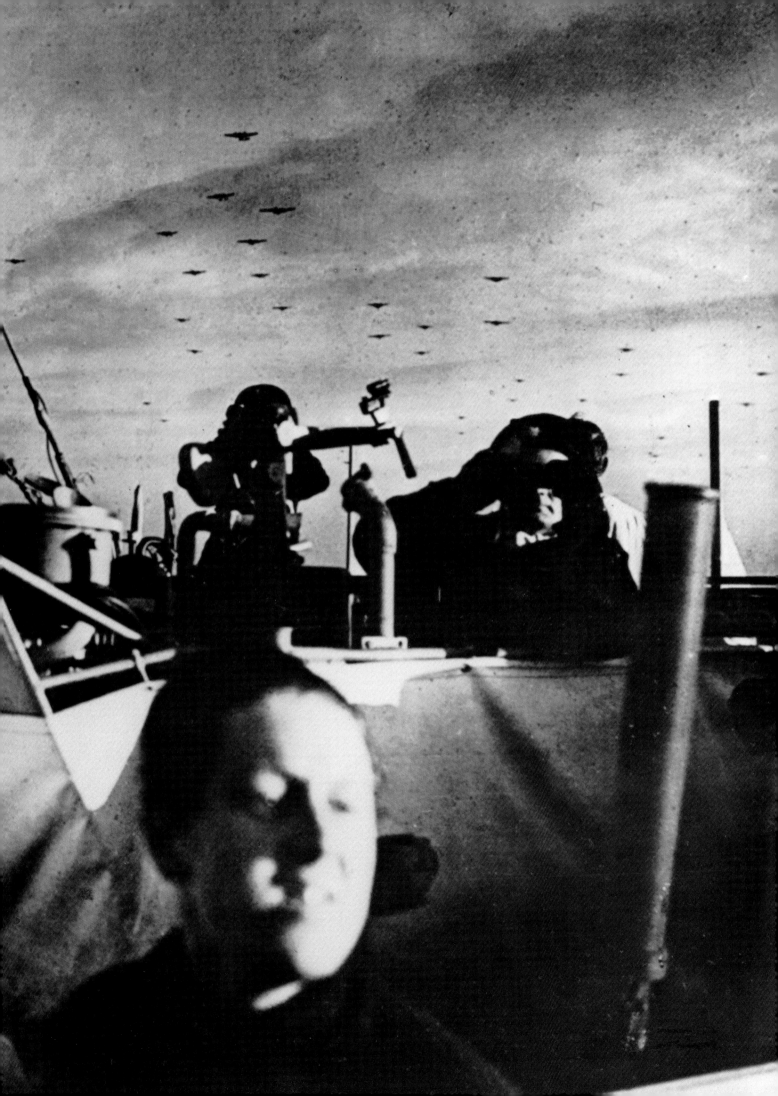

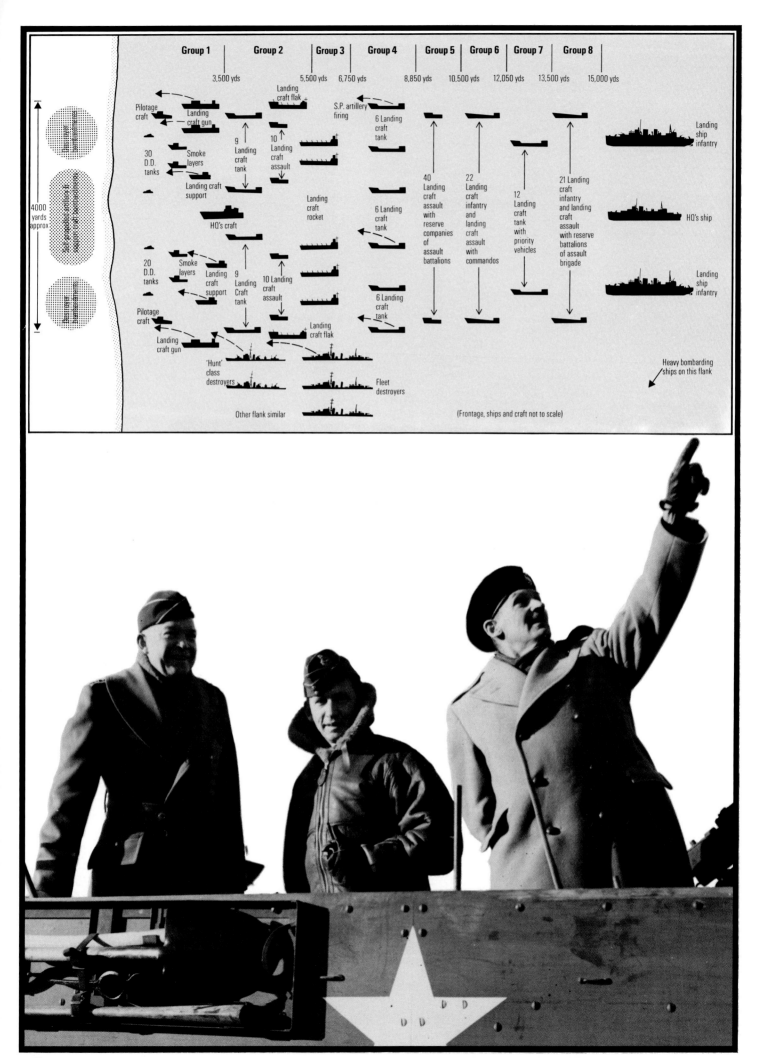

Nothing mattered more, and nothing was harder to decide than 'D-Day' and 'H-Hour', the planners' terms for the movable timetable of the assault. The soldiers asked for landing under cover of darkness but the sailors reminded them that the navigation of landing craft and the preliminary bombardment called for daylight. An additional problem was the demolition of thousands of beach obstacles such as mines and 'hedgehog' barriers; they could only be cleared if they stood in less than two feet of water, and this delicate job could only be done in daylight. The ideal time was 3-4 hours before high water and about 40 minutes after 'nautical twilight', but to complicate matters a moonlit night was needed for the passage of convoys and for the airborne paratroop landings which were to seize the flanks. These contradictory requirements could be met, but only on three or four days in each month.

The Moment of Decision

The first target date chosen was May 31, but on May 8 General Eisenhower provisionally fixed D-Day as June 5, and the whole vast enterprise began to gather momentum. On May 28 the date was revealed to the assault forces, and it became necessary to impose a complete security blackout. Obviously the assault troops could not be kept in their ships indefinitely, and if Operation 'Overlord' was not be launched then a massive stand-down would ensure with all the disorganization and security risks involved. But on Sunday morning, June 4, the weather forecast was so gloomy that General Eisenhower took the dangerous step of postponing D-Day by 24 hours. So complex were the plans that a large American convoy of 138 landing craft did not receive the postponement order, and was only turned back when it was almost within range of German radar. Had this vast assembly, itself only a small part of 'Overlord', been sighted the whole invasion would have been betrayed, but nothing leaked out.

The weather continued to look bad throughout June 5 and Eisenhower faced a terrible dilemma. But the meteorologists forecast a slight improvement for the morning of June 6,

and so the momentous decision was taken to launch 'Overlord'. At last it was possible to fix H-Hour, 7.25am for 'Sword' and 'Gold' beaches, 7.35–7.45 for the two wings of 'Juno' and 6.30am for 'Omaha' and 'Utah'.

On the German side surprise was complete. The poor weather seemed to rule out a landing, but when British bombers started to shower the skies over the Pas de Calais with 'Window', tinfoil strips which jammed German radar, it was assumed that the invasion would come there. Even when paratroops were reported to be landing near the River Orne they were taken to be a diversion. Not until 3am did Admiral Krancke, commanding Group Command West, receive confirmation of ships off Port en Bessin. Another problem for the Germans was that bombing had knocked out the big radar station at Cape Barfluer, while other stations had been swamped by 'Window'. By 5am on June 6 over a thousand bombers had dropped 5000 tons of bombs on the 'Atlantic Wall' and its ancillary defenses.

Half an hour after the aerial bombardment stopped the naval bombardment began along a 55-mile front. Only in the closing stages of the Pacific War were the bombardments actually heavier, but the Normandy defenses were about to suffer the heaviest shellfire yet seen. Just before 'H-Hour' rocket-firing landing craft moved in to drench the beaches with salvoes of 5-inch rockets. Typically, the Headquarters Ship and Landing Ships Infantry (LSIs) would anchor about seven miles offshore, and begin to lower the Assault Landing Craft (LCAs). These small, fast craft would deploy into groups with the accompanying support craft of various types, with the slower craft moving off first. Two hours before H-Hour the Tank Landing Craft (LCTs) carrying amphibious (water-proofed) tanks would move off, with their own screen of control and support craft, and launch their tanks about 5-6000 yards offshore. The tanks would 'swim' ashore about five minutes before H-Hour, while behind them the support craft were engaging the beach defenses. A short way behind the amphibious tanks came more specialized landing craft, some with bomb-

Standard landing craft were fitted to fire salvoes of rockets against enemy gun-positions behind the beaches. Note that she is equipped with a radar aerial over the wheelhouse right aft, to provide accurate navigation in taking up her firing position. Top: a rocket landing craft fires an awe-inspiring salvo.

ordination. Only months of training could avoid the utmost confusion, and the fact that such a vast armada of craft was able to keep to its planned timetable marks 'Neptune' as the most complex seaborne operation in history.

Despite its late start the German Group Command West was able to launch an attack on the Eastern Task Force just as the 'Sword' force was about to lower its LCAs. Suddenly three torpedo boats from Le Havre raced in through a newly-laid smokescreen and fired torpedoes at the bombarding ships on the flanks. The only casualty was the Norwegian destroyer *Svenner*, which broke in two and sank quickly, and the torpedo boats withdrew under cover of the smokescreen without loss. No air attacks took place and the few coastal guns which fired at the shipping scored few hits. All five assaults reached their objectives exactly on time, and only at 'Utah' did a small navigational error put the troops ashore on the wrong beach. However this turned out to be fortunate as the defenses of the designated beach were much tougher. The only other miscalculation that was made was about the height of tide, and as a result the first wave landed among the maze of obstructions rather than short of them. But the high degree of seamanship shown by the landing craft crews enabled them to pick their way through, despite the comparatively rough sea.

The American landings at 'Utah' and 'Omaha' differed in detail from the other beaches. The bombardment started later and the lowering position was four miles further out (11 miles) to reduce exposure to heavy guns on the Cotentin Peninsula. The three-hour passage in rough weather made it very hard to maintain formation, and although this did not affect the 'Utah' force it had a serious effect on the 'Omaha' force under Rear-Admiral Hall USN. By H-Hour at 'Utah' the US Rangers had seized the St. Marcouf Islands four miles out, and the battleship *Nevada*, the cruisers *Tuscaloosa*, *Quincy*, *Hawkins* and *Black Prince* and the monitor *Erebus* had silenced the defenses. The beach obstacles proved easier to clear than in the British sector, and the only serious losses were caused by a belt of delayed-

throwers to blast a way through the barbed wire and obstacles, and others with such weird machines as 'flail' tanks, to beat a path through minefields on the beaches, or 'tank-dozers' to clear roadways. Directly astern of this wave came the assault brigade, due to touch down at H-Hour precisely, followed by rocket-firing LCTs.

About 3000 yards behind the assault brigade came LCTs with self-propelled artillery, which could also fire on beach defenses during the run in. While the assault brigade was landing the other two brigades would be following in nine more groups of LCTs and LCIs. The assault force comprising typically 327 craft of various sizes demanded the highest accuracy and co-

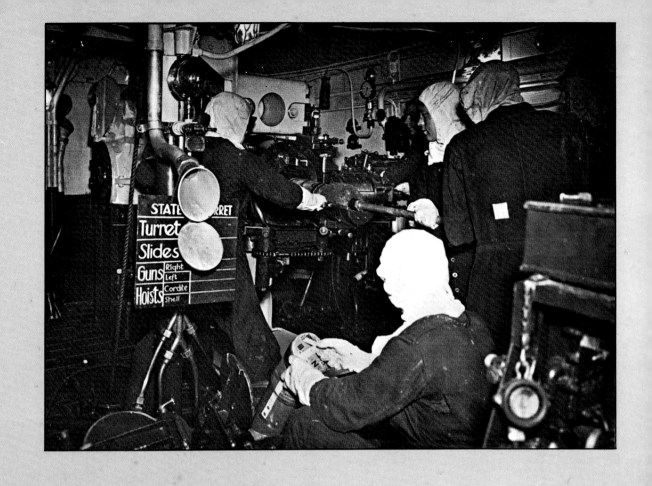

action mines which were not detected during the first assault. By 6pm on D-Day 21,238 men, 1742 vehicles and 1695 tons of stores were ashore at 'Utah'.

Agony at 'Omaha'

The story at 'Omaha' was very different. Heavy surf was breaking over the beaches and by an unhappy coincidence the Germans had allocated more men to that area than the normal density on the Normandy coast. Added to this, the air bombardment had not subdued the defenses, and the batteries were so well sited that the naval bombardment had great difficulty in winkling them out. The battleships *Texas* and *Arkansas*, the French cruisers *George Leygues* and *Montcalm* and HMS *Glasgow* all fired continuously at targets between Port en Bessin and the River Vire, but even with observation from the air they had difficulty in finding their targets, and so the first assault waves were met with murderously accurate fire. 'Omaha' turned into a shambles, with the troops pinned down ashore and much of their artillery lost on the way in. Many of the special support craft were sunk, while the reinforcing LCAs were held off by the obstacles. All this was happening in a short, steep sea which rapidly destroyed the formation of those undamaged landing craft, and soon there was a confused mass of craft, all desperately trying to find a way ashore.

The heavy seas and the long passage had played havoc with the assault. Some small craft had only survived because the GIs had baled them out with their steel helmets. Sea-sickness, that harmless-sounding ailment, soon reduced highly trained and fit soldiers to a condition in which they could barely save themselves, let alone fight. The assault waves that reached 'Omaha' beach were exhausted, soaked to the skin and unutterably wretched. The amphibious DD (Duplex Drive) tanks which should have given the GIs fire support had also been launched prematurely and 27 had foundered. Over 1000 dead and 2000 wounded were suffered by the 'Omaha' assault forces, in comparison with 12 dead at 'Utah'.

Apart from the tactical error in choosing a

The minesweeper USS *Tide* (AM-125) lies wrecked and sinking after being blown up by a mine off 'Omaha' Beach on D-Day. Mines, particularly the new 'oyster' mine, caused most of the naval casualties.

lowering position too far away from the beach, another miscalculation helped to pile up the cruel losses at 'Omaha'. General Omar Bradley had been offered a choice of what were known as 'Hobart's Funnies', the specialized armor developed under the aegis of the gifted British Major General Sir Percy Hobart. Hobart produced a huge range of tracked vehicles to help in eliminating beach obstacles and defensive positions, 'Crab' tanks with flails to explode land mines, 'AVREs' to lob demolition charges at pillboxes, 'Bobbin' tanks to lay tracks, 'Crocodile' flamethrower tanks etc. etc. General Eisenhower was most impressed by this array of gadgetry, but apart from requesting a brigade of DD tanks left the choice of specialized types to Bradley. Unfortunately Bradley rejected the rest, with the result that his men had to face Rommel's own 'funnies' with none of the types which proved so useful on the other beaches, and also under conditions in which the men themselves were at a disadvantage. Many of the casualties at 'Omaha' were caused by mines and the obstacles, which stopped the landing craft from getting through. Even the DD tanks had been accepted with reluctance, and as they had been launched *after* the infantry the few which survived were not available fast enough to help the infantry to storm the German strongpoints on the beach.

Near Disaster at 'Omaha'

It is all the more ironic that Eisenhower, when he came to write his report, said,
'The comparatively light casualties which we sustained on all beaches except Omaha, were in large measure due to the success of the novel mechanical contrivances which we employed....'
For six hours the troops ashore were pinned down just above the high-water mark, but eventually, with destroyers coming in to within 800 yards to hurl 5-inch shells at the strongpoints, the GIs were able to make progress. In the afternoon, as the tide receded, gaps were cleared in the obstacles and more and more troops and vehicles came ashore, but the beaches were not secure until 5.30pm. The US Rangers had also encountered stiff opposition

when they stormed Pointe de Hoe, a position which overlooked 'Omaha'. Although the Rangers eventually scaled the cliffs they were cut off for 48 hours, until the main force was able to advance inland. The near-disaster at 'Omaha' showed only too clearly what could have gone wrong on the other beaches, and the relatively low casualties incurred on D-Day, 4300 men in the British sector and 6000 in the American sector, give a misleading impression of an easy victory.

Victory it was, for the German commanders Rommel and Rundstedt knew that the battle was lost if the Allies gained a foothold. As D-Day drew to a close, some 17 hours after H-Hour, the Allies had 132,715 men ashore. Full details of stores landed were not kept until later, but British records show that some 6000 vehicles, tanks and guns, with 4300 tons of ammunition went ashore, and the figure for the

American sector cannot be much less. The German commanders differed as to the best method of countering a landing; Rundstedt favored a massive counter-attack while the assault troops were still disorganized whereas Rommel wanted to launch his attack before they got ashore. But as we have seen, the Allies' pre-invasion tactics cut off much of the intelligence on which Rommel's plan depended, while Rundstedt's ideas grossly underestimated the weight of attack which the Allies could mount. The German lack of experience in amphibious warfare and the enormous resources of the Allies meant that the build-up of troops and armor ashore was far more rapid than anything foreseen by the defenders. One can cite the apocryphal story of the German prisoner being taken to the beaches, passing enormous parks of tanks, guns and supplies and asking, 'Where do you keep your horses?'

Army trucks head inland from 'Omaha' Beach as the beachhead is consolidated. In the background blockships are being prepared for scuttling to form part of the breakwater. Bottom: the Allied air forces had laid waste the French railroad system, and so locomotives and rolling stock had to be taken over to France in specially converted landing craft.

As night fell the fighting died down ashore, but for the ships a new vigilance was demanded. Attack was expected from German surface warships and from U-Boats, and so the Eastern Task Force stationed a patrol line six miles out. Similar precautions were taken by Admiral Kirk in the western sector, and these effectively kept German attacks away from the invasion fleet. The biggest danger was found to be from air-dropped mines, but once again the pre-invasion bluff worked, and many mines were laid off the Pas de Calais and the Belgian coast, where more landings were expected by the Germans. The new 'oyster' mine was soon in evidence, and proved as deadly as the Germans had hoped. But the Allies soon recovered one intact and were able to issue instructions to ships about safe speeds. Nevertheless mines caused a great deal of trouble, and off 'Utah' beach four destroyers, two minesweepers and 25 other craft were damaged in the first ten days.

Success at Last

There were virtually no daylight raids by S-Boats, thanks to Allied superiority at sea and in the air, and even at night movement was restricted. When it was reported that a large concentration of light forces had been detected at Le Havre RAF Bomber Command mounted a heavy raid on the evening of June 14, with 325 Lancaster bombers. In the words of Admiral Krancke, it would 'hardly be possible to carry out the planned operations with the ships which have survived'. The following night a similar blow fell on Boulogne, sinking 27 vessels, and for the moment German surface forces ceased to be a threat. A new S-Boat flotilla was moved from the Baltic to Ijmuiden on the Dutch coast but throughout the rest of June this force achieved nothing. The larger surface units fared no better, and on the night of June 9/10 a force of British, Canadian and Polish destroyers defeated a force of German destroyers West of Cherbourg, sinking $ZH.1$ and $Z.32$ The U-Boats were harassed by air and sea patrols, and twelve were sunk during the month.

When asked by Hitler what to do after the landings on D-Day his Commander-in-Chief in

Panzergrenadier, Ardennes, 1944. The special SS-pattern eagle is worn on the left sleeve of the camouflage tunic. The helmet cover is made of the same special SS-pattern material, and he is carrying an MP40 sub-machine gun.

the West, Rundstedt advised him to get the best peace terms he could. For this truthful but unwelcome advice Runstedt was to lose his command, but the fact was that the Allies were now ashore and well-established. On the afternoon of June 7 the wind began to drop, and particularly off 'Omaha' beach this enabled the work of consolidation to be speeded up considerably. The beach parties worked frantically to restore order, clearing the beaches and salvaging derelict landing craft. The first convoy of 'Mulberry' components arrived that day, the blockships, and by June 10 they were providing much-needed shelter. The first of the floating pierheads were in place by June 17 despite some of the equipment being lost *en route* through rough weather. It was not only the army that needed logistic support; the bombarding ships had to return to England to replenish their magazines and in many cases replace worn-out guns.

Naval Gunfire Support

One of the outstanding features of the Normandy landings was the volume of fire available from ships; it was not only accurate but it was also available quickly and in quantity. The reason for this was the provision of good shore-to-ship communications to allow Forward Observation Officers (FOOs) to give rapid instructions about the army's requirements. To cite one example, the British battleship *Warspite* was returning to Normandy from Portsmouth on June 10 when she received an urgent call for help from the US forces at 'Utah', so she engaged four different targets. Next day she was off 'Gold', firing in support of the British 50th Division. Later HMS *Rodney* surprised the Germans by locating and firing at armor formations 17 miles inland from 'Gold' beach. Rommel told Hitler that no operations with infantry or armor were possible in areas commanded by naval guns, but Hitler's only advice was to tell the Kriegsmarine to 'eliminate' the naval forces and in particular the dreaded battleships. The overworked forces of Admiral Krancke could work that one out for themselves, but the means were lacking.

By the middle of June the beaches were clear

US troops take over the devastated town of La Haye du Puits. Many small towns in Normandy were almost obliterated by Allied bombing or the fierce German resistance. Right: a long file of German prisoners makes its way to the back areas.

Assault gun Oberleutenant, Normandy 1944. Uniforms for assault artillery and tank-destroyer crews were made of field gray material to the same pattern as the black tank uniform. They were distinguished by a variety of collar patches, in this case an officer's pattern piped in artillery red.

and all the arrears of supplies had been cleared. The 'Mulberries' were steadily progressing, and already provided shelter for large numbers of vessels of all sizes. Half a million soldiers and 77,000 vehicles were ashore, representing eight American infantry divisions, five British infantry divisions, one American and two British armored divisions, and two American and one British airborne division. On June 17 the American 1st Army made the first offensive move to break out of the bridgehead and were on their way to capturing the Cotentin Peninsula and Cherbourg. All seemed to be going well, and the military commanders looked eagerly to the next decisive phase. Unfortunately this optimism was misplaced, for the whole invasion plan was about to suffer a nearly disastrous setback.

The Great Gale

Although the weather had hardly been favorable to Operation 'Overlord' it had been getting steadily better since June 6, and bad storms are not normal in mid-June. On the evening of June 18 everything was calm, but the barometer began to fall ominously and by Monday morning a gale of Force 6-8 was raging. In the evening it blew even harder and losses began to mount. Immense damage was done to shipping, but worst of all, the incomplete Mulberry harbors were wrecked. When the gale blew itself out on the evening of June 22 the beaches were littered with wrecked LCTs, 'Mulberry' pontoons, guns, trucks and drowned bodies. In all about 800 craft had been wrecked or sunk, and the highly intricate supply and ferry service which not only fed but passed every round of ammunition and gallon of gasoline to the armies, no longer existed.

The exertions to get the Normandy invasion working again were even greater than those at the beginning of the assault. On June 21 it proved possible to beach some LSTs in order to land vitally needed ammunition, but the transports could not begin to unload for another 24 hours. Before the gale a daily average of 22,570 tons of stores was being landed but between June 19 and 22 only 3400 tons was coming ashore through the remaining 'Mulberry' and over the open beaches. The American 'Mulberry' at St Laurent was useless, and three divisions were still waiting to disembark. To make matters worse the respite allowed the Germans to move up their reserves, particularly as the bad weather grounded Allied aircraft. Admiral Ramsay and his team assessed the shortfall of supplies as 105,000 tons of supplies and 20,000 vehicles, and so he instituted emergency measures.

By strengthening the salvage organization Ramsay was able to refloat a number of ships and landing craft, which got the ferry service working again. Eventually General Eisenhower vetoed the attempt to repair the American 'Mulberry' harbor at St Laurent, and instead the material which could be salvaged was used to strengthen and enlarge the British 'Mulberry' at Arromanches. The result of these herculean labors was that the first cargoes were delivered through Arromanches on June 29, and ten days later the intake had reached 6000 tons. The special pier for LSTs was used for the first time

on July 19, a date which marks the completion of this remarkable scheme. It reached its designed intake of 7000 tons of cargo, and but for the gale it would have achieved that figure in half the time. By the end of July the intake reached a peak of 11,000 tons. The 'Pluto' scheme did not suffer as grievously because its special ships had been sheltering in Port en Bessin, and by early July it was handling 8000 tons of fuel per day.

'Overlord' Vindicated

The decision to build the two 'Mulberries' was amply vindicated by the experience with Cherbourg, which fell to the American VII Corps on June 26. The demolition of the port facilities shocked the Allies by its thoroughness, and although the first deep-draught ships docked on July 16 it was three months before Cherbourg could handle the armies' needs. But the fall of Cherbourg meant that a large number of warships and landing craft could be released for other operations. As the situation

A wrecked roadway in the Mulberry harbor, wrecked during the gales of 19-22 June 1944. One of the Mulberries was totally wrecked but material was salvaged and used to extend and repair the one at Arromanches.

Only a week after the landing order and tranquility settled over the beaches, to the extent that these GIs could go bathing.

ashore stabilized the naval side of 'Overlord' was progressively run down.

On the German side there were nothing but recriminations. Rommel had been right; the first 24 hours were decisive, but he had been outfought and outwitted. His superior Rundstedt, who had also been right in his own way, and rather more truthful to Hitler, was dismissed as Commander-in-Chief West on July 2. His successor, General von Kluge was given a new string of instructions about how to defeat the Allies, but the time was past for bombast, and everybody knew it. Although Rommel survived he was implicated in the July Plot on Hitler's life, and forced to commit suicide.

The lessons of D-Day were many, but the most important can be summarized briefly. First, the Allies spared no effort to learn from their mistakes. All the successes and failures of the previous four-and-half years of war were

studied during the planning period. And yet, such was the flexibility of the planning that when the unexpected did happen, emergency measures could be put into effect. Second, although the purpose of 'Overlord' was to accomplish the defeat of the German ground forces in Western Europe, it was always dependent on Allied control of sea and air. The Allies' growing seapower and airpower made it possible for them to have much more choice in how they mounted the invasion. One of the most crucial differences between the Allies' plans and the Germans' counter-plans was the lack of German experience in planning a seaborne enterprise on such a scale. By comparison their own 'Sealion' plans of 1940 were unbelievably naive, and had been drawn up in a matter of six weeks!

In retrospect the Allies probably overinsured against the risks. The provision of war-

Despite the calm on the beaches thousands of vehicles continued to pour into Normandy. This truck-driver snatches a rest while waiting to embark.

work in Northern France, in order to disrupt the movements of troops and supplies. But the change from strategic to tactical bombing brought an additional bonus, by forcing the Luftwaffe to send up its defending fighters earlier instead of waiting to deal with the bombers deep inside Germany. This was the sort of air superiority battle which suited the Mustang fighter's qualities superbly, and the Allies began to make serious inroads into the Luftwaffe's fighting strength. As the fighters came up earlier and earlier to engage the bombers, even the Spitfires and Thunderbolts which had been unable to fly with the bombers, came back into the air battle. The result was that the bombers' losses dropped while the German fighters' losses climbed remarkably, giving the Allies the air superiority they had sought after for so long.

In strategic terms the D-Day landings were the start of the final phase of the European War. However many victories were won in North Africa, the Mediterranean and elsewhere, the Allies sooner or later had to defeat the German Army in Western Europe if they were to dictate suitable peace terms. More than that, if the Second Front was not opened the Russians would never forgive their allies, and would almost certainly refuse to make any post-war concessions. But above all the Western Allies wanted to liberate Europe after four years of subjugation. From Norway to the Pyrenees the people of Europe looked to the Americans and the British to redeem the promises they had made.

Although the Allied armies took longer to make their breakout from the Normandy beach-head than had been hoped, it could not be delayed indefinitely. German documents of the period show that their interception of radio traffic depressed them because of the evidence that the Allies were landing many times the amount of material and manpower that they themselves could ever manage. Once that breakout was achieved the Wehrmacht was rolled back steadily, caught in a gigantic vice between East and West. However valiantly his troops were to fight in the next ten months Hitler's defeat was now assured.

ships and landing craft was lavish, and the same results might well have been achieved with fewer ships. Certainly the German Navy never showed any sign of being a threat to the invasion fleet, and the heart had already been cut out of the Luftwaffe in the Spring of 1944. This was due largely to the introduction of the P51 Mustang long-range fighter, and to the change of policy which D-Day forced on the British and American supporters of strategic bombing. Until early in 1944 the US 8th Air Force and RAF Bomber Command had been bombing strategic targets in Germany under the impression that this was the quick way to end the War. The casualties were very heavy, and the Allied bombers were slowly and in-exorably heading for a massive defeat in the skies over Germany. The Normandy invasion provided an opportune diversion, for bombers had to be switched to attacking the railroad net-

INDEX

Figures in italics refer to illustrations

PICTURE CREDITS.

Bibliothek für Zeitgeschichte, Stuttgart: 22/23; **British Official:** 80/81, 228, 229, 230, 234/235, 245; **ECPA, France:** 6/7, 30/31, 34, 42/43, 44, 106/107, 53 (top), 70, 71, 76 (inset), 111, 140/141; **German Archives:** 9, 11, 13, 25; **Imperial War Museum, London:** 224 (top); **National Maritime Museum, London:** 240, 241; **Library of Congress, Washington:** 28; **Novosti:** 118, 119, 120, 126/127, 128, 129 (bottom), 130/131, 138, 139, 142/143, 145, 146/147, 148, 155, 158/159, 164, 166/167, 169, 170/171, 172/173, 174/175, 178, Endpapers; **Popperfoto:** 35, 46/47, 51, 52/53, 54/55, 59, 63 (top), 68, 70/71 (bottom), 87, 89, 90/91, 95, 100, 102/103, 156/157, 180/181, 182, 184, 186/187, 188, 189 (top), 190/191, 192, 196, 200/201, 212, 216, 217 (left and right), 220/221, 224 (bottom), 229 (left), 232/233, 236, 238, 248/249, 252, 253; **St Louis Post-Dispatch:** 143 (inset); **Quarto:** 10, 12, 14, 16, 17, 18, 19, 20/21, 24, 26, 27, 29, 37, 38/39, 40, 41, 48/49, 50, 56, 63 (bottom), 64, 73, 74, 75, 76, 77, 78, 79, 82/83, 92, 93, 97, 98/99, 105, 109, 110, 115, 116/117, 121, 123, 124/125, 128 (bottom), 129 (top), 133, 134/135, 136, 137, 144/145, 149, 151, 162, 163, 176, 177, 189 (bottom), 191 (inset), 194, 198, 202, 204, 206, 207, 210/211, 215, 218, 225, 226/227, 239, 247, Jacket; **US Navy:** 84, 223, 228, 229, 242/243, 244/245, 251.